The Speaker's Treasury

Of Stories

For All Occasions

Lincoln gave me this book
18-8-85

Patricia Henry.
+
Ronnie Henry

Other books by
HERBERT V. PROCHNOW

The Successful Speaker's Handbook
The Toastmaster's Handbook
American Financial Institutions
Term Loans
Practical Bank Credit (with Roy A. Foulke)

The Speaker's Treasury
Of Stories
For All Occasions

Herbert V. Prochnow

PRENTICE-HALL, INC.
Englewood Cliffs, N.J. 07632

PRINTED IN THE UNITED STATES OF AMERICA

82420-T

Foreword

This book is meant for two great groups of persons. First, it is for those who like to read amusing, serious, and inspiring anecdotes and stories for pleasure and entertainment. Second, it is for those persons who like a practical reference book containing hundreds of stories from which they can select those they can use in introductions and speeches, and in their everyday social, civic, professional and business affairs.

Some of these stories are humorous; some are serious. The grave and the gay have here been mingled freely. One story may be sophisticated; another may be so simple it appeals to the shepherd's heart. Many of the anecdotes are unusual incidents from the lives of the world's distinguished men and women. Observations by great leaders on important problems are also included.

Having good stories in mind and being able to tell them well gives one an instrument of great usefulness on many occasions. There is genuine satisfaction, and often real gain, in using stories to illustrate a point convincingly and forcefully. Such occasions may arise when one presides at a meeting and introduces a speaker, when one makes a few remarks or a speech, or when one is in a discussion with a friend or a group of friends.

In some instances stories and comments which are related are grouped in one item. To be helpful to the reader, the items are arranged by subject matter and are further classified in the index.

Preceding the items there is a short chapter outlining rules which it is generally advisable to follow if one is to tell a story with the most gratifying results.

Here then is a book of stories which it is hoped will be a source of pleasure as well as profitable reading.

HERBERT V. PROCHNOW

Using Anecdotes and Stories Effectively

Almost all of us will agree that good stories and anecdotes are interesting to hear and entertaining to read.

But can such stories and anecdotes be helpful to us in a practical way from day to day? The answer is "yes." They can assist us practically in dozens of ways. In fact, they can give encouragement and inspiration.

An anecdote is a narrative, or story, ordinarily brief, of an incident or event of unusual interest. It is often from biography. It may come also from history, autobiography, philosophy, one's experience, or from other sources.

In this book there are scores of such stories and illustrations. In addition, there are humorous, serious and inspiring observations on life taken from many sources and embracing a great diversity of subjects. Many of these stories are included for entertainment and for their humor. Some are included for meditation and reflection; others are a part of this anthology for the intellectual and emotional inspiration they may provide. All of them may, on the proper occasion, be used to make clear some observation to another person, to emphasize a viewpoint, to strengthen a speech, to enliven conversation. We use illustrations and stories in our conversation, in letters, in speeches and in writing of all kinds. The stories of Lincoln and the parables of Christ were illustrations used to present great ideas effectively.

BASIC RULES FOR TELLING STORIES

There are certain basic rules with which we should be familiar if we are to make the best use of anecdotes and stories. Twenty of them are here summarized.

1. Do not over-emphasize to the listener or reader that the story you are about to relate is an extraordinarily good one. Your praise may be too lavish. Let him judge the merit of your story.
2. You must sincerely feel that the story is a good one, and worth telling, or you cannot use it effectively. If you have any doubts, skip it.

3. The length of a story is not too important. If it is a long story, it must have interesting points as you proceed, and the climax at the end must be good enough to justify the length. If the anecdote is long, it is especially important not to have a single unnecessary word. If it is short, it must be sufficiently complete so the listener does not fail to understand the anecdote.

4. Do not add a great deal of unnecessary material that has no close relationship to the story.

5. The story must be closely connected with your subject of discussion or the point you are trying to make in your comments or writing. It must fit snugly into your comments if it is to accomplish your purpose.

6. You should not applaud your own story. If you tell a story you think is humorous, the listener either thinks it is or thinks it is not. You cannot make it funny with your laughter. If you tell a story you think is inspiring, you should permit the listener to judge for himself. You cannot give a signal for the listener to look inspired. Once told, your anecdote must stand without your support. To paraphrase Shakespeare in his *Love's Labour's Lost*:

> *An anecdote's prosperity lies in the ear*
> *Of him that hears it, never in the tongue*
> *Of him that makes it.*

In relation to humorous stories, Keith Preston in *The Humorist* stated it a little differently, but with the same conclusion:

> *He must not laugh at his own wheezes*
> *The snuff box has no right to sneeze.*

7. Your story must be related to subjects which are of interest to the listener. A golf player is interested in stories about golfers. He is probably not interested in soccer or diversified farming. A farmer is more interested in anecdotes about farming than about bookkeeping procedures. To be most effective, anecdotes must touch the fields in which the listener has some interest.

8. If the story you have told has made no impression on the listener,

do not repeat it in a vain effort to get some response. Never waste time trying to salvage or explain an anecdote that has died. A boring person is one who is constantly explaining the obvious.

9. A story is always told because you believe it will interest the listener. It should never be told because you like it or your Uncle Bill thinks it is good.

10. There are some persons who apparently seek attention by off-color anecdotes. They remind one of the lines in William Cowper's translation of the *Iliad:*

> *Might he but set the rabble in a roar*
> *He cared not with what jest.*

Jonathan Swift's comment that wit "disdains to serve ignoble ends" describes the proper use of stories precisely. The person loses who gets the reputation for telling anecdotes which are off-color, of double meaning, or filthy. There are stories of this kind in biography, history and other fields. It pays to forget them and to gain a reputation for colorful expression of one's ideas with the help of interesting, unusual and clean anecdotes.

11. Read widely. As Thomas Carlyle said, "All that mankind has done, thought, gained or been: it is lying as in magic preservation in the pages of books." If you are well-read, you will acquire many stories which you can use profitably. Hundreds are to be found in this book. You may classify some anecdotes in this book as old, including some of those Lincoln told and which have often been repeated. But when an anecdote fits an occasion exactly, even if you think it is old, it may often be used effectively.

12. It is especially important that the listener hear clearly the opening sentences of your story or the whole point may be lost.

13. If you use a story to criticize some type of conduct, it is a good idea to tell it in reference to yourself if you can. Most listeners grow tired quickly of the person who makes himself the hero of his own stories. People like the person who tells a story on himself. He seems more human. Even in the use of anecdotes,

4

humility is "That low, sweet root from which all heavenly virtues shoot."

14. Unless you are very good at it, never use a dialect in telling an anecdote.

15. Unless it is a common form of physical ailment, such as nearsightedness which millions of us have and can often find occasions to laugh about, it is never good to use a story to make fun of persons with serious physical troubles. For example, it is not funny to laugh at people who lisp or stutter or who have lost an arm or an eye. However, anecdotes which tell of achievement in the face of hardship are often inspiring and encourage us to greater accomplishment.

16. If your story was originally told by or about some distinguished person, for example, an author, statesman, or artist, it is highly desirable to associate the story with that person. Any story takes on additional interest if you can associate a name with it.

17. If you tell a humorous anecdote and there is laughter, never repeat the line that brought the laughter. Adults are not little children who cry, "Daddy, do it again." That can become very boresome. Let the listener repeat the humorous line if he wishes, but do not do it yourself.

18. Many anecdotes and stories have a definite point or climax. Decide exactly how that climax should be worded. Tell the story so it builds up interest to this point. The major emphasis should be on this point. No other secondary points should be added after the big point or climax. The story should end precisely at the climax. That's all; there isn't any more.

19. Always be certain you have a story clearly in mind before you try to use it. You will be in trouble if you have to say, "I'm not certain just how the story goes." "No, that wasn't it." "There is something I missed. But anyway, you get some idea of the story." If you do not have the story well in mind, you will probably waste both your time and the listener's. If one does it often, he may get the reputation of being a bore.

20. Remember, people like a good anecdote or story. They like to be inspired. They like to have their hearts touched. They like

to be encouraged. They like to laugh. They like stories that deal with other human beings, their hardships, their struggles to overcome difficulties, their sorrows, and their triumphs.

HOW TO ADAPT STORIES

Every story can be adapted to many different occasions and uses. No extraordinary effort or unusual ability is required to make a story fit a number of situations. And it should be emphasized that no story should ever be used that does not relate itself to the situation in which it is used.

Consider the following story: A young couple was looking forward to the first blessed event. The young man promised he would telephone his mother-in-law as soon as they had the news. Twins were born, and the young man telephoned, saying, "Mother, we have had twins!" The connection was not very good and the mother-in-law said, "Louder, I can't hear you." So he again said, "Mother, we have had twins!" She still couldn't hear him and said, "Could you repeat it?" He said, "Repeat it? I didn't think we could do it the first time!"

To what situations could you adapt this story? The answer is "Many." For example, you are invited to speak for the second time before a particular audience. You will say, after telling the story, "When your chairman wrote to me and asked, 'Could you repeat it?', I told him I didn't think I could do it the first time."

You may also be talking at a golf tournament dinner where someone has just won a first prize for the second year in succession. You may say in giving him the first place prize, "When we asked Bill this evening whether he thought he could repeat last year's score, he said he didn't think he could do it the first time."

When Community Chest, Red Cross, or church budget campaigns go over the top for the second year in succession in raising their quotas, you have opportunities for using a story of this kind. In fact, frequently when you have an event that is repeated, you have an opportunity to use this story. The story is a very effective one.

Let us consider the use of another story. A teacher once asked each eighth-grade student in a spelling test to name his father's occupation and spell the word. The first student said, "Banker. B-A-N-K-E-R." The second said, "Electrician. E-E-L. No, I think it's E-L-R." The teacher said, "Think it over. I'll come back to you." The next student said, "Bookie. B-O-O-K-I-E, and I'll bet you 2 to 1 the other kid can't spell electrician."

This story is a good one because almost every member of an audience will have had the experience of a spelling contest in his elementary school days. The situation is familiar, but the outcome is completely unexpected. Where can you use the story? Whenever you wish to emphasize that something is very unlikely to happen. You may be making a speech on municipal government, and you say that the city should acquire ten more acres of parks. Then you may state, "I am sure we could also bet two to one that the city will not do it unless the citizens actively promote a program for greater recreation facilities.

By stating it in the affirmative, you can even reverse this story if you wish to emphasize that something can or will be done. To illustrate, you may say, in speaking of the possibility of building a community hall in your town, "I think we may bet two to one that our people will be sufficiently public-spirited to make this hall a possibility in Jonesville within one year."

Let us analyze one other story. Assume you have been given only a few minutes to discuss an important subject. You would probably cover the topic as rapidly as you could, omitting some details. At the conclusion you might use the following story: Two buzzards were flying over a western state, when a big jet went by at 500 miles per hour, shooting out flame, smoke and fire. One buzzard turned to the other and said, "Boy, that bird was certainly in a hurry." The other buzzard said, "Listen, son, you'd be in a hurry too if your tail was on fire!" Then you could conclude by saying, "Ladies and gentlemen, I have spoken very hurriedly, but if you had been given this assignment to complete a discussion on the state highways in ten minutes you would have been in a hurry, too."

This story might also be used to introduce your comments. You could begin directly with the story. In that case you will recognize the need for changing the language slightly in the latter part of the story. For example, you would say, "I shall have to speak very hurriedly" instead of "I have spoken very hurriedly." You would also change the words, "You would have been in a hurry, too" to "You would be in a hurry, too." Or after you had told the story, you could simply say, "Ladies and gentlemen, you will understand if I speak rapidly that we have a very large subject to consider in a very short time."

The story might even be used in the middle of your speech if you have occasion to call attention to the hurry with which something has been done.

A little ingenuity will enable you to use almost any story in many different ways. If you have a good story you would like to use, go over the language carefully until the story fits perfectly into your remarks. Then it will help to reinforce the point you wish to emphasize.

BIOGRAPHICAL STORIES

You will find in a number of places in this book short stories from the lives of famous men and women. These stories represent hardship, thrift, persistence and other subjects. Use these stories and others you will get from your own reading of biography. Most persons are greatly interested in unusual incidents from well-known lives. Wide reading in the field of biography will return rich rewards in giving you the ability to cite illustrations from famous lives that will help to make your speeches interesting.

REMEMBERING STORIES

One can learn to remember stories by two simple steps. First, associate the story with an idea. The buzzard story told earlier in this chapter can be associated with the idea of hurrying. When you think of hurrying, think of this story. In that way the story will even come to your mind on occasions in your daily conversation when you can use it in talking with a friend.

Secondly, you can learn to remember stories by telling them upon suitable occasions to friends. Soon they will become a part of the stories you have stored away mentally for use at the right time.

HOW TO TEST A STORY

It is a good idea to test a humorous story before you use it. Tell it to your wife, mother, children or office associates. Of course you must know the story well enough to tell it with the greatest effectiveness. Then watch the reaction carefully. If the response is a sort of polite smile or half-hearted chuckle, you will know you didn't tell the story well or it may not be suitable for the purpose you have in mind. Some persons have little sense of humor. Be certain you tell it to someone who does enjoy a good story. Try it on two or three people to be sure. The best humorous story has an instantaneous, almost explosive reaction.

REPEATING A STORY

If you speak before different audiences over a period of years, never hesitate to use the same good story before different audiences. As you repeat it, you will gradually tell it with the greatest effectiveness. You will tell it with confidence, because you will know from experience that the story is one that gets a good response from an audience. In order to avoid repetition if you make speeches frequently to the same audiences, it is advisable to keep a simple written record of the humorous stories and illustrations you have used. Incidentally, it is also a good idea to keep at least an outline of the major points made in your speeches so you will not repeat them if you speak before the same audience twice.

THE NATURE AND PSYCHOLOGY OF HUMOR

The effective use of humor is an art, but it is an art which one can acquire with modest effort and practice. To use humor with the best effect one must have some understanding of the nature and character of humor. *Webster's Collegiate Dictionary* defines humor as "that quality which appeals to a sense of the ludicrous or absurdly incongruous." The *Oxford Universal English Dictionary* says humor is the "faculty of perceiving what is ludicrous or amusing, or of expressing it."

9

Thomas Carlyle said, "True humor springs not more from the head than from the heart; it is not contempt, its essence is love; it issues not in laughter, but in still smiles, which lie far deeper."

Giles said, "Humor involves sentiment and character. Humor is of a genial quality, dwells in the same character with pathos, and is always mingled with sensibility." In general, true humor does not injure others or cause pain to them.

Humor was very ably defined by George Santayana as follows: "The world is a perpetual caricature of itself; at every moment it is the mockery and the contradiction of what it is pretending to be. But as it nevertheless intends all the time to be something different and highly dignified, at the next moment it corrects and checks and tries to cover up the absurd thing it was; so that a conventional world, a world of masks, is superimposed on the reality, and passes in every sphere of human interest for the reality itself. Humor is the perception of this illusion, whilst the convention continues to be maintained, as if we had not observed its absurdity."

An idea which we recognize as not conforming with what we think or believe has in it the elements of humor. Our ideas of what life should be like may in themselves be humorous to others because they do not agree with our ideas. So stories may be humorous to some persons but not to others. However, there are many standard, accepted ideas and concepts in life to which millions of us conform. Any deviation from these concepts will appear incongruous or inconsistent to large numbers of persons and will therefore contain the possibilities of humor. Situations that are humorous today may not be humorous tomorrow, because the ideas to which we conform change.

The judge says, "Have you a lawyer?" The prisoner responds, "No, and I won't need one because I have some good friends on the jury." The accepted idea is that a prisoner is not supposed to have such friends on a jury. Consequently, the prisoner's answer was a deviation from what we expected.

An unsatisfactory explanation is also a deviation from an expected answer and may be humorous. "Grandpa, to what do you attribute your great age?" Grandpa says, "I can't say quite yet. Several of them advertising fellers are a-dickering with me for testimonials." A husband tells his wife she is extravagant. She replies, "Darling, with the

10

exception of spending money, can you tell me a single way in which I'm extravagant?"

Exaggeration is also a source of humor, as an exaggerated statement is not consistent with what we expect. There is an old story that a manufacturer of boats was trying to impress Abraham Lincoln with the idea that his boats were superior because they would run in very shallow water. "Yes," Lincoln replied, "I've no doubt they'll run anywhere the ground's a little moist." Or there is the comment of the Blue Ridge mountaineer who said of his mule, "that critter is so stubborn that when his hind legs are goin' ahead his front legs are walkin' backwards."

Understatement, or a failure to state the facts for their full value, is fully as good a source of real humor as exaggeration. A brakeman finds a six-foot-six-inch, two-hundred-fifty-pound stranger on a train without a ticket. The brakeman asks for his ticket. The stranger says he has no ticket and displays a revolver he is carrying. The brakeman gently backs away and reports his experience to the conductor in another car. The conductor says, "Did you put him off the train?" The brakeman replies, "No, I found he was a cousin of mine, and I couldn't throw a relative off the train." The conductor then says he will go into the coach and put the man off the train. In a few minutes the conductor returns. The brakeman asks, "Did you put him off?" The conductor replies, "No, he turned out to be a cousin of mine, too."

Most of us like to think of ourselves as generous. Most of us probably believe we are generous. So we laugh at Jack Benny with his portrayal of himself as a penny-pinching individual. He deviates from the concept we want the world to believe we accept, and from the generous, unselfish views we believe we hold. Thus, Jack Benny is so miserly, so funny with his attitude on life. How can one hold such peculiar ideas?

Blunders in the use of words are also a source of humor. Amos and Andy use this device frequently. Instead of saying, "Amos, will you explain this to me?" Andy says, "Amos would you resplain the sitseashun again?" Jimmy Durante also frequently uses the wrong word or mispronounces a word for humorous effect. "Jimmy, do you know what an operetta is?" "Soitinly, an operetta is a goil who woiks for de telephone company."

11

We enjoy humor also when a relatively unintelligent person out-smarts an intelligent person. This type of humor falls in the general pattern of being a deviation from what one normally expects. "I like San Juan," says the person without an education. The "smart" person replies, "The correct pronunciation is San Huan. In California we pronounce the "J" like "H." Then the "dumb" guy says, "Oh, I didn't know that. You see I wasn't in California in Hune and Huly." In humor the "stupid" fellow so often outsmarts the "smart" person.

Humorous definitions are almost invariably illustrations of statements that do not conform to what we consider accepted standards or ideas. For example, "Dancing is defined as the art of pulling your feet away faster than your partner can step on them." "A bore is a person who, when you ask him how he is, tells you." "Tact is the art of letting someone do it your way."

Deviations from what we expect are therefore the principal sources of humor; and when they are entirely unexpected, the element of great surprise adds to the humor.

ABILITY

Rudyard Kipling took a piece of paper worth a cent, dipped his pen in the ink, drove his pen across the page—and a London editor is said to have paid for that piece of paper one thousand dollars. A million men working with a million machines could not have written Kipling's *Recessional,* of which the following is one of the five verses:

> *The tumult and the shouting dies,*
> *The captains and the kings depart:*
> *Still stands thine ancient sacrifice—*
> *An humble and a contrite heart.*
> *Lord God of Hosts, be with us yet,*
> *Lest we forget—lest we forget!*

ABSENT-MINDED

STUPID SHEEP

SHE: "I consider, Henry, that sheep are the stupidest creatures living."
HE (absent-mindedly): "Yes, my lamb."

12

One morning two small parcels appeared upon the professor's desk. As the pupils passed out at the noon hour they noticed the parcels lying there. Later, one of the parcels was missing. When the professor opened the afternoon lecture, he took the remaining parcel in his hand, as he began:

"In the study of vertebrata we have taken the frog as a type. Now, let us examine the gastrocnemius muscle of this dissected specimen."

The professor untied the string of the bundle, and disclosed to the pupils a sandwich and a boiled egg.

He looked up in great surprise, staring blankly. "But I have eaten my lunch," he said, completely bewildered.

Her Work

So absorbed was the professor in his work that he forgot to go to the hospital to wait for the birth of his child.

The telephone rang and the nurse said, "You are now the father of a bouncing baby boy."

"What?" said the professor, slightly impatient at the interruption, "You shouldn't telephone me about it. You know my wife always takes care of such matters."

ACCIDENT

On Purpose

The farmer was being examined by the insurance company doctor. "Ever had a serious illness?" asked the examiner.

"No," was the reply.

"An accident?"

"No."

"Never had a single accident in your life?"

"Well, no, I haven't. But last spring when I was out in the meadow, a bull tossed me over the fence."

"Well, don't you call that an accident?"

"No, I don't. That bull did it on purpose."

13

ACCOMPLISHMENT

The Whole Man

It is said that someone once asked Michelangelo, one of the greatest painters and sculptors of all time, why he led such a lonely life. He replied, "Art is a jealous mistress; she requires the whole man." One remembers Goethe's comment, "The important thing in life is to have a great aim and to possess the aptitude and perserverance to attain it." One thinks also of Adam Smith, the Scottish economist, spending ten years on his great *Wealth of Nations;* Noah Webster, great American lexicographer and author, spending thirty-six years working on his dictionary; Cyrus Field, American financier and promoter, crossing the ocean fifty times to lay a cable; and Edward Gibbon, English historian, working a dozen years on his *The Decline and Fall of the Roman Empire.*

ACHIEVEMENT

The Individual

For nine thousand years society has depended upon its members as individuals for those creative achievements of mind and spirit that have guided it along the path of civilization. The spark from heaven falls. Who picks it up? The crowd? Never. The individual? Always. It is he and he alone, as artist, inventor, explorer, scholar, scientist, spiritual leader, or statesman, who stands nearest to the source of life and transmits its essence to his fellow men. Let them tie his hands or stop his mouth or dragoon him in the name of uniformity, and they cut themselves off from that source in equal measure.

Wisdom and virtue cannot be forced from a crowd as eggs from chickens under electric lights. There is no such thing as general intelligence. There is only individual intelligence communicating itself to other individual intelligences. And there is no such thing as public morality. There is only a composite of private morality.

A. Whitney Griswold, President
Yale University

ACTORS

Tomorrow Night

A road company put on a play in a small town. The acting was bad. The audience shouted and whistled at the actors' attempts to entertain them.

In the final act, the leading man clasped the heroine in his arms and said, "At last, my darling, we are alone."

"No you aren't, son," shouted a voice from the gallery. "But tomorrow night you will be."

ADVERTISING

It Pays

"Do you find advertising brings quick results?"

"Yes, indeed! Why only the other day we advertised for a night watchman, and that very night the safe was robbed."

It Pays to Advertise

A restaurant customer summoned his waiter and said, "Look at this small piece of beef. Last evening I was served with a portion more than twice the size of this."

"Where did you sit?" asked the waiter.

"I believe I sat by the window."

"In that case," said the waiter, "the explanation is simple. We always serve customers by the window large portions."

ADVICE

Watch Out for Insults

His wife had just purchased a grandfather's clock in an antique shop, and he was forced to carry it for several blocks.

As he labored along under the burden a man stopped him and asked, "Wouldn't a watch be more convenient?"

Never Ask Anyone

Never ask anybody, if you mean to write anything. If Schiller had asked me about his *Wallenstein* before he had written it, I should surely have advised him against it; for I could never have dreamed that from such a subject so excellent a drama could be made.

Eckermann: *Conversations*
With Goethe, 1827

AGE

Changeable

"How old are you, little boy?" asked a visitor.
"When I'm home I'm seven, and when I'm on the bus I'm five."

Truth

"Don't you hate to be as old as ninety-six?"
"Nope. If I wasn't this old, I'd be dead."

We Know How He Feels

Discussing his tennis game, a stout bald man panted: "My brain immediately barks out a command to my body. 'Run forward speedily,' it says. 'Start right away! Slam the ball gracefully over the net, then walk slowly back!'"
"And then what happens?" he was asked.
"Then," he replied, "my body says, 'Who, me?'"

Hearsay Evidence

An actress was testifying in New York in a suit for damages, and the cross-examiner plotted to discredit all her testimony by proving that she consistently lied about her age. She was fifty-two, but posed as forty. She did not wish to lie under oath.
"How old are you?" the cross-examiner asked.
"I don't know," she said promptly.
"What! You don't know?"
"No. I never had a birth certificate. I have never looked up the record of my birth."

"But Miss ———," the cross-examiner protested suavely, "surely your parents told you your age. When did they say you were born?"

"That," said the actress firmly, "is hearsay evidence and I am sure you would not ask that it be admitted."

"But . . . but. . . ," the cross-examiner sputtered.

The actress turned to the judge. "Am I right or wrong, Your Honor?"

The judge grinned. "You are correct," he said.

H. E. Cook
Federal Deposit Insurance Corporation

NOT OLD

A young girl was a little doubtful about the advisability of keeping company with a rich, old bachelor.

"Don't you think he is a little too old to be considered eligible?" she asked her aunt.

"My dear," she replied with the wisdom of years of experience, "he is a little too eligible to be considered old."

A LITTLE SHY

An actress was making her first road trip, and her press agent explained to each group of newspaper reporters, "She's an innocent little thing, easily startled. That's because she's so young and shy."

"She's shy, all right," admitted one of the reporters, "about ten years."

LOOKED HEALTHY

The photographer had just taken a picture of a man on his ninety-ninth birthday. He thanked the old gentleman, saying, "I hope I'll be around to take your picture when you're a hundred."

The old man replied, "Why not? You look pretty healthy."

STILL YOUNG

Titian painted his masterpiece, the "Battle of Lepanto," at the age of 98. Verdi wrote his great opera *Otello* at 74, and *Falstaff* at 80. Kant, at 74, wrote his *Anthropology*. Root, at 84, revamped the World Court.

Edison built chemical plants after he was 67. General MacArthur was supreme commander of the occupation in Japan in his 70's.

Women and music should never be dated.
Oliver Goldsmith

The years that a woman subtracts from her age are not lost. They are added to the ages of other women.
Countess Diane of Poitiers

GOOD OR NEVER

At ten, a child; at twenty, wild;
At thirty, tame if ever;
At forty, wise; at fifty, rich;
At sixty, good, or never.
Author Unknown

MIDDLE AGE

With steady foot and even pace
I tread the Milky Way;
I've youth without its levity
And age without decay.
Daniel Defoe, 1712

OLD AGE

The riders in a race do not stop short when they reach the goal. There is a little finishing canter before coming to a standstill. There is time to hear the kind voice of friends and to say to one's self: "The work is done."
Oliver Wendell Holmes on his 91st birthday, 1932

AGE CAN'T BE HIDDEN

An agèd dame may dye her locks of gray,
But not make straight the back which time has bent.
Sadi, c. 1258

BEAUTY

As a white candle in a holy place
So is the beauty of an agèd face.
Joseph Campbell, 1920

Socrates learned to play on musical instruments in his old age. Cato, at eighty, studied Greek; and Plutarch, almost as old, Latin.

Dr. Johnson applied himself to the Dutch language but a few years before his death. One morning in later life he amused himself by committing to memory eight hundred lines of Vergil. At the age of seventy-three, while suffering from an attack of paralysis so severe that it rendered him speechless, he composed a Latin prayer in order to test the condition of his mental faculties.

Chaucer's *Canterbury Tales* were the composition of his later years. They were begun in his fifty-fourth year, and finished in his sixty-first.

Franklin's philosophical pursuits began when he had nearly reached his fiftieth year.

Sir Christopher Wren retired from public life at eight-six; after that he spent five years in literary, astronomical, and religious pursuits.

Necker offers a beautiful instance of the influence of late studies in life; for he tells us, "The era of threescore and ten is an agreeable age for writing: your mind has not lost its vigor, and envy leaves you in peace."

Thomas Hobbes rejoiced that he had outlived his enemies, and was still the same Hobbes; and to demonstrate it he published, in the eighty-seventh year of his life, his translation of *The Odyssey,* and in the following year, *The Iliad.*

AGRICULTURE

Where Are We Going?

I read of a young boy who worked on a farm and he described his troubles with milking. After the milking was done his mother strained the milk and set it in pans for the cream to rise and then he went out and sold it for 5 or 6 cents a quart. The price was a private matter. Regulations were unknown. Now, however, the boy, grown to manhood, writes:

> *The Department of Agriculture is mobilized,*
> *The stable is sterilized,*
> *The cows are immunized,*

The milk is homogenized,
The butter is subsidized,
The dairymen are organized,
The milkmen are unionized,
The voters are anaesthetized,
The public is victimized.

It's progress, I guess, but where are we going?

Edward J. Fox, Jr.
Attorney, Easton, Pennsylvania

AIRPLANE

She was taking her first trip by airplane. "Wait a minute," she said, "I'm afraid we will have to go down again."

"What's wrong?" asked the stewardess.

"I dropped one of the pearl buttons off my jacket. I can see it glistening on the ground."

"Please keep your seat," said the stewardess, "that's Lake Michigan."

ALONE

"ALL I AXES IS, LET ME ALONE"

It was Scipio Africanus who said, about 200 B.C., that he was never less alone than when he was alone. He maintained that when he was alone in some solitary place, "he discoursed many things in his mind." Edward Gibbon said almost the same thing in 1767, "I was never less alone than when by myself." But Ovid, a Latin poet who lived about two thousand years ago, disagreed about the virtues of living alone. He said, "You will be sad if you are alone."

AMBITION

FREE ENTERPRISE

When large numbers of people are ambitious and are free to profit from their ambition, they set off eagerly down a thousand trails and they flush a great many birds.

Benson Ford

20

No Opportunity to Advance

When two industrialists met at their club the other day, one of them said to the other, "Well, John, I suppose now that your boy is graduating from college he will be going to work in your factory."

"No, I'm afraid not," rejoined the other. "He said that he couldn't realize his life's ambition if he worked for me."

"And what is his life's ambition?" asked the first.

"To marry his wealthy employer's daughter," sighed the father.

ANCESTORS

Old Seed

Marconi, of wireless fame, was praising American democracy.

"Over here," he said, "you respect a man for what he is—not for what his family is. You remind me of a gardener in Bologna who helped me with my first wireless apparatus. As we were working on it one day, a young count joined us. While he watched us work, the count boasted of his lineage.

"The gardener, after listening a long while, smiled and said, 'If you come from an old family, it's so much the worse for you. As gardeners say, the older the seed the poorer it is.'"

Just Starting

When Iphicrates, the famous Athenian general (c. 325 B.C.), was twitted by Harmodius, descendant of a long line of illustrious fore bears, for being a shoemaker's son, he replied, "My family history begins with me, but yours ends with you."

Short Trip

It was Eric Johnston who said at a speech at Boston University in 1944, "In the architecture of American Society it's just three jumps from the master bedroom to the doghouse."

ANGELS

Robert Burns, Scotch Poet,

Was in church one Sunday. Seeing his difficulty in finding a seat, a young lady kindly made room for him in her pew. The preacher was strongly denouncing sinners. The lady seemed very attentive, but somewhat agitated. Burns, on perceiving this, wrote with a pencil on the blank leaf of her Bible, the following lines:

> *Fair maid, you need not take the hint,*
> *Nor idle texts pursue;*
> *'Twas only sinners that he meant,*
> *Not angels such as you.*

ANGER

How Could He Stop It?

John and Mary had quarreled. Their mother told them of the Bible verse, "Let not the sun go down upon your wrath."

"Now, John," she pleaded, "are you going to let the sun go down on your wrath?"

He squirmed a little. Then he said, "Well how can I stop it?"

Watch Out

The following admonition was addressed by a Quaker to a man who was using vile language against him, "Have a care, friend, thou mayest run *thy face against my fist.*"

ANIMALS

High Cost of Living

Nowadays when a man bites a dog it isn't news—it's lunch.

Vitamins

Excitement flushed little Willie's countenance as he pointed his fork at the wriggly little worm in his salad.

"Oh, Mother, I see a vitamin!"

Not Ripe

LITTLE SUE (in the country for the first time): "Oh, mamma, look at the cute little green snake."

MOTHER (in the country for the first time): "Put it down at once. It might be as dangerous as a ripe one."

Homesick

A man walked into a restaurant leaving the door open, whereupon another man boomed, "Shut the door! Were you brought up in a barn?"

The little man went back, shut the door, sat down and began to cry.

The other man became uneasy, walked over to the little man and said, "I'm sorry I hurt your feelings."

The little man replied, "You didn't hurt my feelings, but it makes me homesick every time I hear a jackass bray."

Lucky

BORE: "This bear on the floor I shot in Alaska. It was a case of me or him."

BORED: "Well, the bear certainly makes a much better rug."

Useful Lesson

TEACHER: "Every one of God's creatures is here for a useful purpose. Now what do we learn from the mosquito, Willie?"

WILLIE: "We learn from the mosquito how easy it is to get stung."

Of Course

Adam and Eve were naming the animals, when a hippopotamus strolled past.

"Well," said Adam, "what are we going to call it?"

Eve said, "Let's call it a hippopotamus."

"Why?" asked Adam.

"Well," said Eve, "it looks more like a hippopotamus than anything so far."

APPEARANCE

Not Too Bright

> *Nor brighter was his eye, nor moister*
> *Than a too-long-opened oyster.*
> Robert Browning: "The Pied Piper."

And a Sow's Ear As a Silk Purse

> *Things are seldom what they seem,*
> *Skim milk masquerades as cream.*
> W. S. Gilbert: *H.M.S. Pinafore.*

"All Hoods Make Not Monks"

There is a wise Danish proverb which says, "If the beard were all, goats could preach."

APPETITE

No Muffler

"Father's vacation did him so much good," said his daughter. "He looks better, feels better, and as for appetite—honestly, it would just do your heart good to hear him eat!"

APPLE

It Can Be Felt

> *A is an apple, sour and green,*
> *Working in Tommy but cannot be seen.*
> Anonymous

ARCHITECTURE

Up the Ladder

COLLEGE GRADUATE: "I've just graduated as an architect. Have you any positions open in your company?"

CONSTRUCTION COMPANY EXECUTIVE: "Well, we might start you as an architect, and let you work up to a bricklayer's job and salary."

Michelangelo's First Sight of the Pantheon

When Michelangelo first saw the Pantheon at Rome, he said, "I will erect such a building, but I will hang it up in the air." With what truth he spoke, the cupola of St. Peter's indicates. Unhappily for him, it was not executed while he was living.

A Culture of Our Own

I've wanted to build the homes of the people . . . rather than great buildings for the public, because I believe that that's where culture, if it ever comes to us, is going to come from. A witty Frenchman has said that we were the only civilization, the only great nation on record, to have proceeded directly from barbarism to degeneracy with no culture of our own in between. Now I've been working on that line. I've been trying to give our people a culture of its own, and I know it begins with architecture.

Frank Lloyd Wright

Michelangelo

Those who say Michelangelo was a "prisoner" of the Pope and a slave are wrong. Michelangelo was never anybody's slave, least of all the Pope's. There may have been some reason why the Pope wanted Michelangelo's services completely to himself. I don't know. Probably so. But Michelangelo was no slave of the Pope. The man that hurled the Pantheon on top of the Parthenon was nobody's slave. He made *us* all slaves. There isn't a thing done since in the name of authority that hasn't had that miserable dome.

Frank Lloyd Wright

ARGUMENT

Good Reason

A quarreling couple saw a team pulling a heavy load. Asked the wife: "Why can't we get along and pull together in harmony like that team?"

"Because," said the husband, "those horses have only one tongue between them."

"Man!" said the foreman, "what have you been doing to yourself?"

"Me? I ain't been doin' nothin' to myself," explained Sam. "It's lak dis. Yistiddy I got into a kind of ahgyment wid anothah gen'lman, an' one word led to anothah. Putty soon I up an' hi at him wid my fist. Well, seemed lak dat irritated him. So he split my lip, an' he blacked dis eye of mine, an' den, to cap all, he knocked me down and stomped up an' down on my stomach wid his feet. . . . Honest, I never did git so sick of a man in all my life!"

ARMY

GUESS HE TOLD HIM

A young foreigner came to this country before World War II and signed up with the American Army. He had a tough time learning the language. When his outfit was preparing for inspection one day, a buddy took the immigrant in hand and explained things.

"If the guy stops to ask any questions," he said, "it's a safe bet he'll ask you how old you are, how long you've been in the Army, and whether you've been getting good food and good treatment. All you've got to do is remember a couple of short answers."

"Well," came the reply, "whadda I say?"

"If he asks how old you are, just say 'twenty-two years.' If he wants to know how long you've been in the Army, say 'two years.' When he gets around to asking whether you've had good food and good treatment say 'both.' Keep it short and you'll stay out of trouble."

The foreigner nodded assent.

When he was asked how long he'd been in the Army he said twenty-two years. When the inspector remarked that the GI looked mighty young for such a record and asked how old he was, the reply came back, "Two years." And when the officer barked, "Do you take me for a fool or do you think I'm crazy?" there was only one answer left. With the air of a man who had made good under pressure, the soldier murmured, "Both."

ART

Nature Is Learning

Whistler, the famous artist, was complimented on his paintings by an admiring lady.

"Yes," she said, "I was reminded of some of your paintings when I walked along a river the other day. The air was so clear that the trees and foliage looked as if you had painted them."

"That's true," Whistler replied, "even Nature is beginning to get on to the trick."

Tolerable

A young artist persuaded Whistler to view his latest effort. The two stood before the canvas for some moments in silence. Finally the young man asked timidly, "Don't you think, sir, that this painting of mine is—well—er—tolerable?"

Whistler's eyes twinkled. "What is your opinion of a tolerable egg?" he asked.

Wanted a Good Job

Whistler had a French poodle of which he was very fond. One day the poodle had an infection of the throat, and Whistler had the audacity to send for the great throat specialist, Mackenzie.

When Mackenzie saw that he had been called to treat a dog, he was incensed but said nothing. He prescribed, pocketed his fee, and drove away.

The next day he sent hurriedly for Whistler. Whistler, thinking he had been summoned on some matter connected with his beloved dog, dropped his work and rushed to the home of Mackenzie.

On his arrival, the medical specialist said, gravely, "How do you do, Mr. Whistler? I wanted to see you about having my front door painted."

ARTIST

THE TRUE ARTIST

George Bernard Shaw wrote in *Man and Superman*, "The true artist will let his wife starve, his children go barefoot, his mother drudge for his living at seventy, sooner than work at anything but his art."

IT SMOKED

A French prince once sent an aide-de-camp to a painter, remarkable for his love of jokes and his idleness, and commanded his presence. The officer brought the painter to the prince. A picture was given him to copy, and he took it away with him. It was the painting of a house. In a few days the officer went to the artist to see what progress he had made. He found it was all done but one chimney, on which the painter was then working.

Some days passed, and the picture was not returned. The prince decided to go himself. He found the painter still at the unfinished chimney. "Why, how is this? All this time employed at one chimney?"

"I have been obliged to do and undo it several times," said the artist.

"For what reason?" inquired the prince.

"I found," replied the artist, "that it smoked."

ATHLETICS

EXPECTING TOO MUCH

VISITOR: "Can you tell me where the science building is?"

COLLEGE BOY: "I'm sorry, but I'm just here on an athletic scholarship."

ATTORNEY

TACTICS

PROFESSOR: "If you have the facts on your side, hammer them into the jury, and if you have the law on your side, hammer it into the judge."

STUDENT: "But if you have neither the facts nor the law?"

PROFESSOR: "Then hammer on the table."

"You seem to have plenty of intelligence for a man in your position," sneered the lawyer, cross-examining a witness.

"If I wasn't under oath I'd return the compliment," replied the witness.

LAW AT ITS HIGHEST

Immediately after that fateful evening in the early spring of 1770, when the streets of Boston were crimsoned by the blood of the first American martyrs in the name of freedom, an indictment was found in the courts of the Colony of Massachusetts charging the British soldiers—whose reckless and intemperate acts resulted in the Boston Massacre—with murder.

Upon their arraignment, inquiry was made of the defendants as to whether or not they had counsel.

They replied in the negative.

They then requested that counsel be assigned and expressed a preference for John Adams.

At this time Adams was at the height of his legal career, the foremost advocate of the Massachusetts Bar.

With tongue in cheek, the court assigned Adams and Josiah Quincy, Jr., as defense counsel.

Adams' patriotism was well known, his love of freedom was a byword, he had been in the forefront of the fight against the Stamp Act and of every movement to prevent British oppression.

So numerous were the inquiries as to why he had accepted, Adams was forced to make a public statement on the subject.

He uttered the words that should, in my opinion, not only adorn the walls of every lawyer's office but also be engraved upon the hearts of every member of our Bar.

Adams said: "Counsel ought to be the very last thing an accused person should want for in a free country. The Bar ought, in my opinion, to be independent and impartial at all times and in every circumstance, and persons whose lives are at stake should have the counsel they prefer."

Adams meant exactly what he said.

So vigorously did he present his defense that the commander of the detachment and all but two of the soldiers were acquitted, and the two who were found guilty of manslaughter

29

owed their very lives to the fervor and eloquence of his plea. This was the practice of law at its highest and in its most honorable estate.

Miles McDonald, District Attorney
Brooklyn, New York

How's That?

A young lawyer was presenting his first case in court. It was a simple damage suit of a farmer against a railroad company whose train had killed twenty-four of his hogs, but the young man was trying to dramatize it.

"Just think of it, gentlemen, twenty-four hogs," he stated impressively, "twenty-four! That's twice the number there are on the jury!"

For the Judges

A lawyer who prided himself on his knowledge of the law was caught one afternoon carrying a number of law books under his arm.

"With your knowledge and memory, I thought you had no need for those things," a friend chided him.

"I don't," the lawyer said. "These are for the judges."

Setting Hens Lay No Eggs

A judge who presided in a county court was fond of indulging in a joke at the expense of a practicing attorney in the same court, for whom he had a high regard. On a certain occasion, when pleading a cause at the bar, the attorney observed that he would conclude his remarks on the following day unless the court would consent to *set* late enough for him to finish that evening. "*Sit*, sir," said the judge, "not *set*. Hens set."

"I stand corrected, sir," said the attorney.

Not long after, while giving an opinion, the judge remarked that, under such circumstances, an action would not *lay*.

"*Lie*, may it please your Honor," said the attorney, "not *lay*. Hens lay."

AUTHOR

WE'VE READ THEM

"I dream my stories," said the well-known novelist.
"How you must dread going to bed!" replied the literary critic.

BETTER TASTE

"You know," said an author, fishing for compliments, to William Dean Howells, "my books are selling better and better, but I think my work is falling off. My new work is not so good as my old."

"Oh, nonsense!" said Howells. "You write just as well as you ever did. Your taste is improving, that's all."

TO THE HEAD OF THE CLASS

Asked to write a composition about geese, this is what Bill turned in: "Geese is a low, heavy-set bird which is mostly meat and feathers. Geese can't sing much on account of the dampness of the moisture. He ain't got no between-the-toes and he's got a little balloon in his stummick to keep from sinking. Some geese when they get big has curls on their tails and is called ganders. Ganders don't haff to sit and hatch but just eat and loaf and go swimming. If I was a goose, I'd rather be a gander."

EXPERIENCE

WRITER: "Here's the manuscript I offered you last year."
EDITOR: "What's the idea bringing this thing back when I rejected it last year?"
WRITER: "Well, you've had a year's experience since then."

COMPETENT

"I am going to write a book called *Popular Ignorance*," said a young man to a much older person.
"I know no one more competent," was the reply.

AUTOGRAPH

TALLEYRAND, FRENCH STATESMAN

Talleyrand was once asked for his autograph by an English nobleman. He promised to send him one in a few days, and kept his word in the following manner. He sent him an invitation to dinner which read: "Dear sir, will you oblige me with your company to dinner, on Wednesday next, at eight o'clock? I have invited a number of exceedingly clever persons, and do not like to be the only fool among them!"

HOW HE REFUSED

The great agitator and Irish leader, Daniel O'Connell, being pestered by a stranger for his autograph, returned the following answer: "Sir: Yours, requesting my autograph, is received. I have been so bothered with similar impertinences, that I'll be blest if I send it. Your ob'd't servant, Daniel O'Connell."

AUTOMOBILES

GIVING CREDIT

COP: "And just how did the accident happen?"
MOTORIST: "My wife fell asleep in the back seat."

WARNING

A man stopped at a small town garage and told the mechanic, "Whenever I hit eighty, there's a knocking in the engine."

The mechanic gave the car a lengthy examination and, after much testing, wiped the grease from his hands and drawled, "I don't see nothin' wrong, mister. It must be the good Lord a-warning you."

NEXT CASE

Two judges were arrested for speeding. When they arrived in court, no other judge was present, so they decided to try each other. The first judge went up to the bench and said, "You are charged with exceeding the speed limit. How do you plead?"

"Guilty," was the answer.

"You are hereby fined five dollars."

"Hmm," said the other judge, "these cases are becoming far too common. This is the second case of this sort we've had this morning. I hereby fine you ten dollars or ten days in jail."

JUDGE, YOU SAID IT

MAGISTRATE: "You cannot drive now for two years; you're a danger to pedestrians."

DEFENDANT: "But, your Honor, my living depends on it."

MAGISTRATE: "So does theirs."

THE JONESES

BILL: "What is worse than keeping up with the Joneses?"

SAM: "Trying to pass them at seventy miles an hour."

BROADER VIEWPOINTS

The social changes brought about by the automobile have been enormous. People who formerly spent their entire lives in a single community now circulate all over the continent— sectional barriers have long since disappeared.

In the War Between the States, it was estimated that not one combatant in a hundred on either side had ever been outside his own county, much less a visitor in the territory of the opposing forces. Today it seems inconceivable that North and South should regard themselves as separate nations, with Virginians summering in Maine, New Yorkers touring the Great Smokies in October, and Pennsylvanians vacationing at Miami or Sea Island. No statecraft, no oratory, no legislation, could achieve this singleness of purpose half so well as has the steering wheel on the family car.

Lives everywhere have been enriched and enlarged by the automobile in a manner impossible to achieve through law. The wonders and attractions of the big city are available to the remote farm; the peace and beauty of the country are there for all to enjoy. We have acquired fuller understanding of each other, greater tolerance of different races and creeds, a broadened national viewpoint.

From an address by Harold Brayman
Director, Public Relations Department
E. I. du Pont de Nemours & Company

PHOPHECY

Carriages without horses shall go,
And accidents fill the world with woe.
Anonymous, 1862

A Chariot for Every Man

Centuries ago only the Roman emperors could ride in their chariots, and they could only travel at a snail's pace. Today over forty million Americans have their own chariots, and they can travel over the entire United States at sixty to seventy miles per hour.

Wham!

While driving about the business section of town one morning, a truck driver attempted to edge past a woman driver who seemed uncertain whether to park or proceed. Suddenly, her mind made up, she clashed gears and crashed backwards into his fender.

Exasperated, she stumbled from her car. "You knew I was going to do something stupid," she screamed at the dazed truck driver. "Why didn't you wait and see what it was?"

Making Progress

"How are you getting along in your driving?"

"Oh, fine," she bragged. "Yesterday I went fifty miles an hour, and tomorrow I'm going to try opening my eyes when I pass another car."

Speeding Up Traffic

"Why do you have that horrible shrieking horn?"

"For humane reasons. If I can paralyze a person with fear, he will keep still and I can drive to one side of him."

34

UNAVOIDABLE

A truck driver had a collision. In filling out the required form, he stated that the accident was unavoidable. Under remarks, he wrote, "The woman in front of me signaled a left turn and made a left turn."

VERY CLEARLY

Woman driver explaining auto crash: "And then I very clearly signaled that I'd changed my mind."

AVERAGE

TIP

A sightseer was just emerging from a cave. "What's the average tip you receive from each person you take through this cave?" he asked confidentially of the native guide.

"The average tip, boss, is a dollar."

This seemed a little high for the short time it took to go through, but not wanting to be ungenerous the sightseer produced a dollar bill. "Thanks, boss, thanks kindly! You are the only gentleman that has reached the average in my whole experience."

COMFORTABLE

An Englishman said that if a man has one foot inside an electric refrigerator and one foot in a hot oven, then on the average he is comfortable.

BABIES

ONE TO ENJOY

MRS. FUSSY: "But why adopt a baby when you have three children of your own under five years old?"

MRS. JONES: "My own are being brought up properly. The adopted one is to enjoy."

He Had Seen Babies

Tommie was told by the nurse that a stork had left him a little baby sister, and he was asked if he did not wish to see her.

"I don't care about the baby," said Tommie, "but I'd like to see the stork."

BACHELOR

Not That Lonely

"Is Jim a confirmed bachelor?"

"He is now. He sent his picture to a lonely hearts club, and they sent it back with a note saying, 'We're not that lonely!'"

Difficult Task

"You have only yourself to please," said a married friend to an old bachelor.

"True," he replied, "but you don't know what a difficult task I find it."

BANK

Taking No Chances

Chlorine, the cook, approached the bank teller's window with an air of determination.

"I wants yo' to take care of dis yeah cash fo' a while," she remarked, handing over her savings.

"Why, Chlorine," said the banker, who knew her, "I thought you always said you'd never trust a bank."

"Dat's all right, dat's all right, but the circumfrances suroundin' de matter makes me change mah mind. You see, I'se gwine to get married, an' Ah don't want dat much money round de house with a strange man on de premises."

BANKING

CONFIDENCE

An old banker who pioneered in a small western town was being interviewed about his career.

INTERVIEWER: "How did you get started in banking?"

OLD BANKER: "It was simple. I put up a sign saying, 'Bank.' A man came in and gave me one hundred dollars. Another came in with two hundred dollars. By that time my confidence reached such a point that I put in fifty dollars of my own money."

ANSWER: NO MORE

HE: "Dear, you must be more careful. The bank has just returned the last check you wrote."

SHE: "Darling, that's wonderful. What shall we buy with it this time?"

IN CHARGE OF LIQUID ASSETS

The city banker was visiting the farm. "I suppose," he said, nodding to a figure in the farm yard, "that's the hired man."

"No," replied the farmer, "that's the first vice president in charge of cows."

SIMPLE INTEREST?

TEACHER: "Now, Henry, suppose I borrowed one hundred dollars from your father and paid him ten dollars a month for ten months. How much would I then owe him?"

HENRY (the banker's son): "About six dollars' interest."

BANKRUPTCY

ALL TAXPAYERS IN FAVOR SAY "AYE"

If the nation is living within its income its credit is good. If in some crisis it lives beyond its income for a year or two it can usually borrow temporarily on reasonable terms. But if, like the spendthrift, it throws discretion to the winds, is willing to make no sacrifice at all in spending, extends its taxing up to the limit of the people's power to pay, and continues to pile up deficits, it is on the road to bankruptcy.

From a speech at Pittsburgh
by Franklin D. Roosevelt, October 19, 1932

BARBERS

Tough Luck

A moron decided to shave. As he was poised with his razor, ready to start, the mirror fell unnoticed to the floor. "Just my luck," said he, staring at the empty wall. "I cut my head off."

Any Leaks

The barber was not very good. After being shaved, the customer asked for a drink of water.

"Are you thirsty, sir?" asked the barber.

"No," answered the customer weakly. "I just want to see if my face still holds water."

Be Careful

Barber (whispering to new helper): "Here comes a man for a shave."

Apprentice: "Let me practice on him."

Barber: "All right, but be careful and don't cut yourself."

H. E. Cook, Director
Federal Deposit Insurance Corp., Washington, D.C.

In Reverse

In the early days in San Francisco, a Chinaman called at the home of his neighbor and said, "Ching Lee, I have come to take you to a Labor Day barbecue."

"I dare not be seen in public," said Ching Lee miserably, as he exposed a shorn head. "Last night two drunken sailors took my cue to a barber."

38

BARGAIN

Not so Green a Buyer

A boy walked into a farmer's melon patch and asked the price of a fine big melon.

"That's forty cents," said the farmer.

"I have only four cents," the boy told him.

"Well," smiled the farmer and winked at his hired hand as he pointed to a very small and very green melon, "how about that one?"

"Fine. I'll take it," the boy said, "but don't cut it off the vine yet. I'll call for it in a week or so."

BASEBALL

He's a Ferocious Bum, Honey

BRIDE: "Who is the man in the blue coat, darling?"
GROOM: "That's the umpire, dear."
BRIDE: "Why does he wear that funny wire thing over his face?"
GROOM: "To keep from biting the ball players, precious."

Don't Do as I Do

A baseball team had had a terrific batting slump. The coach called a special batting practice and watched with disgust as his players bounced slow grounders and short pop flies to the infield.

Grabbing a bat, he charged out of the dugout and said, "I'll show you what I want." He ordered the pitcher to toss them in as hard as he could. But he did no better than his men. After ten futile swipes at the horsehide, he flung his bat to the ground and shouted, "See, that's what you guys have been doing. Now get up there and slug the ball."

Calamity

Oh, somewhere in this favored land the sun is shining bright,
The band is playing somewhere, and somewhere hearts are light.
And somewhere men are laughing, and somewhere children shout:
But there is no joy in Mudville—mighty Casey has struck out.

From "Casey at the Bat,"
by Ernest L. Thayer, 1888

BEAUTY

It Never Does Them Any Good

"I'll admit she's snobbish," said the farmer's wife, "but she's pretty."
"She's the village belle, all right," said her husband, "but she shouldn't have been tolled."

BEHAVIOR

Everybody Can Have Some

MAMA: "Let's buy Junior a bicycle."
PAPA: "Do you think it will improve his behavior?"
MAMA: "No. But it will spread his meanness over a wider area."

Well-behaved

MOTHER: "You were a very tidy boy to throw your orange peel on the floor of the bus. Where did you put it?"
JOHNNY: "In the pocket of the man next to me."

BIBLE

The Best Gift

Abraham Lincoln once said to a delegation which came to give him a Bible, "This great book . . . is the best gift God has given to man. . . . But for it we could not know right from wrong."

BIGOTRY

Willing to Be Reasonable

They had been having a series of temperance revivals and Pat had signed the pledge. Not long afterward he was seen coming out of a saloon.
A friend said, "Pat, I thought you were a teetotaler."
"Indeed," said Pat, "I am the same, but I am no *bigoted* taytotaler."

BIRTHDAY

THAT'S DIFFERENT

TRAMP: "Beg pardon, ma'am, but do you have some pie or cake you could spare an unfortunate wanderer?"

LADY: "No, I'm afraid not. But wouldn't some bread and butter do?"

TRAMP: "As a general rule it would, ma'am—but you see, this is my birthday."

STILL THIRTY

"This is my birthday, you know," said the young miss.

"Many happy returns," replied her friend. "How old aren't you?"

BLUFFING

PASS FOR THE AUTHOR

A man without any money, wishing to see a Shakespearean play, stepped up to the box office and said: "Pass me in, please."

"Pass you in? What for?" the attendant asked.

The applicant drew himself up haughtily: "What for? Why, because I am William Shakespeare, author of the play."

"Oh, I beg your pardon, sir," replied the attendant and hurriedly wrote out an order for a ticket.

BLUNDER

THE LIGHTNING BUG

The lightning bug is brilliant,
But it hasn't any mind;
It blunders through existence,
With its headlight on behind.

BOASTING

SLOW TRAINS

A tall Texan was touring England. Whenever he got a chance, he would kid the Britishers about their "midget" country. He irritated one man who asked him to give the dimensions of his wonderful State.

41

"Waal," drawled the Texan. "I don't rightly know just how big she is, but I do know that you can board a train, and twenty-four hours later you will still be in the Lone Star State."

"But what does that prove?" the Englishman replied. "We have trains like that here, too."

On the Radio

MEL BLANC: "I'm a proud Texan. I come from Texas, the biggest cattle state in the Union. We ship cattle all over the world."

JUDY CANOVA: "Yeah, but I'm from California. Do you ship oranges all over the world like we do?"

MEL BLANC: "We can't ship oranges out of Texas; they refuse to leave."

Attention, D.A.R.

They're telling of the Boston salesman who visited Texas and heard one particular Texan boasting about heroes of the Alamo who, almost alone, held off whole armies.

"I'll bet you never had anybody so brave around Boston," challenged the Texan.

"Did you ever hear of Paul Revere?" asked the Bostonian.

"Paul Revere?" said the Texan. "Isn't that the guy that ran for help?"

Texas

A group of Chicagoans were showing the town to a visiting Texan "What do you think of our stock yards?" they asked.

"Man, we got brandin' corrals in Texas bigger'n this."

"Well, what do you think of the imposing skyscrapers of the Chicago skyline?"

"Why, man, we got tombstones in Boot Hill bigger than those."

That night they put some snapping turtles in his bed. When he turned down the covers and asked what they were, he was told, "Illinois bedbugs."

He looked at them a moment. "So they are," he agreed. "Young 'uns, ain't they?"

Just Tosses Them Away

A boastful woman was talking about her jewelry. "I clean my diamonds with ammonia," she said, "my rubies with Bordeaux wine, my emeralds with Danzig brandy, and my sapphires with fresh milk."

"Oh, I don't clean mine," said the other woman. "When they get dirty, I just throw them away."

Just Medals

Two veterans were boasting about their old outfits.

"Why, our company was so well drilled," said one, "that when we presented arms, all you could hear was slap, slap, click."

"Pretty fair," said the other, "but when our company presented arms, you could hear slap, slap, jingle."

"Jingle?" said the other. "What did that?"

Came the reply, "Oh, just our medals."

First and Only Performance

"Do you have any theatrical attractions in Bear Valley?"

"Theatrical attractions? Well, I guess! Why, stranger, we have plays here that you never see in New York."

A Touching Story

"What sort of person is he?"

"Well, after a beggar has touched him for a dime, he'll tell you he gave a little dinner to an acquaintance of his."

Cut Down to Size

A famous author was attending a party. An unsuccessful writer came up to him and belittled himself to the author, admitting he was a poor writer, a hack, who shouldn't even be included in the great man's company.

The famous author listened patiently for five minutes, and then said, "Why do you make yourself so small? You were never that big."

SPEED

A New Yorker was boasting to a visitor.

"Look at that skyscraper going up! The workmen putting the finishing touches on the upper twenty stories have gone down to the fiftieth floor for lunch while the tenants on the first forty floors are moving out because the building is old-fashioned!"

BOATS

OLD JOKE—STILL GOOD

A magician performed every evening on a luxury liner. Also on this ship was a parrot which belonged to an old sailor. Every time the magician went into his act, the parrot screamed, "Phoney! Phoney!" One day the ship sank. All that was left was the parrot sitting on one end of a long board and the magician on the other. One day passed. They said nothing. Finally, the parrot looked suspiciously at the magician and said, "All right, wise guy, what did you do with the ship?"

ON THE UP AND UP

He was making his first ocean voyage and was in his cabin, groaning with seasickness.

"Shall I send you some dinner, sir?" the steward asked.

"No," was the reply. "Just throw it overboard and save me the trouble."

BOLD

LUCKY GIRL

When the bold young man noticed the attractive waitress he announced himself in a breezy manner: "Hi, sweetheart! Where have you been all of my life?"

The waitress scrutinized him coldly in silence for a moment, then replied: "Out of it—thank heaven!"

BOOKS

BUSINESS SENSE

The owner of a book-rental business noticed that when people had held a book out too long, they were slow to return it and pay up. Often he lost both the book and future business. So he tried a new angle. For a long-overdue book he would send a card saying the borrower owed only twenty-five cents in rental. Thinking he was getting the better of a mistake, the customer quickly paid up and became a customer again.

PROGRESS

In the tenth century the Countess of Anjou gave two hundred sheep, a load of wheat, a load of rye, and a load of millet, with several skins of costly fur, for a single book written in longhand. Now the printing press has transformed the world, enabling millions of men and women to own books at low prices.

TO THOSE WHO KEEP BOOKS

> Steal not this book, for fear or shame,
> For it is in its owner's name;
> And when you're dead, the Lord will say,
> "Where is that book you stole away?"

MANUSCRIPT OF ROBINSON CRUSOE

There is an old story that Robinson Crusoe, in manuscript form, was not accepted by any book publisher, though the writer, Defoe, was in good repute as an author. One bookseller, at last, remarkable not for his discernment but for his speculative turn, published the book in 1719. This bookseller got more than a thousand guineas ($5,110 at that time) from it. Booksellers now make money almost every hour through sales of the various editions of the book.

BORE

WE'VE MET HIM

"What kind of a man is Duncan? I don't believe I have met him."
"Well, if you see two men off in a corner anywhere and one of them looks bored to death, the other one is Duncan."

AFTER-DINNER SPEECHES

A Frenchman once remarked at a dinner that was to be followed by speeches, "The table is the only place where one is not bored for the first hour."

SPEECH

During the delivery of one of those tedious and interminable speeches that are often inflicted upon the House of Representatives, a member who had occupied the floor for many hours was called to order, on the ground that his remarks were not pertinent to the question before the House. "I know it," said he. "I am not speaking for the benefit of the House, but for posterity."

"Speak a little longer," said Representative John Randolph in an undertone, "and you will have your audience before you."

THAT WILL HELP

GUEST: "This party's dull. Think I'll leave."
HOST: "Yes, do. That'll help some."

BOYS

ALL THE MEADOWS AND FIELDS

I devise to boys, jointly, all the idle fields and commons, where ball may be played, all pleasant waters where one may swim, all snow-clad hills where one may coast, and all streams and ponds where one may fish, or where, when winter comes, one may skate, and to hold the same for the period of their boyhood. And all the meadows with the clover-blossoms and butterflies thereof, the woods with their appurtenances, the

46

birds and squirrels and echoes and strange noises, and all distant places which may be visited, together with the adventures there to be found.

From the "Last Will and Testament"
Charles Lunsbury, c. 1875

BRAINS

WOUND ONLY ONCE

Our brains are seventy-year clocks. The angel of life winds them up once for all, then closes the case, and gives the key into the hands of the angel of the resurrection.

From "The Autocrat of the Breakfast Table"
O. W. Holmes, 1858

ANY IMPROVEMENT?

HE: "I've changed my mind."
SHE: "Does your new mind work any better than your old one?"

DANTE

The secret of the poet Dante's struggle through life was in the sarcasm of his answer to the Prince of Verona, who once asked him how he could account for the fact that, among princes, the court fool was in greater favor than the philosopher.

"Similarity of mind," said Dante, "is all over the world the source of friendship."

GOOD MIXTURE

An eminent painter was once asked what he mixed his colors with in order to produce so extraordinary an effect.

"I mix them with brains, sir," was his answer.

BRAVE

ALMOST YELLED ONCE

A New Englander took his wife to a country fair where plane flights were made daily. He asked the price of a trip. The aviator told him it was ten dollars.

47

"Ten dollars!" exclaimed the New Englander. "There wouldn't be no pleasure in that for me."

"Well, I'll tell you what I'll do," replied the aviator. "Since you want to go up so much, why I'll take you and your wife up for nothing if you'll agree not to say a word all the time we're in the air. But if you say anything while we're up there, it's going to cost you the full price."

So the New Englander and his wife entered the little plane and a few minutes later they were soaring over the countryside. When the plane had reached an altitude of five thousand feet, the aviator began his efforts to make the Yankee shout. He gave them all the thrills that he could command. But the farmer and his wife remained silent. At last the aviator returned to the ground.

"Well," he said, stretching out his hand, "you've won, and the ride's yours, free of charge. I congratulate you on your pluck."

The New Englander smiled and replied, "Yep, I suppose I was brave—but I tell you, you almost caught me there once, when Ma fell out!"

BREVITY

THE LONG AND SHORT OF IT

FATHER: "I'm busy. Be short."
SON: "I will. I am."

No P.S.

A remarkable example of concise writing took place between two Quakers. An Edinburgh Quaker sent to a brother Quaker in London a letter containing nothing whatever except a question mark, thus— (?). His friend returned the sheet, adding as his sole reply a zero—(0). The meaning of the question and answer is as follows: "What news?" "Nothing."

BRIDE

SHE'LL LEARN

The old commercial traveler was relating his experiences to a young man. "And don't forget," he said, "never try to sell an encyclopedia to a bride."

"Why not?" asked the young man.

The older man smiled cynically. "She always thinks her husband knows everything."

BURGLARS

YOU FIRST

A man returning home in the small hours of the night found a burglar jimmying the lock on the front door. Thinking quickly, the man whispered to the prowler, "I'll open the door if you'll go in first."

BUS

TRUTH

RIDER: "How many does this bus carry comfortably?"

BUS DRIVER: "None!"

BUSINESS

VERY BUSY

An office manager was asking an applicant if she had any unusual talents. She said she had won several prizes in crossword-puzzle and slogan-writing contests.

"Sounds good," the manager told her, "but we want somebody who will be smart during office hours."

"Oh," said the girl, "that was during office hours."

No Profit Motive

It had taken the entire morning for Ezra to tow the tourists' car to town. When he finally returned home with his weary old mules his wife asked, "How much did you charge that city fellow for towin' him?"

"Fifty cents," Ezra answered. "Guess it wasn't too much. Leastwise, he didn't kick up no fuss."

"Fifty cents? Ezra, sometimes I wish you'd do the pullin' and let them mules handle the executive end of the deals."

Start Easy!

A movie producer was giving his script writers a pep talk. He wanted a super-colossal picture, one that would be sure to draw audiences. One of the men asked whether he had any suggestions.

"Sure! Start with an earthquake," he replied. "Then work up to a climax!"

Almost Perfect

NEW STENOGRAPHER (following dictation): "Mr. Jones, I got everything, except what you said between 'Dear Sir' and 'Sincerely yours.'"

BUSINESS

Don't Lose Your Head

It seemed as though there was no end to the money needed to carry on and develop the business. As our successes began to come, I seldom put my head upon the pillow at night without speaking a few words to myself in this wise:

"Now a little success, soon you will fall down, soon you will be overthrown. Because you have got a start, you think you are quite a merchant; look out, or you will lose your head—go steady." These intimate conversations with myself, I am sure, had a great influence on my life.

John D. Rockefeller

A "foreigner" with just an academic knowledge of the American business man's lingo would have a tough time. For the benefit of our foreign readership—and maybe for you, too—we publish this handy glossary:

A program—Any assignment that can't be completed by one telephone call.

To expedite—To confound confusion with commotion.

Channels—The trail left by interoffice memos.

Co-ordinator—The guy who has a desk between two expediters.

Consultant (or expert)—Any ordinary guy more than 50 miles from home.

To activate—To make carbons and add more names to the memo.

To implement a program—Hire more people and expand the office.

Under consideration—Never heard of it.

Under active consideration—We're looking in the files for it.

A conference—A place where conversation is substituted for the dreariness of labor and the loneliness of thought.

Reorientation—Getting used to working again.

Reliable source—The guy you just met.

Informed source—The guy who told the guy you just met.

Unimpeachable source—The guy who started the rumor originally.

A clarification—To fill the background with so many details that the foreground goes underground.

We are making a survey—We need more time to think of an answer.

Note and initial—Let's spread the responsibility for this.

See me, or let's discuss—Come down to my office. I'm lonesome.

Give us the benefit of your present thinking—We'll listen to what you have to say as long as it doesn't interfere with what we've already decided to do.

Will advise you in due course—If we figure it out, we'll let you know.

To give someone the picture—A long, confused, and inaccurate statement to a newcomer.

Steel, June 1951

Big Business

"Big" business: There are 240,000 manufacturing companies in the U. S. About one five-hundredth, or 504 to be exact, employ more than 2,500 men and women. So, there's one good-sized company for every 480 little ones.

The Employment Counselor
Employment Counselors Association
Columbus, Ohio, July 1951

Consider the Crab

Consider the crab. He can move backward or forward instantly with equal ease. That may be why he has survived for so many millions of years. To keep alive today, any business may have to move fast—just like the crab. But which way?

George F. Trundle, Jr., in "Trundle Talks" No. 141
Trundle Engineering Company

How About Duller?

TEACHER: "How many seasons are there?"
SAM: "Two. Busy and dull."

Nothing, Apparently

EMPLOYER (to office boy, who is half an hour late): "You should have been in here at nine o'clock."
OFFICE BOY: "Why, what happened?"

Piccolo Player and the Cook

An unknown author is responsible for the statement: "When I hear artists or authors making fun of businessmen I think of a regiment in which the band makes fun of the cooks."

Spiritual Life

Business underlies everything in our national life, including our spiritual life. Witness the fact that in the Lord's Prayer, the first petition is for daily bread. No one can worship God or love his neighbor on an empty stomach.

From a speech by Woodrow Wilson in New York, 1912

According to a study made by Notre Dame University, 73 per cent of all income on property—all income from stocks, bonds, and rent payments to individuals—goes to people making under $100 a week.

The Management Review, July 1951

MASS PRODUCTION

We all like the fruits of mass production—we get more and better products at lower cost than through any other method, and more and more people can enjoy the fruits of our productive system. However, mass production by its very nature requires huge formations of capital, large congregations of employees, and highly skilled management. This leads to social problems which tend to become political problems. So, we avidly grasp the good things that flow from the system then "cuss" the system for being so big and productive. We are the only people in the world whose major troubles arise from an inability to agree on the division of an adequate supply of the necessities and luxuries of life, and from an ineptness in the disposal of the surplus.

Everybody else, the world over, or practically so, has the problem in reverse—how to get enough to live on with perhaps just a litle sweetening in the way of luxuries.

From an address by Benjamin E. Young
General Vice President, National Bank of Detroit

BUSY

GOING PLACES

A very ordinary fellow got rich suddenly by striking oil, and got awfully swell-headed, always trying to impress others with his great importance.

One day he rushed into the railway station, laid one hundred dollars down at the ticket-seller's window, and said:

"Gimmie a ticket."

"Where to?" asked the ticket-agent.

"Anywhere. It doesn't make any difference. I got business all over."

CAMPING

WE WENT WITH HIM ONCE

"What sort of fellow is Jones to camp out with?"
"He's one of those fellows who always takes down a guitar about the time it's up to somebody to get busy with the frying pan."

CANDID

HEAR! HEAR!

"I rise for a point of information," said a member of the legislature.
"I am very glad to hear it," said a critic, "for no man needs it more."

CAPITALISM

MILLIONS OF CAPITALISTS

Who are capitalists? American Telephone and Telegraph Company? General Motors? United States Steel? Big Business? Yes! But also there are approximately 4,000,000 recorded corporations and partnerships, not to mention possibly 1,000,000 or more individuals operating their own small businesses. Add to this over 3,500,000 professional men, doctors, dentists, lawyers, etc., all businessmen, and 5,275,000 farm owners and operators, and this does not include tenant farmers operating their own businesses with the farm owner as a 50 per cent stockholder, of which there are at least 2,000,000 more. Then there are approximately 4,000,000 men, women, or children owning stock in the corporations whose stock is available to the public. . . . We estimate 20,000,000 families are full-fledged capitalists. By the same reasoning, many millions of working men who are not in the categories I have mentioned share in the profits of their employers, through bonus plans and profit-sharing trusts for employees; thus they, too, become capitalists. Yes, all are capitalists. Yet the adherents and fellow-travelers for some other type of government, whatever "ism" it be, refer to "Big Business" and "Wall Street" as capitalism.

George O. Brown, past President, Optimist International.

54

CARPENTER

AMATEUR

CARPENTER: "Say, you really hammer nails like lightning."
APPRENTICE (eagerly): "You mean I'm fast?"
CARPENTER: "I mean you rarely strike twice in the same place."

CAUTION

LOOKING AHEAD

"Say, jedge," an indignant gentleman declared, "Ah wants fo' to git a conjunction out again mah wife. She don th'owed me clean out o'mah secon'-story winder, right on a pile ob bricks."

"But you don't seem to be any worse for the fall, Amos," replied the judge. "Not hurt any, are you?"

"No, suh, Ah ain't hurt," was the reply, "but 'sposin' she does it agin, an' dem bricks ain't dere?"

HE EATS MEAT TOO

An extra employed at one of the movie studios in Los Angeles was asked by a director to do a comedy scene with a lion.

"You get in this bed," said the director, "and we'll bring the lion in and put him in bed with you. It will be a scream."

"Put a lion in bed with me!" yelled the extra. "No, sah! Not a-tall. I quits right here and now."

"But," protested the director, "this lion won't hurt you. This lion was brought up on milk."

"So was I brung up on milk," wailed the extra, "but I eats meat now."

CHANGE

WANTED: A CHANGE

A waiter asked the customer, "Will you have your cup filled again with tea or coffee?"

The customer replied, "If what I had last was coffee, I want tea; and if tea, I want coffee. At any rate I want a change."

CHARACTER

HUMAN LOSS

An inscription over an old German schoolhouse reads:

If you have lost wealth, you have lost nothing.
If you have lost health, you have lost something.
If you have lost character, you have lost all.

GREATNESS

When Washington agreed to act as commander-in-chief, some felt that the strength of the American forces had been more than doubled. Years later, in 1798, when Washington had withdrawn from public life and was living in retirement at Mount Vernon, and when it seemed that France might declare war against the United States, President Adams wrote to him, saying, "We must have your name, if you will permit us to use it; there will be more efficacy in it than in many an army."

INDIVIDUALS COUNT

When someone says, "But what can a mere individual do now?" I answer: Look at what mere individuals *are* doing now. Who supports the gambling rackets that take billions every year from the pockets of the people and shamefully debauch our local government? Individuals.

Who elect our public officials? Inidividuals.

Who encourage the glamorizing of sexual license in public entertainers? Individuals.

Who stand aside and let rotten conditions in our slums beget the tragic shame of dope peddling? Individuals.

Who tempt the tax-gatherers to the shameful betrayal of their trust? Individuals.

Who accept government largesse which dishonest officials sell? Individuals.

Believe me, in our present situation, personal character counts. As another put it, "No rearrangement of bad eggs can make a good omelet."

From an address by Dr. Harry Emerson Fosdick

Education preserves the American heritage through the development of character. Character to some extent is a little different from education. In education you always take what is best in a pupil. For example, education would never take hold of me and teach me to be a singer. When I first instructed Grace Moore, she said after the first ten minutes, "You have a wonderful voice." I said, "If I do have a wonderful voice, why can't I sing?"

She said, "Have you ever tried?" (What priest hasn't?) "What is your favorite duet?"

I said, *"Anges Pures* from *Faust."*

She said, "Let's sing it."

Well, we sang it. It goes up about eight octaves each verse. She finally stopped and said, "You are right. You can't sing."

From a speech by the Rt. Rev. Monsignor Fulton J. Sheen

CHARITY

Giving

We all know about the Negro preacher who said that "It takes three books to run a church—a hymn book, a prayer book, and a pocket book." However, the latter "book," so many feel, is just a man-added nuisance. Is it?

No, the giving of money is not a man-made rule at all. It is born in the heart of our God. And if I know that I have been forgiven much, how can I give except in the measure of "much"? I say that I "love" God. Love is giving. God also "loved," and He gave that of which He only had one—His only begotten son. Christ "loved me and gave Himself for me." When we say we love God, then it ought to be more than just lip service. Love dare not stop at the edge of the pocket. It must open the pocket book, and let the surrendered heart dictate the terms of giving. Our Lord said: "Give."

Dr. R. R. Belter, President, The Wartburg Synod
United Lutheran Church in America

CHEMISTRY

No Chance

"Suppose," said the chemistry professor, "that you were summoned to the side of a patient who had accidentally swallowed oxalic acid. What would you administer?"

The student, studying for the ministry, took chemistry because it was obligatory in the course. He replied, "I would administer the sacrament."

CHILDREN

His Fault

"Jimmy, how dare you kick your little brother in the stomach!"
"It was his own fault, Mother. He turned around."

He Has Problems

The car was crowded and the conductor was irritable. "Where is the fare for the boy?" he snapped, as the father handed him one fare.
"The boy is only three years old."
"Three years! Why, look at him. He's seven if he's a day."
The father leaned over and gazed at the boy's face, then turned to the conductor and said, "Can I help it if he worries?"

Will Please Everyone

Visitor: "Well, Billy, what are you going to be when you grow up?"
Billy: "Well after I've been a lawyer a while to please Daddy, and President for a while to please Mama, I'm going to be an aviator to please myself."

Expecting Too Much

Mother: "Johnny, did you fall down in your good pants?"
Johnny: "Yes, ma'am. I didn't have time to take them off."

It Won't Be Long

Jerry, six years of age, was getting ready for the first day of school. He wasn't very anxious to start and his mother's tear-filled eyes only added to his reluctance. As they drove toward the school and his mother's tears continued to flow, he said consolingly, "Aw, Mom, don't take it so hard. Just as soon as I learn to read comics I'll quit."

No Fair Comparison

Two small boys at a dinner put their dirty hands up on the table-cloth for inspection. "Mine's dirtier'n your'n," one exclaimed triumphantly.

"Yeh, but you're two years older'n me," said the other disdainfully.

Looking Ahead

The children had all been photographed and the teacher was trying to persuade them each to buy a copy of the group picture. "Just think how nice it will be to look at it when you are all grown up and say, 'There's Rose; she's married,' or 'That's Billy; he's a banker.'"

A small voice at the back of the room piped up, "And there's teacher; she's dead."

His Fault

Little Sue ran into the house crying as though her heart would break.
"What's wrong, dear?" asked her mother.
"My dolly—Billy broke it," she sobbed.
"How did he break it, dear?" asked mother.
"I hit him on the head with it!"

Air Minded

"I am Red Eagle," said the Indian chieftain to his paleface visitor. "This is my son, Big Bird. And here," he added, "is my grandson, DC-6."

He Learned 'Em

MOTHER: "What did Mama's little baby learn at school today?"
SONNY: "I learned two fellows not to call me 'mama's little baby.'"

Experienced

COUNSEL (to woman witness): "I hope I haven't bothered you with all these questions."
WITNESS: "Not at all, sir, I have a small boy aged ten at home."

Full-grown

Army paratroopers were practicing their jumps in a backwoods region. A parachutist started to come down on a field near the home of an old mountaineer and fifteen children. One of the youngsters saw the parachute floating down with a man attached to it, and he ran into the house yelling, "Bring your shotgun, Pappy—the stork is bringin' 'em full-grown now!"

Power and Influence of the Child

Shortly after the victory of the Athenians over the Persian fleet at Salamis in 480 B.C., Themistocles, the great admiral, was met on the street by a fellow citizen who hailed the victory and called the hero the most powerful person in the world.

"You are wrong," said Themistocles, "my little son here is the most powerful."

Puzzled, the man asked, "How so?"

"Well," said the admiral, "'tis thus: the Athenians rule the world, I rule the Athenians, my wife rules me, and this little boy rules his mother."

Dr. George P. Rice, Jr., Chairman
Department of Speech and Drama
Butler University, Indianapolis

Dried Off Wet

FATHER: "What on earth are you doing?"

HERBIE (in bathtub): "I dropped the towel in the tub, and I've dried myself wetter than ever."

It's a Small World

"Dad, where were you born?"

"Chicago, dear."

"Where was Mommy born?"

"Dallas."

"And where was I born?"

"Philadelphia."

"Certainly is funny how we three people got together, isn't it?"

CHRISTMAS

He Remembered Him

Little six-year-old Jimmie was asked by his Sunday-school teacher: "And Jimmie, what are you going to give your little brother for Christmas this year?"

"I dunno," said Jimmie, "I gave him the measles last year."

How Many Candles

A three-year-old youngster was told that Christmas was Jesus' birthday.

"How many candles does He have on His cake?" he asked.

CHURCH

Seeking God First

When the *Mayflower* cast anchor in Plymouth Harbor, with its weary load of storm-tossed human beings who, after years of exile in Holland, had suffered for weeks in their tiny bark on the stormy Atlantic, how eagerly they must have looked at the solid ground, their new home. It was Saturday afternoon, but in spite of their hunger they remained on board, continuing their preparation for observing the Sabbath day. For forty-two hours, Saturday afternoon and evening and all day Sunday, they remained on board worshipping God and remembering to keep the Sabbath day holy. Not until Monday morning did they set foot on land. They were in dead earnest in seeking the Kingdom of God first.

The way to make a beginning toward restoring our country to a sound basis is to dust off our Bibles and read them, to get down on our knees and ask God to forgive us for our neglect, indifference, and sinfulness, and get back into our churches—worshipping God, singing the great hymns, and listening to the voices of our ministers.

William Penn truly said, "If we will not be governed by God, we must be governed by tyrants."

Such are the ideological conflicts we are facing. Some are

new, some are very old. Let us face them with high courage and dedication and with renewed determination to find the truth and make it known

From an address by Howard E. Kershner
President of Christian Freedom Foundation, Inc.

OPPORTUNITY

Perhaps we are too much like the prominent businessman who only went to church occasionally. One beautiful Easter morning he and the family decided to go to church. I suppose the fact that his wife and daughters had some new hats may have had something to do with that decision. I don't know. But in any event they decided to go to church, and like people who don't go regularly they had sort of forgotten just what time church started. The result was they got there a little late, and they had to take seats right down in the front pew. As the minister came out in the pulpit he looked down, and there in the front pew, as big as life, was this distinguished business-man, and the minister's heart swelled with pride to see him there. And then he looked out over the fine audience that had turned out this beautiful Easter morning and his heart swelled with pride again at the splendid turnout. Finally it came time for him to make his announcements and he said, "I want all you folks to know how much I appreciate this excellent turnout on this beautiful Easter morning. And I want you to know that I observe some people here whom I have not seen recently, and lest the opportunity does not present itself again soon, may I take this occasion to wish them a Merry Christmas and a Happy New Year."

From an address by Bruce F. Gates
President, Gates College, Waterloo, Iowa

CHURCHES AND MEN ON FIRE

Our Western liberties had their historic source in profound conviction about God and about man as the child of God, and so from the essential human values and dignities, from major elements in the Jewish-Christian faith concerning God and man, backed by the insights of the great seers, our democracy came.

And we have been drifting into neglect of these deep origins. That is what the professor of physics meant when he

said, "We can have no moral revival without a living relig.
I wish our churches would wake up to this, and I wish th.
you would help them.

In one of our communities the church building burned down,
and two neighbors found themselves standing side by side,
watching the blaze. One said to the other, "This is the first
time I ever saw you in church." To which the other retorted,
"This is the first time I ever saw the church on fire."

Well, the churches had better be on fire.

From an address by Dr. Harry Emerson Fosdick

CIRCUMSTANCES

Creating Favorable Circumstances

Johann Goethe: "He who has a firm will molds the world to
himself."

Victor Hugo: "People do not lack strength, they lack will."

Benjamin Disraeli: "Man is not the creature of circumstances. Circumstances are the creatures of men."

William Shakespeare: "Men at some time are masters of their fates:
The fault, dear Brutus, is not in our stars,
But in ourselves, that we are underlings."

CIRCUS

Excitement

Willie to the circus went,
He thought it was immense;
His little heart went pitter-pat,
For the excitement was in tents.
Harvard Lampoon

Helping Dad

"Well, little boy, did you go to the circus the other day?"
"Yes'm. Dad wanted to go, so I had to go with him."

CITY LIFE

CALL THE FIRE DEPARTMENT

After fifty years in a country village a couple sold their farm and went to live in a large city where they could enjoy more conveniences. On their first morning the wife arose before sunrise as usual and said: "Isn't it about time you were getting up and lighting the fire?"

"No," yawned the old man. "I'll call the fire department. We might as well get used to these city conveniences right away."

CIVILIZATION

CIVILIZATION ON A TIGHTROPE

On August 19, 1859, Charles Blondin walked a tightrope over Niagara Falls. On his back he carried another man. When Blondin was half-way across, the tightrope slackened and began to wobble. Blondin instantly surmised the reason. Heavy bets had been wagered that the daredevil would tumble from the high, suspended rope. When his success seemed assured, the gamblers were panic-stricken.

There he was on a sagging rope. Below were the raging, churning falls of Niagara. And on his back was another human being. The tightrope began to sway. What could he do? Blondin did two things. Though ordinarily not a praying man, he prayed, and he prayed hard and fast. And then he went into double-quick action, figuring the faster he moved, the better his chances. Spectators later declared that at the end of that "walk," Blondin was actually running. The parable is obvious: Civilization's on a tight rope, and we are the riders. Below, waiting a misstep, is catastrophe's yawning chasm. "We are wandering between two worlds," said Matthew Arnold. "One is dead. The other is waiting to be born."

Through World War I and again in World War II we dreamed of a bright, new, shiny world, of Brotherhood, Peace. "One World," we called it. The millennium did not come. It seems to have completely eluded us. Between the "world that is" and the "world that might be" civilization today is putting on a "ropewalking act." Will it make the trip safely? The answer depends upon *you* and *me,* and what we do to help, now. Only five of the twenty-one major civilizations on earth have made the grade, says Toynbee, the historian.

All the others have gone down to oblivion. And of the five surviving, declares Toynbee, only our western civilization is vitally alive.

Dr. Eva Anderson
Chelan County Member of Washington State Legislature

The Fall of Nations

Toynbee, in his great history, tells us that since the birth of Christ, we have had twenty-one major civilizations and almost every one is dead. That's right. Up and down in order: the Near East, Greece, Rome, Northern Europe, Britain. When I was in high school and college, "Britain ruled the world." How I envied London. You had to have her support . . . for political or economic or military power or opportunity. And in my lifetime, I have seen that great nation topple and become dependent on America. And now the torch of civilization has been passed to America. . . . A people like we are, made of all peoples of the earth, the richest in the world, motivated by a great spiritual ideal, must lead now or go the way all others have gone.

From an address by U. G. Dubach
Head, Political Science Department
Lewis and Clark College, Portland, Oregon

CLOCKS

Fooled the Clock

PAT (in bed, to alarm clock as it goes off): "I fooled yez that time. I was not aslape at all."

Just Like That

The farmer gave the new man an alarm clock and told him that he was expected to get up at four o'clock each morning. The first morning the alarm failed to ring, and the new man was an hour late.

"Why didn't you get up at four o'clock?" the farmer asked him.

"The alarm didn't ring," the new man replied.

"I meant to tell you about that," said the farmer. "Sometimes it gets stuck, and won't ring. You've got to shake it a bit, and she'll ring all right. Now if she don't ring by five past four tomorrow mornin', give her a shake."

65

CLOTHES

PARTICULAR

MR.: "You must be careful about packing away your winter clothes. The moths might get into them."

MRS.: "Oh, don't worry about the moths. They're not going to bother with my seal when they can get Persian lamb at the Browns' next door."

SAY THAT AGAIN, PLEASE

"The evening wore on," continued the man who was telling the story.

"Excuse me," interrupted the wit, "but can you tell us what the evening wore on that occasion?"

"I don't know that it is important," replied the storyteller. "But if you must know, it was the close of a summer day."

DOUBTLESS SOMETHING WE ATE

Men's clothing look so spick-and-span
On haberdasher's dummy—
I wonder why the suits I buy
So seldom fit my tummy?
William A. Philpott, Jr.

COFFEE

WITH OR WITHOUT CREAM?

"What do you call this, tea or coffee?" demanded the angry customer. "It tastes more like castor oil."

"If it tastes like castor oil," said the waiter, "I can guarantee it's coffee, because our tea tastes like dishwater."

66

LUCKY

SOPHOMORE: "Dad, you're a lucky man."

FATHER: "How is that?"

SOPHOMORE: "You won't have to buy new books for me next semester. I am taking last year's work over again."

TAKING A CHANCE

FRESHMAN: "What'll we do tonight?"

SOPHOMORE: "We'll toss a coin. If it's heads we'll get dates; if it's tails, we'll go to the movies alone; if it stands on edge, we'll study."

A FRESHMAN KNOWS THE ANSWERS

"Can't I take your order for one of our encyclopedias?" asked the salesman.

"No," said the busy man. "I might be able to use it a few times, but my son will be home from college in June."

O.K., YALE, TELL IT YOUR WAY

Three young men from Yale, Princeton, and Harvard were in a room when a lady entered. The Yale boy asked casually if someone ought not to give a chair to the lady; the Princeton lad slowly brought one; and the Harvard boy deliberately sat down in it.

NO ADMITTANCE

The Freshman dean had dark circles under his eyes. His face was pallid, he wore a hunted expression.

"You look ill," said his wife. "What is wrong, dear?"

"Nothing much," he replied. "But—I— had a fearful dream last night."

"What was the dream?" asked his wife.

"I dreamed the trustees required that—that I should—that I should pass the freshman examination for—admission!" sighed the dean.

HE'LL HAVE TO WORK TWICE AS HARD

"You know," said the high school graduate, "I have half a mind to go to college."

"Well," his teacher decided, "that's as good as most."

TUT-TUT

"You know, professor, the word 'reviver' is spelled the same way backward and forward. Can you tell me another?"

"Tut-tut!" said the professor. "Why does the student mind waste time on such easy questions?"

DON'T FOOL WITH THE PROFESSOR

The professor put the following notice on the bulletin board:

PROFESSOR JONES WILL NOT MEET HIS CLASSES TOMORROW.

A student came along, and rubbed out the letter *c* from the word "classes."

The professor noticed what had been done to his announcement, and promptly rubbed out the initial letter of "lasses."

THIS DEFINITION WILL STICK

TEACHER: "Use the word 'coercion' in a sentence."

STUDENT: "Some things like waffles and syrup have a wonderful coercion."

HARD WORK

PARENT: "Are you working hard on your history course?"

COLLEGE SON: "Yes, I am constantly on the verge of mental exertion."

HIGHER MATHEMATICS

MATHEMATICS TEACHER: "What is a circle?"

STUDENT: "A circle is a straight curved line running around a dot."

68

COMPASSION

A few weeks before the Continent was plunged into the bloody bath of World War II, it was my privilege to stand before the magnificent cathedral of St. Paul's in London, the masterpiece of the great architect, Sir Christopher Wren. I cannot describe the feeling of awe and reverence that stirred my soul as I passed through the portals of that great Protestant cathedral of worship. Scarcely had I entered when my attention was call to Holman Hunt's original painting, "The Light of the World." It was not the cost of the canvas, or the dobs of paint upon it that challenged my attention. Oh no, it seemed that the soul and genius of the artist had combined to portray in far more eloquent language than I could utter, the tender compassion of a seeking Saviour. The vision enthralled me. I slipped into the shadows to watch the varied crowd pass by.

At first it was an old white-haired man that caught my attention; then a middle-aged woman; and last, an inspiring youth. They paused before the mellow light thrown on the painting, drew closer in rapt attention, then quietly moved on. Not infrequently did I see a hand lift to wipe a falling tear or lips move as if in silent prayer. It was a sight I shall never forget. *Jesus, the Light of the World,* standing there, was moving the hearts of men.

Then I remembered! This Man of Galilee went about doing good. He was unjustly brought to trial; He was scourged and beaten—spat upon. Pricking thorns were pressed hard upon His brow. A purple robe in mock derision was given Him. Then up that lonely ascending trail He bore His own cross. The dull thud of pounding nails against human flesh was heard. The uplifted cross with the Christ upon it was dropped in its prepared socket. Softly the thief, the only fit being to associate with the King, so His enemies thought, cried out, "Remember me." And when the man on the middle cross said, "It is finished," He remembered not only the thief, but all men everywhere gone astray. He remembered you and me.

From an address by Dr. S. T. Ludwig
Executive Secretary, Department of Education
Church of the Nazarene, Kansas City, Missouri

69

COMMUTERS

WE COULD USE THAT BRAND

"I see you are carrying home a new kind of breakfast food," said the first commuter.

"Yes," said the second commuter, "I was missing too many trains. The old brand took three seconds to prepare. You can fix this new brand in a second and a half."

COMPETITION

NO SUBSTITUTE FOR COMPETITION

There is no substitute in my opinion for competition. We all need the spur of competition. Sometimes it hurts but it is the only road to security for the nation and for the people. Competition in a world of freedom and opportunity has put the tremendous driving power into our national economy and made us strong. It is the force which has made our country today the hope of the world.

Henry Ford II

COMPLAIN

RELATIVES

There was a dead mule in front of the minister's house for two days. He called up the local board of health to complain. "This is Reverend Jones. There's a dead mule in front of my house."

The man in the board of health office thought he would be smart. "I thought you ministers took care of the dead?"

"We do," said Reverend Jones. "But first we get in touch with their relatives."

SHE DIDN'T TREAT HIM RIGHT

"Jedge, yo'honah," complained an irate lady to the court, "dis yeah no 'count husban' o' mine drinks."

"Yessuh, jedge, you' honah, Ah does drink some," admitted the husband. "But, jedge, dat woman don' treat me right. Why, Ah pawns de kitchen stove t' git a li'l money an' she don' miss it fo' two weeks."

70

COMPLIMENTS

THAT WILL HOLD THEM

"I always make it a rule," said the preacher at the close of the sermon during which there had been some misbehavior in the audience, "to thank my audience for their attention; and I now thank you for your attention. It is true," he added, "there has been some disturbance, nevertheless I will thank you for behaving as well as you knew how."

CONCEIT

COULDN'T REACH IT

A pompous person was staying at a small country hotel. As he entered the breakfast-room in the morning, the only other visitor rose from his seat.

"Sit down, sit down!" boomed the great man condescendingly.

"Why?" asked the other, surprised. "Can't I get the marmalade from the next table?"

NEVER MISSED

A conceited young man asked a friend what apology he should make for not having attended a party the day before to which he had been invited. "Oh, my dear sir," replied the friend, "say nothing about it; you were not missed."

OBSERVATIONS ON CONCEIT

Benjamin Whichcote, in 1753, said, "Take away the self-conceited, and there will be elbow room in the world"; and George Eliot (real name, Mary Ann Evans), English novelist, 1819-1880, commented, "I've never any pity for conceited people, because I think they carry their comfort about with them."

71

They Won't Try That Again

Three conceited young men who were walking along an old road near Oxford, England, met an old gentleman.

"Good morrow, father Abraham," said one.

"Good morrow, father Isaac," said the next.

"Good morrow, father Jacob," cried the last.

"I am neither Abraham, Isaac, nor Jacob," replied the old gentleman, "but Saul, who went out to seek his father's asses, and lo! here I have found them."

CONCLUSION

School Is Out

The university president was delivering the commencement address. In the audience were an elderly couple, obviously foreigners, who were having some trouble understanding the address to the class, of which their daughter was a member.

"What did he say?" finally demanded the mother, frowning.

"Who?" asked the father.

"The beega fella in black robes. What did he say?"

"He say school is out."

CONFIDENCE

He Will Try Anything

The smiling, confident young man entered a large bank. He stepped up to the manager's desk and began. "Good day, sir. Has your bank any need of a highly intelligent, college-trained man?"

The manager poised over a form. "Your name?"

"Harold Jones."

"Experience?"

"Just out of college."

"And what kind of a position are you seeking?"

"Well," mused the young man, "I want something in the executive line, such as a vice-presidency, for example."

The manager put down his pencil. "I'm really very sorry," he said, "but we already have twelve vice-presidents."

The young man waved a hand, then said happily, "Oh, that's all right; I'm not superstitious!"

CONGRESS

SEMANTICS

One congressman called another a jackass. The expression was unparliamentary, and in retraction he said: "While I withdraw the unfortunate word, Mr. Speaker, I must insist that the gentleman is out of order."

"How am I out of order?" yelled the other.

"Probably a veterinary surgeon could tell you," answered the first congressman, and that was parliamentary enough to stay on the record.

CONSCIENCE

REFLECTIONS ON CONSCIENCE

NIETZSCHE: "One may so train one's conscience that it kisses one when it bites."

SCHILLER: "The worm of conscience keeps the same hours as the owl."

COLERIDGE: "Conscience is but the pulse of reason."

BROWNE: "There is another man within me that's angry with me."

CONSERVATIVE

CROSBY ON THE RADIO

BING CROSBY: "Television is really here to stay. My brother Everett bought a set last week."

KEN CARPENTER: "Is that a sure sign?"

CROSBY: "Infallible. Everett didn't buy a shoehorn until 1948."

CARPENTER: "He waited to see if shoehorns were really going to stay?"

CROSBY "He wanted to make sure that shoes were going to stay."

What Is a Conservative?

Franklin D. Roosevelt: "A Conservative is a man with two perfectly good legs who, however, has never learned to walk."

Ambrose Bierce: "A statesman who is enamored of existing evils, as distinguished from the Liberal, who wishes to replace them with others."

CONTEMPT

Hard to Conceal

One day when Thaddeus Stevens was practicing in the courts, he didn't like the ruling of the presiding judge. The third time the judge ruled against Stevens, the old man got up with scarlet face and quivering lips and commenced tying up his papers as if to quit the courtroom.

"Do I understand, Mr. Stevens," asked the judge, eying him, "that you wish to show your contempt for this court?"

"No, sir; no, sir," replied Stevens, "I don't want to show my contempt; I'm trying to conceal it."

CONTRIBUTIONS

They Came

"I advertised that the poor were welcome in this church," said the preacher to his congregation, "and as the offertory amounts to two dollars, I see that they have come."

The Face Is Familiar

Mr. Jones stared in a puzzled way at Mr. Clark, to whom he had just been introduced. "You look like a man I've seen somewhere, Mr. Clark," he said. "Your face seems familiar. I fancy you have a double. A funny thing about it is that I remember I formed a strong prejudice against the man who looks like you—but I'm quite sure, we never met."

Mr. Clark laughed. "I'm the man," he answered, "and I know why you formed the prejudice. I passed the contribution plate for two years in the church you attended."

CONVENIENT

ONE ADVANTAGE

Irvin Cobb used to tell of walking along a road in Georgia one day after a hard rainstorm when he came upon Henry sitting in an easy chair by his kitchen door, fishing in a puddle of water.

"Henry, you old fool," said Cobb, "what are you doing there?"

"Boss," said Henry, "I'se jes' fishin' a little."

"Well, don't you know there are no fish there?" demanded Cobb.

"Yes, suh," said Henry, "I knows dat, but dis yere place is so handy!"

CONVENTIONS

THEY LOVE A CROWD

There are those who are naturally gregarious and who take a peculiar delight in belonging to something. Americans are the greatest "joiners" in the world, and, as Will Rogers once said, "When Gabriel blows his horn, half of the American people will be at a convention and the other half will be packing their bags in preparation for one."

Dr. Edward Hughes Pruden, Minister
First Baptist Church, Washington, D. C.

CONVERSATION

LEARNING FROM OTHERS

John Locke, English philosopher, was asked how he had accumulated a mine of knowledge so rich. He replied that he attributed what little he knew to not having been ashamed to ask for information, and to the rule he had laid down of conversing with all descriptions of men on those topics chiefly that formed their own peculiar professions or pursuits.

Sir Walter Scott said that he never met with any man, let his calling be what it might, even the most stupid fellow that ever rubbed down a horse, from whom he could not, by a few moments' conversation, learn something which he did not know before, and which was valuable to him. He seemed to have knowledge of everything.

Conversation of the Great

In conversation, the sublime Dante was taciturn or satirical. Butler was sullen or biting. Thomas Gray seldom talked or smiled. Milton was unsociable, and even irritable when much pressed by the talk of others. Vergil was heavy in conversation, and resembled more an ordinary man than an enchanting poet. La Bruyère, French author, appeared coarse, heavy, and stupid; he could not speak or describe what he had just seen; but when he wrote, he was the model of poetry. John Dryden, English poet, said of himself, "My conversation is slow and dull, my humor saturnine and reserved. In short, I am none of those who endeavor to break jests in company, or make repartee." Descartes, French philosopher, whose habits were formed in solitude and meditation, was silent in mixed company. James Smith, English humorist, said, "I don't fancy painters. I know nothing about which they talk, and they know nothing else."

Sounds Like a Bridge Party

> *"The time has come," the Walrus said,*
> *"To talk of many things:*
> *Of shoes—and ships—and sealing wax—*
> *Of cabbages—and kings—*
> *And why the sea is boiling hot—*
> *And whether pigs have wings."*

From Through the Looking-Glass
by C. L. Dodgson (Lewis Carroll)

Flashes of Silence

Sidney Smith said of Macaulay, "He once talked too much; but now he has occasional flashes of silence that make his conversation perfectly delightful."

Quiet Please!

"How do you like your hair cut?" asked the barber, who was anxious to please.

"Off," replied the customer, who was a man of few words.

He Knew

The talkative lady was telling her husband about the bad manners of a recent visitor. "If that woman yawned once while I was talking to her," she said, "she yawned ten times."

"Perhaps she wasn't yawning, dear," the husband said. "Maybe she wanted to say something."

COOKING

Burns on Gracie's Cooking

GEORGE BURNS: "Whenever we have a roast, Gracie always buys two —a big one and a little one. She puts them both in the oven, and when the little roast starts burning, the smoke reminds her that the big one is done."

Let Them Worry

"Harry," whispered his wife, poking her sleeping husband. "Wake up. There are burglars in the kitchen and they're eating my mince pies."

"Well, what do we care," mumbled Harry, rolling over, "so long as they don't die in the house?"

Can't Live Without 'Em

We may live without poetry, music and art;
We may live without conscience, and live without heart;
We may live without friends, we may live without books;
But civilized man cannot live without cooks.

E. R. Bulwer-Lytton

Some Views on Cooks

An old English proverb says that "It's a bad cook who can't lick his own fingers."

Seneca said, about 63 B.C., "It is no wonder that diseases are innumerable: count the cooks."

Nietzsche, the cynical philosopher, believed that "Woman does not understand what food means, and yet she insists upon being a cook!"

Some evidence of mistrust is evident in the Polish proverb, "When a cook cooks a fly, he keeps the best wing for himself."

Correct

KINDERGARTEN TEACHER: "Johnnie, what do zebras have that no other animals have?"

JOHNNIE: "Little zebras."

That Ends It

DOTTIE: "Mother, you know that vase you said had been handed down from generation to generation?"

MOTHER: "Yes, dear."

DOTTIE: "Well, this generation has just dropped it."

COURAGE

Better Example

He was the young son of a bishop, and his mother was teaching him the meaning of courage.

"Suppose," she said, "there were ten boys in one bedroom, and nine got into bed at once, while the other knelt down to say his prayers. That boy would show true courage."

"Oh!" said the youngster. "I know something even more courageous! Supposing there were ten bishops in one bedroom, and one got into bed without saying his prayers!"

Let Him at Least Bark

Dr. Samuel Johnson, English poet and man of letters, hated to hear others complain. He once said, "I hate a fellow whom pride, or cowardice, or laziness drives into a corner, and does nothing, when he is there, but sit and *growl;* let him come out as I do, and *bark.*"

Not How Many

The Spartans did not inquire how many the enemy are, but where are they.

Agis II

Only a Few More

We all know that the Greeks put Socrates to death, but most people don't know how it was done. On the jury that condemned Socrates were 500 men; 280 of them voted for death, 220 voted for acquittal. If only a few individuals more had had insight, courage enough to see and stand their ground, what a crime might have been avoided! Now, that is a parable of all history, and every last man-jack of us is on the jury.

From an address by Dr. Harry Emerson Fosdick

COURTESY

Ouch!

The butcher was waiting on a customer when a woman rushed in and said, "Give me a pound of cat food, quick!"

Turning to the other customer, she said, "I hope you don't mind my getting waited on before you."

"Not if you're that hungry," the other woman replied.

Means Nothing

The District Attorney was questioning a Kentucky colonel. Unable to shake his testimony, he tried sarcasm. "They call you colonel," he sneered. "In what regiment are you a colonel?"

"Well," drawled the colonel, "it's like this. The 'Colonel' in front of my name is like the 'Honorable' in front of yours. It doesn't mean a thing."

Ordinary Courtesy

A young lady refused to hang any mistletoe at Christmas, and when asked why, she said, "I've got too much pride to advertise for the ordinary courtesies a lady has a perfect right to expect."

OH, YEH?

His car and her car met head-on. The drivers got out and, with the fine courtesy so characteristic of motorists nowadays, both began to apologize profusely. "I'm so sorry," said the woman. "It was all my fault."

"Not at all, madam," the man responded with a gallant gesture. "I was to blame myself."

"But I insist the fault was mine. I was on your side of the road."

"That may be true; but, my dear madam, I am responsible for the collision. I saw you coming blocks away, and I had ample opportunity to dart down a side street."

COW

WHAT IS A COW?

A cow is an angular feminine bovine with four legs, an alto voice, a well-established milk route, and a face that inspires confidence.

A cow's husband is a bull. A cow's brat is known as a calf. Calves are generally used in the manufacture of chicken salad. Calves' brains can't be distinguished from scrambled eggs. When part of a calf gets breaded, it is called a "cutlet."

A cow has four stomachs. The one on the ground floor is used as a storehouse for grass, loco weed, corn stalks, rock salt, and the neighbor's cabbage. When her storehouse reaches a state of either over-production or under-consumption, she reclines in the shade of a tree and then belches like Henry VIII at a coronation banquet. This social error on the part of the cow makes some of the hay and stuff do a return trip from the storehouse, back up to the region of the cow's kind face, where it is "fletcherized." This is quite a chore, because a cow has no upper front teeth. They are all in the lower part of her countenance.

After this second-hand meal has been sufficiently gummed up, she sends it on to another stomach, from whence it goes along the milk route or is turned into cow meat.

An old cow has a tough time of it. In the end she gets skinned by those she has benefited, even as you and I.

A slice of the cow's rear end is very valuable to a cow, but it is worth only a dime to a farmer, 16 cents to a meat packer, 46 cents to a retail butcher, and $1.75 in a restaurant, not counting the tips.

—Oregon Cattleman

CREDIT

PLEASE STAND STILL

An aggressive firm advertised: "All persons indebted to our store are requested to call and settle. Those indebted to our store and not knowing it will please call and find out. Those knowing themselves indebted and not wishing to call, are requested to stay in one place long enough for us to catch them."

CRITIC

OTHERWISE SHE WAS O.K.

She had the appearance of a sergeant-major in the guards, and her voice did nothing to dispel that illusion. Her adoption of the concert platform must have been a distinct loss to the coal trade. As to her execution, it was a pity there was no way of bringing it about. The whole thing was stunning. Her low notes were like the rumbling of Vesuvius when about to erupt, and her high notes the shrieks of a wild motor bus calling to its mate.

Anonymous

THEY CAN REVIEW

Nature fits all her children with something to do:
He who would write and can't write can surely review.
J. R. Lowell, 1848

CRITICISM

A LONG TIME

Perhaps one of the most severe criticisms ever uttered was made by Professor Richard Porson, English classical scholar (1759-1808), a short time before his death, to a conceited author. Porson said, "I will tell you, sir, what I think of your poetical works: they will be read when Shakespeare's and Milton's are forgotten—but not till then!"

How Would You Describe Criticism?

Criticism is a study by which men grow important and formidable at very small expense.

Samuel Johnson, 1759

The most agreeable of all amusements.

H. H. Kermes, 1762

Criticism strips the tree of both caterpillars and blossoms.

Jean Paul Richter, 1803

It is much easier to be critical than to be correct.

Benjamin Disraeli, 1860

Advice to an Author

An acquaintance of Sir Thomas More, English statesman and author, having taken great pains in writing a book, which he intended to publish, brought it to Sir Thomas for his opinion. Sir Thomas, finding it a foolish, trifling performance, told the writer, with a grave face, that it would be worth more if it were in verse. The man, upon this, took it home and set about turning it into verse. When he had finished it, he carried it again to Sir Thomas, who, having looked it over, said to him, "It is now something; it is now rhyme, but before it was neither rhyme nor reason."

CURIOUS

In the Front Pew

A preacher noticed a lone man sitting in the front pew of his church. It was so unusual that he called the man aside as he left the church, telling him he was curious to know why he sat in the front pew. "Well," said the man, "it's like this. I'm a bus driver, and I just wanted to find out what your secret was in getting folks to move to the back."

Harry D. Harrison
past President of the Nelson Board of Trade
Nelson, B.C., Canada

DAMAGES

BEST HE COULD DO

Ole Swanson's cow was killed by a railroad train. The claim agent for the railroad telephoned and said, "We understand that the deceased was a docile and valuable animal, and we sympathize with you and your family in your loss. But, Mr. Swanson, you must remember that your cow had no business on our tracks. The tracks are private property, and she was a trespasser. Technically speaking, you, as her owner, became a trespasser also. But we have no wish to carry the matter into court and give you trouble. Now then, what would you regard as a fair settlement between you and the railroad company?"

"Vall," said Swanson, "Ay bane poor farmer. Would you be satisfied if I give you two dollars?"

HARD CHOICE

"I educated one of my boys to be a doctor and the other to be a lawyer," said the father.

"You should be very proud of them," replied his friend. "That seems like an excellent arrangement."

"I don't know about that," replied the father. "It looks as if it is going to break up the family. I got run into by a locomotive, and the doctor wants to cure me, and the lawyer wants me to go lame so he can sue for damages."

DEATH

BAD ACCIDENT

Two men were traveling on a motorcycle on a winter day. One of them put his overcoat on backwards, to keep the wind from the opening. A few miles farther on, the motorcycle hit a tree, killing the driver and stunning the man with the reversed overcoat. When the coroner visited the scene, he found a rookie policeman standing nearby.

"What happened?" the doctor asked.

"Well," the officer replied, "one of them was dead when I got here, and by the time I got the head of the other one straightened around, he was dead too."

JUDGMENT OF THE NEIGHBORS

Funeral services were being held for a man who had been thoroughly disliked in his community. He had a violent, explosive disposition: he nagged his wife, drove the children mercilessly, and quarreled with the neighbors.

The day was warm, and as the service ended a storm broke furiously. There was a blinding flash followed by a terrific clap of thunder.

"Waal, he *got* there!" a mourner said.

SUMMARIZED

The old-time preacher, who can still be found in the South, is a lover of big words, most of which he may but vaguely understand and seldom use rightly. Yet the wrong word he uses often turns out to be just the right one.

Down in South Alabama, Jim, a farmhand, was plowing corn, when a sudden thunder shower drove him to shelter under a tree. There his Maker suddenly summoned him home with a bolt of lightning.

Over the shattered remains of the defunct Jim the local pastor preached, concluding with this moving climax:

"De call for our pore brother wuz swift and suddin. He did not linger for long months on de bed of pain and affliction. He did not suffer and waste away. No, suh, de Lawd just teched an electric button in de skies and summarized Jim."

LIKED IT NOT

When Sir Albert Morton died, his wife's grief was so complete that she shortly followed him, and was laid by his side. Wotton's (English diplomat and poet, 1568-1639) two lines on the event have been celebrated as containing a volume in seventeen words:

> *He first deceased; she for a little tried*
> *To live without him, liked it not, and died.*

The Market-place

> *This world's a city full of straying streets,*
> *And death's the market-place where each one meets.*
> Shakespeare and John Fletcher

All That We Have

> *All buildings are but monuments of death,*
> *All clothes but winding sheets for our last knell,*
> *All dainty fattings for the worms beneath,*
> *All curious music but our passing bell;*
> *Thus death is nobly waited on, for why?*
> *All that we have is but death's livery.*
> Anonymous, 1640

No Vestige

> *Man grows old, and dwindles, and decays,*
> *And countless generations of mankind*
> *Depart, and leave no vestige where they trod.*
> William Wordsworth, 1814

"Death Keeps No Calendar"

"God's finger touch'd him, and he slept," said Alfred Tennyson.

A Russian proverb says of death, "The greatest king must at last be put to death with a shovel."

An Irish proverb gives death a lighter touch: "What is the world to a man when his wife is a widow?"

"Graves Are of All Sizes" (Thomas Fuller)

A piece of a churchyard fits everybody.
> George Herbert, 1651

The bodies of those that made such a noise and tumult when alive, when dead, lie as quietly among the graves of their neighbors as any others.
> Jonathan Edwards, 1740

The Death of Raleigh

Walter Raleigh was one of the most remarkable men of the sixteenth century—less a poet, indeed, than a prose writer, and less a scholar than a warrior. He was known both in the old world and the new.

His busy life was closed by a violent death, probably an unjust one. He was beheaded October 29, 1618.

On the scaffold, after addressing the people in justification of his character and conduct, he took up the axe, and observed to the sheriff, "This is a sharp medicine, but a sound cure for all diseases." Having tried how the block fitted his head, he told the executioner that he would give the signal by lifting his hand, and then added, "Fear not, but strike home."

He then laid himself down, and was requested by the executioner to alter the position of his head. "So the heart be right," was his reply, "it is no matter which way the head lies." On the signal being given, the executioner failed to act with promptitude, which caused Raleigh to exclaim, "Why dost thou not strike? Strike, man!" By two strokes, which he received without shrinking, the head of this intrepid man was severed from his body.

Be a Good Man

"My dear," said Sir Walter Scott to his son on his deathbed, "be a good man; be virtuous, be religious, be a good man. Nothing else can give you comfort when you come to lie here."

Life Flies Swiftly

This is our life, while we enjoy it. We lose it like the sun, which flies swifter than an arrow; and yet no man perceives that it moves. . . . Is not earth turned to earth; and shall not our sun set like theirs when the night comes?

Henry Smith

As the End of Life Came

Sir Thomas More remarked to the executioner that the scaffold was extremely weak. "I pray you see me up safe," said he, "and for my coming down let me shift for myself."

Chaucer breathed his last while composing a ballad. His last production is called, "A Ballad Made by Geoffrey Chaucer, on His Death-Bed, Lying in Great Pain."

"I could wish this tragic scene were over," said Thomas Quin, the Irish tragic actor, "but I hope to go through it with becoming dignity."

Petrarch was found dead in his library, leaning on a book.

Rousseau, when dying, ordered his attendants to remove him and place him before the window, that he might look upon his garden and gladden his eyes with the sight of nature.

Pope tells us he found Sir Godfrey Kneller, portrait painter (whom he visited a few days prior to his end), sitting up and forming plans for his own monument. His vanity was conspicuous even in death!

Lord Chesterfield's good breeding only left him at death. "Give Drysdale a chair," said he to his valet, when that person was announced.

William Pitt, great British statesman, died alone in a solitary house on Wimbledon Common.

THE DRAMA OF DEATH

Copernicus, the great astronomer, died on the day of the appearance of his famous book from the press. The closing scene of his life would furnish a subject for an artist. For thirty-five years he studied his system of the heavens. A mildness of disposition, bordering on timidity, a reluctance to encounter controversy, and a dread of persecution led him to withhold his work from the press, and to make known his system only to a few confidential friends and disciples.

At length he draws near his end; he is seventy-three years of age and he gives his work on the "revolutions of the heavenly orbs" to his friends for publication. The day at last has come on which it is to be ushered into the world. It is the 24th of May, 1543. On that day, the effect, no doubt, of the intense excitement of his mind operating upon an exhausted frame, brought him near to death. His last hour is come; he lies stretched upon the couch from which he will never rise, in his apartment at the Canonry at Frauenberg, in East Prussia. The beams of the setting sun glance through the Gothic windows of his chamber; near his bedside is the armillary sphere, on which he has contrived to represent his theory of the heavens; his picture painted by himself, the amusement of his earlier years hangs before him; beneath it his astrolabe and other imperfect astronomical instruments; and around him are gathered his sorrowing disciples. The door of the apartment opens; the eye of the departing sage is turned to see who enters; it is a friend who brings him the first printed copy of his immortal treatise. He knows that in that book he contradicts all that had ever been distinctly taught by former philosophers; he knows that he has rebelled against the sway of Ptolemy, which the scientific world had acknowledged for a thousand years; he knows that the popular mind will be shocked by his innovations; he knows that attempts will be made to press even religion into the service against him; but he knows that his book is true. He is dying, but he leaves a glorious truth, as his dying bequest, to the world. He bids the friend who has brought it place himself between the window and his bedside, that the sun's rays may fall upon the precious volume and he may behold it once before his eye grows dim. He looks upon it, takes it in his hands, presses it to his breast, and expires. But no, he is not wholly gone. A smile lights up his dying countenance; a beam of returning intelligence kindles in his eye; his lips move; and the friend who leans over him can hear him faintly murmur the beautiful sentiments which the Christian lyrist of a later age has so finely expressed in verse:

Ye golden lamps of heaven, farewell, with all your feeble light!
Farewell, thou ever-changing moon, pale empress of the night!
And thou, refulgent orb of day, in brighter flames arrayed,
My soul, which springs beyond thy sphere, no more demands thy aid.
Ye stars are but the shining dust of my divine abode,
The pavement of those heavenly courts, where I shall reign with God.

So died the great Columbus of the heavens.

DEBT

ONE QUESTION

Harry MacGregor was a young Scot anxious to get married. The local newspaper told of a young woman who had agreed to marry any man who would pay her father's debts.

88

Harry called on the money-minded lady, found her to be very pretty and most agreeable. A match seemed very much in prospect, until he asked a question the young woman dared not answer.

"Lassie," the cagey suitor remarked, "before I marry you and pay your father's debts, tell me, who got your old man in debt in the first place?"

The Presidents and Public Debt

If a national debt is considered a national blessing, then we can get on by borrowing. But as I believe it is a national curse, my vow shall be to pay the national debt.

Andrew Jackson, 1824

I place economy among the first and most important of republican virtues, and public debt as the greatest of the dangers to be feared.

Thomas Jefferson, 1816

Let us have the courage to stop borrowing to meet continuing deficits. Stop the deficits.

Franklin D. Roosevelt, 1932

DECEIVE

Fooling 'em

There was a chap who worked in a factory of some kind. He came very highly recommended, and the guard at the gate was surprised to see him coming out of the main gate one evening with a wheelbarrow full of sawdust.

The guard asked him what he had, and the man said he had a load of sawdust and was going to see if he could make it burn in the fireplace.

"Did you get permission?" asked the guard.

"Yes," said the man.

"Very well," said the guard and allowed the man to leave the gate.

Not long afterward they discovered him coming out with another wheelbarrow filled with sawdust. The usual questions and answers ensued, and finally they let him go on his way. The fourth time he came out with a load of sawdust, they began to get suspicious, and they analyzed the sawdust to see if there were anything valuable in it. There was not, and he was again allowed to leave the gate.

One of his friends said, "What is this racket of yours? What are you doing with this sawdust?"

Not a word.

"Are you stealing sawdust?" asked the friend.

"No, I'm not stealing sawdust," said the man. "I'm stealing wheelbarrows."

Edward Everett Horton Distinguished Actor

DECEPTION

INGENUITY

Henry, on his tenth birthday, had a party. It was over, and he was now gazing at the remains of the cake. "Mother," he said, "may I have a piece of cake, please?"

"No," replied his mother, "you've had enough."

"Well, may I sleep with a little under my pillow?" asked the boy.

"Very well, here you are. Remember to keep it under your pillow. Now run along to bed."

On going up to Henry's room some time later, his mother was amazed to see Henry sleeping peacefully with the pillow over his stomach.

SOMEONE ELSE PAID THE COST

A certain woman thinks she played a very smart trick. Her husband left their summer cottage to drive home some 150 miles distant. That evening she placed a person-to-person telephone call to herself at her home. Her husband, of course, answered and reported that his wife would not be home for another week. She had learned that her husband arrived home safely without any cost to her.

From an address by S. Guernsey Jones, Vice President
National Newark and Essex Banking Company
Newark, New Jersey

DEFENSE

"Adam, Where Art Thou?"

Even God himself did not pass sentence upon Adam before he was called upon to make his defense. "Adam," says God, "where art thou? Hast thou not eaten of the tree whereof I commanded thee that thou shouldst not eat?" And the same question was put to Eve also.

John Fortescue, c. 1462

Humanity Left Out

Voltaire, when on his estate of Ferney, was fond of assuming the air of nobility, and displayed a hatred of transgressors. One of the poor fellows was caught and brought before him. Voltaire determined to try him in the form of law, and took his seat as judge, directing his secretary to act as attorney for the prisoner. The attorney made a long speech in his favor, and suddenly stopped short.

"Why do you hesitate?" asked Voltaire.

"I wish to read a passage from a volume in your library."

He procured the book, and kept turning over the leaves, for some time, without saying a word. Voltaire became impatient, and asked him what book he was looking at.

"It is your *Philosophical Dictionary*," was the answer.

"Well."

"I have been looking for the word 'humanity,' and I see you have omitted it."

Voltaire thought the argument so forcible, that the culprit was set free at once.

Difference

There is a difference between a blunder and a mistake. When a man puts down a bad umbrella and takes a good one, he makes a mistake. When he puts down a good one and takes up a bad one, he makes a blunder.

DEFINITIONS

The acid soliloguised on cooling.

A circle is a figure with no corners and only one side.

Typhoid fever may be prevented by fascination.

When you breathe you inspire. When you do not breathe you expire.

The cuckoo does not lay its own eggs.

Acrobats have subtle spines.

An aquarium is a man who collects old things.

A senator is half horse and half man.

A brunette is a young bear.

Kreisler can play the violin to distraction.

When you cross a busy street you must have all your fatilities about you.

Killing a man in cold blood means killing him when he is dead.

Matrimony is a place where souls suffer for a time on account of their sins.

Liberty of conscience means being able to do wrong without bothering about it afterwards.

Iron mould can be removed by using a cold chisel.

Sugar is used in tea and coffee to make them sweat.

The American School Board Journal

Next Question, Please

The teacher, having spent some time telling a new geography class the facts about food and natural resources said:

"Now, Johnny, can you tell me what sugar is?"

Johnny replied, "Sugar is the stuff that makes the grapefruit taste sour when you don't put any on."

DEMAGOGUE

They Still Are

Aristophanes wrote, about 424 B.C., "Agitators are like those who fish for eels. When the water is tranquil they catch nothing, but if they stir up the mud they make a haul."

Only the People Make Demagogues Possible

The demagogue, puffing up the people with words, sways them to his interest. When calamity follows he escapes from justice.

Euripides, way back in 421 B.C.

A new race of men is springing up to govern the nation; they are the hunters after popularity, men ambitious not of the honor so much as of the profits of office—the demagogues, whose principles hang laxly upon them, and who follow not so much what is right as what leads to a temporary vulgar applause.

Joseph Story
Professor of Law at Harvard, 1829-1845

Demagogues and agitators are very unpleasant, but they are incident to a free and constitutional country, and you must put up with these inconveniences or do without many important advantages.

Benjamin Disraeli, British House of Commons, 1867

The shortest way to ruin a country is to give power to demagogues.

Dionysius of Halicarnassus, 20 B.C.

DEMOCRACY

A Democracy and a Republic

In a democracy the people meet and exercise the government in person; in a republic, they assemble and administer it by their representatives and agents. A democracy, consequently, will be confined to a small spot. A republic may be extended over a large region.

James Madison in *The Federalist*, XIII, 1788

DENTIST

Anything to Please

PATIENT: "Five dollars seems like a lot of money for pulling a tooth It's only about two seconds' work."
DENTIST: "Well, if you wish, I can pull it very slowly."

93

DEPORTMENT

No Guessing

FATHER: "Jimmy, don't you know the difference between right and wrong?"
JIMMY: "Sure!"
FATHER: "But you always do wrong."
JIMMY: "Well, that shows it isn't guesswork."

DESCRIPTION

Distinction

A father was once informed that his son had been disrespectful to some neighbors. He called the youngster into his study. "My boy, is it true that you called Mrs. Smith a fool?"

The boy hung his head. "Yes, father."

"And did you call Mr. Smith a worse fool?"

"Yes, father."

The father pondered for a minute. Then he said: "Well, my son, that is just about the distinction I should make."

DESSERT

Hush! Child

"Mother," asked the little one, when a number of guests were present at dinner, "will the dessert hurt me, or is there enough to go around?"

DETERMINATION

Improvement

A toast I heard recently goes like this: "I'm not as good as I ought to be; I'm not as good as I'm going to be; but I'm better than I was."

From an address by Benson Ford
Vice President and General Manager
Lincoln-Mercury Division, Ford Motor Company

"I am a man of strong determination," he confided to his fellow benedicts. "Whenever I make up my mind to tell my wife to do something, I do it!"

DIET

NO FAIR

A portly executive who hadn't gone shopping with his wife for ten years wanted to know where all the grocery money was going to.

She told him to stand sideways in front of the mirror.

TWO CAN LIVE AS CHEAPLY

When Jones met his old friend, Smith, whom he hadn't seen in six months, he was shocked by his altered appearance. His face looked haggard, his eyes held a glassy stare, and the way his clothes draped his frame spoke eloquently of a considerable weight loss.

"Good heavens, man!" Jones exclaimed. "Have you been ill?"

"No," Smith answered wearily, "but my wife is on a reducing diet."

DILEMMA

POOR ADVICE

When buffalo grazed in the western mountains, two prospectors met a wild one. One of the prospectors climbed a tree and the other ran into a cave. The buffalo bellowed at the entrance of the cave and then turned toward the tree. Out came the man from the cave, and the buffalo took after him again. The man made another run for the hole. After this had been repeated several times, the man in the tree called to his comrade, who was trembling at the mouth of the cave.

"Stay in the cave, you fool!"

"You don't know anything about this hole," yelled the other. "There's a bear in it!"

DINNER

How Greatness Is Achieved

> *The family that dines the latest*
> *Is in our street esteemed the greatest.*
> Henry Fielding, 1743

All Human History Attests

> *That happiness for man—the hungry sinner!—*
> *Since Eve ate apples, much depends on dinner.*
> Byron, 1823

DIPLOMAT

Otherwise a Good Letter

Sam's wife cautioned him to control his temper in the letter he was about to write to a man who owed him for a diamond he had bought for his wife many months before.

"Be diplomatic, Sam," she warned. "Don't write notting dot might offend him."

"All right, Momma," he agreed.

Sam finished the letter and showed it to his wife for her approval.

"A verry, verry nize ledder," she admitted. "But, dollink, skunk ain't spelt vith two k's."

DISAPPOINTMENT

Hardship

Try as we may, none of us can be free of conflict and woe. Even the greatest men have had to accept disappointment as their daily bread.

Woodrow Wilson was a striking example. The disappointment in not being able to put over the League of Nations broke him physically. His hands had held the peace of the world in their grasp; but his last days were spent, looking at empty hands.

Clemenceau—the tiger of France—did so much for his country. Yet in the evening of his life he was denied the presidency of the French Republic—denied it by one vote in the French

Senate. His election could have done no harm—not even to his enemies—for the powers of the French president are sharply limited.

From an address by Bernard M. Baruch

DISTINCTION

Among all excellent and illustrious men those are most praise worthy who have been the authors of religion and divine worship; next come the founders of states; then come successful generals who have enlarged their own kingdom or the dominion of their country. To these are to be added literary men of all kinds, according to their several degrees; and lastly, as being the greatest number, come the artificers and mechanics.

Machiavelli, 1531

That you have enemies you must not doubt, when you reflect that you have made yourself eminent.

Thomas Jefferson, 1782

They that stand high have many blasts to shake them.

Shakespeare, 1592

That last infirmity of noble minds.

John Milton, 1638

Fame is but wind.

Thomas Coryate, 1611

Fame is no sure test of merit, but only a probability of such: it is an accident, not a property of a man.

Thomas Carlyle, 1828

DOCTORS

Yes

FATHER: "You can ask a question, but make it short."

SMALL SON: "Well, when a doctor gets sick and another doctor doctors him, does the doctor doing the doctoring have to doctor the doctor the way the doctor being doctored wants to be doctored, or does the doctor doing the doctoring of the doctor doctor as he wants to doctor?"

97

Mistake

A doctor rushed into the coroner's office: "I want to change that death certificate I gave you yesterday. I put my name down in the space marked 'Cause of Death.'"

Not Worth Anything

"How is your aunt?" asked a family friend of the small boy.

"She had her appendix taken out the other day," the lad informed her.

"Did they give her anything for it?"

"No," answered the lad, "it wasn't worth anything."

Table of Contents

While the diagnosis of the patient, who had eaten too heavily, was proceeding, the sick man asked, "Doctor, do you think the trouble is in the appendix?"

"Oh, no," said the doctor, "not at all. The trouble is with your table of contents."

Lucky

PATIENT: "Man, what an awful bill just for one week's treatment."

DOCTOR: "My good fellow, if you knew what an interesting case yours was, and how strangely I was tempted to let it go to a postmortem, you wouldn't grumble at a bill three times as large."

Ah, That's Different

"Say, 'ah,'" said the doctor.

"I do not want to be examined. I want to pay my bill."

"Ah," said the doctor.

That Will Put Them on a Diet

YOUNG DOCTOR: "Why do you always ask your patients what they have for dinner?"

OLD DOCTOR: "It's a most important question, for according to their menus I make out my bills."

He Will Sweat

At the bedside of a patient, five doctors were consulting as to the best means of producing a perspiration.

Finally an old doctor said, "Just send in our bills, gentlemen; that will bring it on at once."

Sometimes We Do

KINDERGARTEN TEACHER: "What do you do when you are sick?"
YOUNSTER: "Mommie says we should insult the doctor."

Curiosity

An insurance agent was filling out an application blank.

"Have you ever had appendicitis?" he asked the applicant.

"Well," he answered, "I was operated on, but I have never felt quite sure whether it was appendicitis or professional curiosity."

It Should Be

DOCTOR: "Your cold sounds much better today."
PATIENT: "It should be. I practiced on it all night."

Leave Well Enough Alone

A doctor fell in a well,
And broke his collar-bone.
The doctor should attend the sick
And leave the well alone.

Nothing Old-fashioned, Please

The fashionable physician walked in and nodded smilingly at his patient. "Well, here I am, Mrs. Cedric. What do you think is the matter with you this morning?"

"Doctor, I really wouldn't know," murmured the fashionable patient. "What is new?"

WE'VE ALL FELT LIKE THAT

A patient in the doctor's office who had waited two hours to see the doctor finally left for home, but before leaving he wrote this note: "Dear Doc: I've gone home to die a natural death."

DOG

SMART DOG

A couple owned a bright-eyed cocker spaniel that always became excited when the telephone rang. At the sound of the bell, the dog would run through the apartment. So his owners fell into the habit of calling home when they were out for any length of time, knowing that the bell would awaken their pet and give him a few moments of exercise.

One evening during their absence, a friend who knew about the arrangement let himself into their apartment. He seated himself and waited, sure the telephone would ring sooner or later. When it did, he let it ring several times. Then he lifted the receiver, panted enthusiastically for a few seconds, barked once, and quietly replaced it.

The couple is still wondering.

IT WON'T HURT HIM

He was about nine years old and extremely fond of his dog, who reciprocated the affection. The other evening they were romping on the floor when the dog stood up, put its paws on the boy's shoulders, and plastered him with wet affection.

To the mother's horror, the boy planted a kiss right on the dog's nose.

"Aw, what you worryin' about?" he said when she remonstrated. "It won't hurt him. I got over my cold a week ago."

NO DISCRIMINATION

A woman with a dog was preparing to board a train. "I suppose," she said to the train conductor, "if I pay fare for my dog, he will be treated the same as other passengers and be allowed to occupy a seat."

"Of course, madam," the conductor replied politely, "he will be treated the same as other passengers, and can occupy a seat, provided he does not put his feet on it."

Hard Job

Two old coon hunters were swapping tall stories about their dogs. "Well," said one of them, "I had a hound once and every time just before I went hunting I'd whittle out a board in the shape of a coon-hide stretcher, just to show him the size of the one I wanted; then I'd set it outside where he could see it. Well, sir, one day my wife set the ironing board outside, and that dog ain't come back yet!"

He Doesn't Say Much Either

Strolling through the card room of a businessmen's club, a member was surprised to see three men and a dog playing poker. He commented on the extraordinary performance of the dog.

"He's not so smart," the dog's owner said in disgust. "Every time he gets a good hand he wags his tail."

Almost Set

"I once owned a setter," said Mr. Jones, "which was very intelligent. I had him on the street one day, and he acted so queerly about a man we met that I asked the man his name, and—"

"Oh, that's an old story!" said Mr. Smith. "The man's name was Partridge, of course, and because of that the dog came to a set."

"You're mistaken," replied Jones. "The dog didn't come quite to a set. The man's name was Quayle, and the dog hesitated on account of the spelling!"

One Friend

Byron's dislike of mankind vented itself in an epitaph on his Newfoundland dog, which he concluded with the following lines:

> To mark a friend's remains these stones arise
> I never knew but one, and here he lies.

DOUBT

THE POOR WORM

A centipede was happy quite,
Until a frog, in fun,
Said, "Pray, which leg comes after which?"
This raised her mind to such a pitch
She lay distracted in a ditch,
Considering how to run.

FULTON'S FOLLY

On August 4, 1807, the crowd that watched Robert Fulton's *Clermont,* the first American steamboat, contained many doubters. "It will burn up"; "the thing will bust"; "all on board will be drowned"; "it can never go upstream."

But it did go upstream 150 miles from New York to Albany in 32 hours.

DUTY

A GREAT JOY

Over the doorway of an old hospital in Philadelphia there is the following inscription:

Think not the beautiful doings of thy soul
Shall perish unremembered; they abide forever.
And the good thou doest nobly, truth and love
    approve.
Each pure and gentle deed of mercy brings an honest
    recompense
And from it looms the sovereign knowledge of thy
    duty done,
A joy beyond all dignities of earth.

That is an inscription worth remembering, worth cherishing.

From an address by Mrs. James Bush-Brown, Director
Pennsylvania School of Horticulture for Women

ECONOMICS

NEW DEFINITION

"According to the law of supply and demand . . . ," began the husband, who liked to explain things.

"No one demands anything at a store now, dear," she interrupted, "it's the law of supply and request."

PATERNALISM

Take your choice: To keep you from starving after paying taxes, the U. S. Government Printing Office has, at the taxpayers' expense, published just the thing for you—*Recipes for Cooking Muskrat.* You don't care much for muskrat? Very well, how about *Attracting Birds,* or *Directions for Poisoning Thirteen-striped Ground Squirrels?* (Serve with truffles and antidotes on the side.)

The Controller

THE DISMAL SCIENCE

Way back in 1790, Edmund Burke, English statesman, said, "The age of chivalry is gone; that of sophisters, economists, and calculators has succeeded."

Fifty-nine years later Thomas Carlyle called economics "the dismal science."

ECONOMIST

WHITHER AND WHY?

Today, there are 5,000 economists in America sporting doctors' degrees. Of this number, about 1,000 are in government service, 1,000 in business and research, and 3,000 in colleges and universities. The 1,000 in government keep the remaining 4,000 busy trying to find out where our national economic policies are actually leading us.

Thomas H. Coulter, President
American Bildrok Company, and
past President, The Executives Club of Chicago

EDUCATION

PERFECTLY CLEAR

PROFESSOR: "I say, you in the motor car—your tubular air container has lost its rotundity."

MOTORIST: "Who?"

PROFESSOR: "The elastic fabric surrounding the circular frame whose successive revolutions bear you onward in space has not retained its pristine roundness."

MOTORIST: "What?"

PROFESSOR: "I say, the cylindrical apparatus which supports your vehicle is no longer inflated."

MOTORIST: "How's that?"

SMALL BOY: "Hey, mister, you got a flat tire!"

OUI, OUI

Someone asked the French poet, François Coppée, whether he knew any foreign languages.

"No," he answered, "I am still engaged in studying French."

DICTIONARY

The New York Times once referred to Noah Webster as "that astute scholar who wrote a perennial best seller by the efficacious expedient of placing words in alphabetical sequence."

DISCRETION

WILLIE: "Paw, what is discretion?"

PAW: "It's something, Son, that comes to a person after he's too old for it to do him any good."

TEACHER, WHAT ARE YOU SAYING?

A high school principal declared in an assembly that he and Miss Jones, the English teacher, were going to stop "necking" in the school.

Little Johnny and his father were sitting in front of the fire. Johnny was reading the paper. He looked up to his father and said, "Say, Pop, is the Empire State Building the tallest building in the world?"

His father looked down and said, "You know I am not an architect. Why do you ask me that question? Are you trying to embarrass me?"

Johnny returned to his paper and in a few minutes he looked up at his father and said, "Pop, why is grass green?"

His father said, "Listen, you know I am not a botanist. Why do you ask me that question? Are you trying to embarrass me?"

Johnny returned to his paper, and in a few minutes he looked up at his father and said, "Pop, why is this paper so slick?"

His father looked down and said, "Johnny, you know I am not a chemist. Why ask me that question? Are you trying to embarrass me?"

Well, Johnny, almost with tears in his eyes looked up to his father and said, "You don't mind my asking you questions?"

"Oh, no, Son, how do you ever expect to learn anything if you don't ask questions?"

Frank Pace, Jr., former Secretary of the Army

Bright Boy

Willie was to take an examination to determine his intelligence quotient. The teacher took a notebook and pencil and said, "Now, Willie, I want to ask you a few questions. Answer me whatever you think the answer should be. Willie, if I cut off your right ear, what will happen?"

"Well, I couldn't hear out of my right ear."

"And if I cut off your left ear, what would happen?"

"Well, I couldn't hear with my left ear."

The teacher continued, "Suppose I cut off both of your ears?"

Willie replied, "I couldn't see."

That was very important to the teacher, and he wrote down a lot of notes. He asked Willie again, "Answer me truthfully now. If I cut off both your ears, what will happen?"

"I couldn't see," replied Willie.

"Why do you say that?" asked the teacher.

"Well," said Willie, "my hat would fall down over my eyes."

Lieutenant General Edward M. Almond

It's I

A Harvard man and a Yale man heard a knock at the door. The Yale man said: "Who's there?"

A voice said: "It's me."

The Harvard man, with a pained expression asked: "What is that oaf trying to say?"

No Use

A little boy came home from his first day at school.

"Ain't going tomorrow," he said.

"Why not, dear?" asked his mother.

"Well, I can't read 'n' I can't write 'n' they won't let me talk—so what's the use?"

Modern Toys

Mother (examining toy): "Isn't this rather complicated for a small child?"

Clerk: "It's an educational toy designed to adjust a child to live in the world today; any way he puts it together it's wrong."

I Will

The speaker was speaking eloquently, and after his peroration on woman's rights he said: "When they take our girls, as they threaten to, away from the co-educational colleges, what will follow? What will follow, I repeat?"

And a loud, masculine voice in the audience replied: "Brother, I will!"

Real Students

One day a touring educator visited the expanding campus of a large western university. He watched construction work on half a dozen new buildings; inspected new laboratories and attended classes in modern study rooms; walked across miles of tree-lined lawns and athletic fields with one of the deans. He was impressed.

"My!" he exclaimed, "just how many students do you have here?"

"Let me see . . .," the dean answered thoughtfully. "I'd say about one in a hundred."

GLAD AND SORRY

One night, in ancient times, three horsemen were riding across a desert. As they crossed the dry bed of a river, out of the darkness a voice called, "Halt!"

They obeyed. The voice then told them to dismount, pick up a handful of pebbles, put the pebbles in their pockets and remount.

The voice then said, "You have done as I commanded. To-morrow at sun-up you will be both glad and sorry." Mystified, the horsemen rode on.

When the sun rose, they reached into their pockets and found that a miracle had happened. The pebbles had been transformed into diamonds, rubies, and other precious stones. They remembered the warning. They were both glad and sorry—glad they had taken some, and sorry they had not taken more. . . .

And this is a story of Education.

Dr. L. H. Adolfson, Director
Extension Division, University of Wisconsin

ARISTOTLE ON LEARNING

Aristotle was asked what were the advantages of learning. He replied, "It is an ornament to a man in prosperity, and a refuge to him in adversity."

IT'S SIMPLE

The philosophy student was talking to a very pretty coed and was trying to impress her with his views on life, death, history, and civilization.

"For instance," he was saying, "one trouble with modern society is that we are too specialized. Now, I happen to have a good background

107

liberal arts, but I must confess I haven't the faintest idea of how ~ radio works."

"My goodness!" exclaimed the sweet young coed. "It's awful easy. You just turn the knobs and it plays."

GO TO STEAL IDEALS

A great art teacher always sent his advanced students to Italy to study art there with these words of admonition: "Go my students, go, and remember you enter Italy to steal."

HE DIDN'T DO NO GOOD

"Well, Billie, how did you get along in the examination in English grammar?"

"Oh, I done fine, Dad. I only made one mistake and I seen that as soon as I done it."

WAY BACK THEN

TEACHER: "Billie, I'm ashamed of you. When I was no older than you, I could reel all the Presidents off in order."

BILLIE: "Yeah, but there were only three or four of them then."

MAKING UP FOR LOST TIME

Dean Jonathan Swift, author of *Gulliver's Travels,* when he received the degree of A.B., was so deficient as to obtain it only "by special favor," a term used to denote want of merit. He was so ashamed, that he resolved from that time to study eight hours a day, and continued his industry for seven years, with what improvement we now know.

OUT OF NOTHING

A certain pedantic gentleman once presented himself at Cambridge for a doctor's degree, and, as is usual on such occasions, the questioning was commenced in Latin, and exhibited the following classical wit:

QUESTIONER: *"Quid est creare?* (What is it to create?)"

PEDANT: *"Ex nihil facere.* (To make out of nothing.)"

QUESTIONER: *"Ergo, te doctorem creamus!* (Therefore, we make you a doctor!)"

108

THE ROYAL ROAD TO KNOWLEDGE

Patrick Henry learned to write by filling a box with white sand and making the letters in the sand with a round stick. Then he would erase the letters by rubbing the stick over the sand and making it smooth again.

Henry Clay made his ink by scraping the soot from the bottom of his mother's soap kettle. He mixed the soot with a few drops of melted tallow and a little water. He took a quill from the wing of a goose in the barnyard and had a pen. His paper was a pine shingle. When he had written his lesson, he shaved away the writing with his hunter's knife.

TO LIVE BY

Dean Luther Weigle of Yale Divinity School relates this story about his elder son, who had just graduated from Yale. "Dick," he queried, "out of what course do you think you got the most these four years?"

To his surprise, the answer came: "Billy's T & B." (He meant the course of Tennyson and Browning taught by Professor William Lyon Phelps.)

He asked his son, "Why?"

After a few moments the reply came: "I suppose because it gave me more to tie to and live by."

From an address by Dr. S. T. Ludwig
Executive Secretary, Department of Education
Church of the Nazarene, Kansas City, Missouri

COLLEGE GRADS DO BETTER

A college boy once wrote a verse which included these lines:
There'll come graduation,
I'll find occupation,
Existence that's meager and lean;
While he who digs ditches
Has cash in his breeches
And rides in a big limousine.
More than half of all young people finish high school today, compared to six per cent fifty years ago; and ten per cent finish

109

college—the old figure was two per cent. The business and industrial demand for educated workers is apparently growing even faster.

Many fields that previously required a high school diploma now require a college education. In others, where a standard four-year course once served, a worker today does better if he has five or six years of college.

This trend is reflected at the New York University School of Business Administration, where the number of candidates studying for the Doctor of Philosophy degree increased thirty-five per cent in one academic year.

Nation's Business, March 1952

Too Fast

TEACHER: "Can you tell me how fast light travels?"

JOHNNIE: "I don't know how fast, but I know it gets here too early in the morning."

Failing Successfully

A study made a number of years ago said the more education a man has, the less likely he is to be an inventor. Now the reason for that is quite simple. From the time the boy, or girl, starts in school he is examined three or four times a year, and, of course, it is a very, very disastrous thing if he fails. An inventor fails all the time and it is a triumph if he succeeds once. Consequently, if education is an inhibition to invention, it is due entirely to the form by which we rate things and not because of any intellectual differential.

I can take any group of young people any place, and teach them to be inventors, if I can get them to throw off the hazard of being afraid to fail. You fail because your ideas aren't right. You shouldn't be afraid to fail, but you should learn to fail intelligently. By that I mean, when you fail, find out why you failed, and each time you fail it will bring you up nearer to the goal.

From an address by Charles Franklin Kettering
Director and Research Consultant
General Motors Company

EFFICIENCY

THE HARD JOB DONE THE EASY WAY

When I have a tough job in the plant and can't find an easy way to do it, I have a lazy man put on it. He'll find an easy way to do it in ten days. Then we adopt that method.

Clarence E. Bleicher

ELECTRICITY

CIRCUS

When visitors came, Sonny, age five, took them to see the pigs in their electric fence enclosure, explaining, "When the piggies back into the 'lectric fence there'll be a short circus."

ELEVATOR

UPS AND DOWNS

A boy got a job running an elevator. The first time he ran it, it went up all right, but when he came down he stopped it too suddenly.

"Man," he exclaimed, turning to the passengers, "did I stop too quickly?"

"No, no," said a six footer, "you didn't stop too quickly. I always wear my necktie around my hips."

EMBEZZLEMENT

FALSE REPORT

There is an old story that when a Mr. Alexander Gun was dismissed from the Customs Office of Edinburgh, the entry made against his name in the books was "A. Gun was discharged for making a false report."

111

EMPLOYEE

Everyone Was Satisfied

One Saturday evening last summer a young boy went into a drug store in Alliance, Ohio, and asked permission of the proprietor to use his telephone. The boy called a number and all that the druggist could hear was one side of the ensuing conversation: "Hello. Is dat Mr. Brown's residence? Yes? Is Mr. Brown dere? This, Mr. Brown? Yes? Well, Mr. Brown, is you lookin' for a boy to mow yure grass, and look after yure garden, and to wash yure automobile? No? You got a boy now? You say dat boy you got is doin' a good job? No, you don't want no other boy? All right, good-by."

As the boy started to leave the store, the druggist called after him, "Sam, I am sorry you didn't get that job."

"Laws, Mr. Jones, I don't want dat job. I's got dat job now. I'se just checkin' myself up!"

EMPLOYER

He Only Laughs at Real Humor

CHIEF CLERK: "Why don't you laugh when the boss tells a joke?"
OFFICE BOY: "I don't have to; I quit on Saturday."

Fair Boss

The office boy came sniffling into the office to ask for the afternoon off so that he might attend his grandmother's funeral. The boss handled the situation masterly.

"Why, certainly, Johnnie. What's more, son, if you'll wait for me I'll go with you."

Look What Happened

"You want more salary? Why, my boy, I worked three years for fifteen dollars a month right in this store, and now I'm owner of it."

"Well, you see what happened to your boss. No man who treats his help that way can hang on to his business."

EMPTY

At dinner a friend asked the poet, Heine, why he was so silent, when usually he was so full of witty remarks.

"Quite right," responded Heine, "but tonight I have exchanged views with some friends, and my head is fearfully empty."

ENCORES

BRAVO

The first encore on record was that given to Livius Andronicus, a Roman actor, who, it is said, was called back so often to repeat his speeches, that, in self-defense, he brought a boy to speak for him, while he himself supplied the gestures.

ENCOURAGEMENT

IF HE HAD MET YOU

Once there was a man, according to an old tale, who was so filled with despondency that he decided to commit suicide. He started on his long walk across the city toward the bridge which was to be his jumping-off place. But he promised himself that if he met one smiling, happy, friendly-looking person on the way, he would turn back from his bitter errand. Oddly, the story ends without answering the question whether or not the mission ended with suicide. The tale, however, poses a question, one of those haunting personal questions which pop into the mind now and then: If that man had met you, would he have turned back and taken up his life with a measure of courage? Well, would he?

Dr. Harold Blake Walker

ENGLISH

TOO BAD HE SEEN IT

As I was laying on the green,
A small English book I seen.
Carlyle's Essay on Burns was the edition,
So I left it laying in the same position.

Anonymous

It Happened in Boston

A motorist, driving through Boston, asked one of the natives: "My good man, could you tell me where I might stop at?"

"I would advise," said the native coldly, "stopping just before the 'at.'"

That's All It Deserves

"Is this a picture of you?"
"Yes. That's me."
"That's bad grammar."
"I know it. But it's a bad picture."

How's That?

Mr. Speaker, I smell at rat. I see him floating in the air. But mark me, sir, I will nip him in the bud.
Boyle Roche, Speech in Irish Parliament, about 1790

ENTHUSIASM

Complete Confidence

The pleasure enthusiasm inspires is the greatest remuneration that men of genius receive for their efforts. Donatello, the great Florentine sculptor (about 1386-1466), had been long at work on his statue of Judith; and, on giving the last stroke of the chisel to it, he was heard to exclaim, "Speak now! I am sure you can!"

EPITAPHS

Greentree's Resurrection

Upon the tomb of one Isaac Greentree, in Harrow Churchyard, England, is inscribed the following:

There is a time when these green trees shall fall,
And Isaac Greentree rise above them all.

For All of Us

In Luton Churchyard, Bedfordshire, England, a voice from the dead to the living speaks as follows:

> *Reader! I have left a world*
> *In which I had much to do,*
> *Sweating and fretting to get rich.*
> *Just such a fool as you.*

Something Appropriate

King Charles II once said over his bottle that he supposed some stupid peasant would write a nonsensical epitaph on him when he was gone. "Now," says His Majesty, "I should like to have something appropriate and witty. Rochester, let's have a touch of your pen on the subject." His Lordship instantly obeyed the command, and produced the following:

> *Here lies our sovereign Lord the King,*
> *Whose word no man relied on;*
> *Who never said a foolish thing,*
> *And never did a wise one.*

ERROR

He Will Pay

A woman, called for jury duty, refused to serve because she didn't believe in capital punishment.

The judge explained: "This is a case where a wife is suing her husband because she gave him one thousand dollars to pay for a fur coat and he lost the money in a poker game."

"I'll serve," said the lady. "I could be wrong about capital punishment."

In the News

If sometimes you think our little newspaper has too many typographical errors, consider some of the many we manage to catch before going to press. We almost said this week that

115

the Legion bowlers attended a Legion bowling tournament during the "lost week end," instead of "last week end."

One week we nearly went to press with: "church services will be hel at 10:00 o'clock." The letter "d" didn't come down on the machine.

We have been feeling apologetic to the Mindoro bowling team for some time for actually going to press with "Mindoro Boosers" instead of "Mindoro Boosters," in the Bangor bowling news.

West Salem Journal, West Salem, Wisconsin

ANACHRONISMS OF SHAKESPEARE

In *Coriolanus,* reference is made to Alexander, Cato, and Galen— all of whom lived long subsequent to his day.

In *Julius Caesar,* Cassius speaks of a clock striking. He must have been endowed with remarkable vision to have known that there would be clocks that would someday strike.

In *King Lear* Gloucester speaks of not being compelled to the use of spectacles! Surely it must have been Shakespeare who was short-sighted.

ETIQUETTE

MOTHER KNEW

The young man who had been calling frequently at last spoke to Mabel's father about marrying his daughter.

"It's a mere formality, I know," he began, "but we thought it would be pleasing to you if it were observed in the usual way."

"And may I inquire," the father asked, "who suggested that asking my consent to Mabel's marriage was a mere formality?"

"Mabel's mother."

DEFINITION

BUD: "What's etiquette?"

HANK: "It's saying 'No, thank you, I've had enough ice cream,' when you want more."

EVIDENCE

MODERN MAID

> *Maud Muller, on a summer night,*
> *Turned down the only parlor light.*
> *The judge, beside her, whispered things*
> *Of wedding bells and diamond rings.*
> *He spoke his love in burning phrase,*
> *And acted foolish forty ways.*
> *When he had gone Maud gave a laugh*
> *And then turned off the dictagraph.*
>
> Milwaukee Sentinel

EVIL

AN OLD SAYING

There is an old Blue Ridge saying, "You cannot measure a snake until it is dead."

Harry F. Byrd, U.S. Senator from Virginia

EXAGGERATION

SMALL CROP

Speaking of wheat crops in Montana, a Montana farmer remarked: "I don't know just how many bushels we raised, but my men stacked all they could out of doors and then stored the rest of the crop in the barn."

EXAMPLE

YOU TELL HIM, I'M BUSY

"Dad!"

"Well, what is it?"

"It says here, 'A man is known by the company he keeps.' Is that so, Dad?"

"Yes."

"Well, Dad, if a good man keeps company with a bad man, is the good man bad because he keeps company with the bad man, or is the bad man good because he keeps company with the good man?"

EXECUTIVE

It Isn't Easy

"What is executive ability, Father?" asked the serious lad.

"Executive ability, my boy, is the art of getting the credit for all the hard work that somebody else does."

Defining the Executive

Since it's quite possible for executives to take themselves too seriously, here are a few current definitions of executives that are worth noting.

One goes: "An executive is a fellow who goes out and finds something that needs to be done. He then finds somebody willing to pay for it. Then he hires somebody to do it."

Another: "An executive is a man who goes around with a worried look on the face of his assistant."

Among non-executive cynics, the favorite definition appears to be: "An executive is a big gun—that hasn't been fired yet."

Public Relations Journal

EXCITEMENT

Experience

A father was asked by one of his sons to go with him to a boxing exhibition.

Son: "You'll see more excitement for your two dollars than you've ever seen in your life before."

Father: "I've got my doubts about that. Two dollars is all that my marriage license cost me."

EXPENSIVE

Correct

Customer: "You're giving me a piece of bone."

Butcher: "On the contrary, madam, you are paying for it."

SCIENTIST: "From our studies we find that other planets may not be able to support life."

HARD-WORKING BUSINESSMAN: "It isn't exactly easy on this one either."

EXPERIENCE

"Are you the man who was married in a cage of lions?"
"Yes, I'm the man."
"Did it seem exciting?"
"It did then. It wouldn't now."

Longer Experience

"I am sorry my car bumped you," the lady driver said. "But you should take more care when you are walking. I am an experienced driver. I have been driving a car for ten years."

"Well," replied the victim, "I'm not a novice myself. I've been walking for fifty-five years."

Father Knew

SHE: "Darling, I saw the sweetest little hat in the store today."
HE: "Put it on and let's see what it looks like."

Experience Keeps a Dear School

A wise old German proverb says, "He who has burnt his mouth blows his soup."

Coleridge put it differently in *The Ancient Mariner,* "A sadder and a wiser man, he rose the morrow morn."

Marcus Aurelius (c. 170) was not so certain about the value of experience, for he observed, "The stone that is thrown into the air is none the worse for falling down, and none the better for going up."

EXPERTS

That'll Fool 'em

One night two burglars entered a store. One approached the safe, sat down on the floor, took off his shoes and socks, and started to turn the dial of the safe with his toes.

"What's the matter?" said his pal. "Let's open this thing and get out of here."

"Naw, it'll only take a minute longer and we'll drive them finger-print experts nuts."

He Knows

What is an expert? An expert is a man who has stopped thinking He knows!

From an address by Frank Lloyd Wright

FAITH

Different Kinds

"As I understand it, Doctor, if I believe I'm well, I'll be well. Is that correct?"

"It is."

"Then, if you believe you are paid, I suppose you'll be paid."

"Not necessarily."

"But why shouldn't faith work as well in one case as in the other?"

"Well, you see, there is considerable difference between having faith in Providence and having faith in you."

No Unbelief

There is no unbelief;
Whoever plants a seed beneath the sod
And waits to see it push away the clod,
He trusts in God.

Lizzie York Case, c. 1850

FAITHFUL

His Servant

When Michelangelo's servant, Urbino, lay on his death-bed, the aged sculptor watched over him constantly, notwithstanding his own infirmities. He wrote as follows to Vassari: "My friend, I shall write ill, but I must reply to your letter. Urbino, you know, is dead. That has been both a favor to me from God, and a subject of bitter grief—a favor, because he who in his life took care of me has taught me in dying, not alone to die without regret, but to desire death. He lived with me for twenty-six years, always good, intelligent, and faithful. I had enriched him, and the moment when I thought to find in him a staff for my old age, he escapes, leaving me only the hope of seeing him again in heaven."

FALL

Melancholy Daze

> *The melancholy days have come.*
> *The saddest in our annals,*
> *It's far too cold for B.V.D.'s*
> *And far too hot for flannels.*
> Amherst *Lord Jeff*

FALSEHOOD

Gossip

"What," asked the teacher, "is meant by bearing false witness against one's neighbor?"

"It's telling falsehoods about them," said one small youngster.

"Partly right," said the teacher.

"I know," said a little girl. "It's when nobody did anything and somebody told about it."

FAME

Glad to Meet You

"No man is so well known as he thinks he is," said Enrico Caruso, the world-famed tenor. "While motoring, the automobile broke down and I sought refuge in a farmhouse while the car was being repaired. The farmer asked me my name, and I told him it was Caruso.

"He leaped to his feet and seized me by the hand. 'Little did I think I would see a man like you in this humble kitchen, sir!' he exclaimed. 'Caruso. The great traveler, Robinson Caruso!'"

But Yesterday

> But yesterday the word of Caeser might
> Have stood against the world; now lies he there,
> And none so poor to do him reverence.
> Shakespeare, *Julius Caesar*, III-2.

Background of Famous Men

Epictetus, the celebrated stoic philosopher, was born a slave, and spent many years of his life in servitude.

The father of Haydn, the great musical composer, was a wheelwright, and filled also the humble occupation of a sexton, while his mother was at the same time a servant in the establishment of a neighboring nobleman.

The father of John Opie, the great English portrait painter, was a working carpenter in Cornwall. Opie rose from being a woodcutter to the professorship of painting in the Royal Academy.

Vergil's father was a potter or brickmaker.

Luther was the son of a poor miner and Calvin's father was not distinguished either for affluence or learning.

Columbus was the son of a weaver, and originally a weaver himself.

Bunyan was the son of a traveling tinker, Shakespeare of a wool stapler and butcher, Milton of a notary, and Thomas Moore of a grocer.

Defoe, author of *Robinson Crusoe,* was the son of a butcher.

122

Rabelais was the son of an apothecary, Molière of a tapestry maker, and Rousseau of a watchmaker.

Linnaeus, the founder of the science of botany, was apprenticed to a shoemaker in Sweden, but went afterwards to college.

Fox, the founder of the sect called Quakers, was the son of a weaver, and was apprenticed to a shoemaker.

The husband and father of the woman that nursed Michelangelo were stonemasons, and the chisel was often put into the hands of the child as a plaything.

WITHOUT FAME AT HOME

A young man went away from his small home town, achieved distinction, and came back. The mayor of the village, a man not of letters but of great earnestness, introduced him as follows: "Our home town hero rose from obscurity. Now he brings it back to us."

From an address by Reverend Daniel A. Poling, D.D.

FARMING

NEEDED RAIN

Last summer a fruit grower who owns fifty acres of orchards in a dry area was rejoicing because of a fairly heavy rain when his hired man came into the house. "Why don't you stay in out of the rain?" asked the fruit grower.

"I don't mind a little fog like this," said the man. "I can work along just the same."

"Oh, I'm not talking about that," exclaimed the farmer. "The next time it rains, you come into the house. I want that water on the land."

HE FOOLED 'EM

"You don't want to plant these seeds. It says on the packet it will take them two years to bloom."

"That's all right. I took them out of last year's catalog."

123

SIMPLE MATTER

The stranger was greeted by the farmer. The visitor produced his card and remarked: "I am a government inspector and am entitled to inspect your farm."

A little later the farmer heard screams from his alfalfa patch, where the inspector was being chased by a bull. Leaning over the gate as the inspector drew near, the farmer cried: "Show him your card, mister—show him your card!"

COST OF FARMING

"Farm products," complained the customer, "cost a good deal more than they used to."

"Sure, they do!" agreed Farmer Brown. "When a farmer has to know the botanical name of what he is raising, the zoological name of the insect that eats it, and the chemical name of what kills it, somebody's got to pay."

FARM PROGRESS

This country has been hearing of agrarian reform since its earliest days. We have gone through many phases of it, from the first Homestead Acts to the Populist Revolt and on to the slaughter of the little pigs in the thirties.

For thousands of years, farming was done chiefly by peasants, serfs, and slaves, and their methods in 1800 A.D. had been substantially unchanged since the times of Nebuchadnezzar. When this country was founded it took nine people on the farm to feed themselves plus one city dweller. Today, in contrast, one man on a farm feeds himself, four city people and one person overseas.

In the inventive environment of the early 1800's, change came to the farm in the shape of new tools. One was the iron and later the steel plow, which opened up whole new acreages formerly lying fallow. The reaper was invented in 1830, replacing the laborious practice of cutting grain with a scythe. In that year, the human labor factor required to produce one bushel of grain was three hours and thirty minutes. By 1896, this had fallen to ten minutes, and we had not yet come to the next great phase of development.

As we got into the gasoline age, the tractor became as important to the farm as the south meadow, and mechanization proceeded to every chore, from milking the cows to trimming the lawn. Today's farmer is indistinguishable from any other businessman, and bears no more resemblance to the cartoonists' picture of the hay-chewing rustic than does the businessman to *The Daily Worker's* drawings of him.

We often hear that the farmers are the beneficiaries of an active lobby and that their favor is regarded lovingly by political candidates. And so it is. But I leave it to you as to whether the farmer's advancement has been due to laws, legislation or bold speeches in Congress, or to the inventions and developments that today enable a single tractor to plow ten acres of land in a single day—as much as an 18th Century settler could handle in months of hard, crushing toil.

Or, as a sidelight on this field, one of the notable inventions giving rise to a social change was, of all things, barbed wire. All the title and claim laws defining property in the western states had little validity to the farmer or rancher prior to 1875. There was no way to keep his cattle on his own land or the other fellow's off, for there were no fencing materials at hand. Cattle ranged far and wide, the round-up was expensive and the meat tough and stringy. Settlement of many areas was retarded. Not until Joseph Glidden fashioned the first barbed fence, taking his cue from a rosebush in his front yard, was it possible to develop the beef cattle business on a production basis. I hope whenever you eat a nice thick steak you will pay a silent tribute to the inventor who helped place it before you.

From an address by Harold Brayman, Director
Public Relations Dept., E. I. du Pont de Nemours & Co.

There's Always a Reason

City visitor: "I see you raise hogs almost exclusively. Do they pay better than potatoes?"

Farmer: "Well, no; but you see, stranger, hogs don't need no hoeing."

Times Have Changed

Farmer Smith was old-fashioned. He believed in "Early to bed, early to rise." But he decided to be generous to his new hired man.

Accordingly, the first morning he waited until four o'clock before he called the new man for breakfast.

"Hurry if you want anything to eat," he said.

"Thanks very much," said the new hired man, "but I never eat just before going to sleep."

Diversified Farming

One farmer asked his neighbor the old question, "How's crops?"

"Waaal," drawled the second farmer, "the fillin' station an' the hot dog stand ain't doing so good, but they're a-gonna hold over Shakespeare's play for a second week in my barn."

"Hope Sustains the Farmer"

Even if a farmer intends to loaf, he gets up in time to get an early start.

E. W. Howe, 1911

The first receipt to farm well is to be rich.

Sydney Smith, 1818

Farming is a senseless pursuit, a mere laboring in a circle. You sow that you may reap, and then you reap that you may sow. Nothing ever comes of it.

Joannes Strobaeus, c. 500

150 Years Ago

A century and a half ago the farmer's house was a log cabin, his team was a yoke of oxen, his wheat was cut with a sickle or scythe. He had no matches; he used flint and steel to make sparks. There were no iron stoves, no gas, no kerosene, no electricity, no automobiles, tractors, trucks, or railroads. The farmer fought wild beasts, hunger, cold, and sickness in a wilderness. His wife spun yarn on the spinning wheel. Every other baby died before it was three months old. For wedding presents there were an axe and a gun for the groom, a spinning wheel for the bride. It was a heroic age.

Lucky Guy

Back in New England we are not as fortunate as you in the great lush prairies that I flew over this morning, coming up here to Chicago from Purdue. We have rather rocky hillsides there. Well, a fellow was plowing one of those Vermont hillsides, a rocky one, when a New Yorker rode up in a cosmopolitan, shiny car, and said, "I don't see how you make a living on this farm."

The old farmer said to him, "Well, Mister, let me tell you something. I ain't as poor as you think. I don't own this farm."

From an address by Owen Brewster
United States Senator from Maine

FASHION

It Costs Money

A woman was astonished at the high price of a new hat. "Why, there's nothing to this hat. Why should it cost so much?" The saleswoman replied, "Madam, nowadays you pay for the restraint."

Now Girls?

First fashion model: "I can't get into my shoes."
Second fashion model: "What! Feet swelled too?"

"Fashion Wears Out More Apparel Than the Man"

To be in fashion one ought perhaps to follow the advice in the lines from Alexander Pope's *An Essay on Criticism, 1711*:

> *Be not the first by whom the new are tried,*
> *Nor yet the last to lay the old aside.*

FATHER

Acquainted Now

The best description of a father in a recent contest came from a youngster who wrote. "We have such good fun with my daddy that I wish I had knew him sooner."

Twins

The teacher was trying to impress her pupils with the life of George Washington.

"Now," she said, "if the Southern states had succeeded in making the Confederacy an independent country, what would Washington have been the father of?"

"Twins!" a little boy promptly replied.

Some Views About Father

A father is a banker provided by nature.

French Proverb

Fathers should be neither seen nor heard. That is the only proper basis for family life.

Oscar Wilde, 1895

What a father says to his children is not heard by the world, but it will be heard by posterity.

Jean Paul Richter, 1807

A father, when punishing, is always a father; a slight punishment suffices for his anger.

Jean Racine, 1677

FAULTS

"Faults are Thick Where Love Is Thin"

La Rochefoucauld (1613-80) left us some great maxims, such as: "If we had no faults, we should not take so much pleasure in noting those of others."

"We confess to small faults to persuade others that we are free of great ones."

"We often take credit for faults opposite to those we have; when we are weak we boast of being obstinate."

FEAR

ROBESPIERRE

The following is a brief and striking sketch of Robespierre, the leader in the French Revolution who was responsible for the "Reign of Terror":

"I had two private conversations with Robespierre," says Dumont. "He had a sinister aspect; he never looked one in the face; he had a twinkling, winking motion in his eyes, which was continual and painful. Once I saw him on some business relating to Geneva. He asked some explanations from me, and I pressed him to speak: he told me that he was *as timid as a child;* that he always trembled when he rose to speak in public, and from the moment he so began speaking, he could not hear his own voice."

FIRE

COLLEGE PRANKS

The English poet, Gray, whose most famous poem is *Elegy in a Country Churchyard* (1751), was fearful of fire and always kept a ladder of ropes in his bedroom. Some mischievous collegians at Cambridge knew this, and in the middle of a dark night roused him with the cry of fire! The staircase, they said, was in flames.

Up went the window, and Gray hastened down his rope ladder, as quickly as possible, into a tub of water, which had been placed at the bottom to receive him. The joke cured Gray of his fears, but he would not forgive it, and immediately changed his college.

FIREMEN

LOOK OUT FOR THE PAINTERS

The fire engines came down the street. A visitor from a small village, who was driving in the city for the first time, pulled out of the way, but then got hit by the hook and ladder truck. The policeman yelled, "Why didn't you get out of the way of the fire engine?"

The visitor explained, "I did get out of the way of the fire engine, but I wasn't expecting that bunch of drunken painters on the other truck."

FISHING

It Only Sank

SWEET YOUNG THING (on first fishing trip): "How much did that red and green thing cost?"

BOY FRIEND: "You mean the float? Oh, about a dime, I guess."

SWEET YOUNG THING: "Then that's what I owe you—mine just sank."

Teaching 'Em

An old-timer sat on the river bank, obviously awaiting a nibble though the fishing season had not officially opened. The game warden stood behind him quietly for several minutes. "You a game warden?" the old-timer inquired.

"Yep."

Unruffled the old man began to move the fishing pole from side to side. Finally, he lifted the line out of the water.

"Just teaching him how to swim," he explained, pointing to a minnow wriggling on the end of the line.

Far-sighted

An old guide was cutting a fishing line part-way through. He explained, "Every week-end I get some fisherman from downstate. We'll go out on the lake and he'll hook a pretty fair fish. When he tries to lift the fish out of the water, the line's sure to break. And that feller'll go home and brag till next season about the big one that got away. What's more, he'll come back every summer for the rest of his life trying to catch that big one."

Correct

"Rastus, give me a sentence with the word 'amphibious.'"

"Yassum. 'Mos' fish stories am fibious.'"

HONEST FISHERMAN?

He had been fishing with no luck. On his way home he entered a fish market and spoke to the clerk. "John," said he, "stand over at that side of the store and throw me five of your biggest trout."

"Throw them? What's the big idea?"

"Just so that I can tell the family I caught them. I may be a poor fisherman, but I'm no liar."

TOO DANGEROUS

A fisherman was telling some friends about a fishing trip to a lake in the West.

"Are there any trout out there?" asked one friend.

"Thousands of 'em," replied the fisherman.

"Will they bite easily?" asked another friend.

"Bite? Why, they're absolutely vicious. A man has to hide behind a tree just to bait his hook."

"A STICK AND A STRING WITH A FLY"

When the wind is in the east,
Then the fishes bite the least;
When the wind is in the west,
Then the fishes bite the best;
When the wind is in the north,
Then the fishes do come forth;
When the wind is in the south,
It blows the bait in the fish's mouth.
Old English Verse

AT LEAST THEY DON'T GET AWAY

In other localities certain places in the streams are much better than others, but at Niagara one place is just as good as another, for the reason that the fish do not bite anywhere.
S. L. Clemens (Mark Twain, 1875)

FLATTERY

How's That?

They were canoeing in the starlight.

"How bright the stars are tonight," he said. "Almost as bright as—"

"Oh, you flatterer!" she replied.

"As they were last night," he finished, calmly.

At Least One Left

SHE: "The day of great men is gone forever."

HE: "But the day of beautiful women is not," he responded.

SHE (smiling and blushing): "I was only joking," she explained.

Never Inhale

I profoundly appreciate that all too generous introduction. I don't deserve it. But then I am comforted by the remark of a friend of mine, that "Flattery never hurts any man unless he inhales."

From an address by Dr. Harry Emerson Fosdick

FOOD

We've Been There

HE: "I'm so hungry I could eat a horse."

WAITER: "Well, you've come to the right place."

Why?

The child took a helping of turkey. "Now," said the hostess, "would you like some of this nice stuffing?"

"No, thank you," the child replied, "and I don't see why the turkeys eat it either!"

Of Course Not

A restaurant owner wanted to run an entirely different restaurant. He advertised: "CUTLETS FROM EVERY ANIMAL IN THE WORLD."

The first customer asked for an elephant cutlet. The chef said, "Madam, I am very sorry, but for one cutlet we cannot cut up our elephant."

Politeness

Nine-year-old Bill hurried off to Sunday-school one morning before his mother inspected his wash job. When he sat down in the classroom, breakfast was still visible on his face.

The teacher frowned and said reprovingly: "Bill, you didn't wash your face. What would you say if I came to Sunday-school with egg and jam around my mouth?"

"Nothing," he replied. "Nothing at all. I'd be too polite."

Help

WAITER: "May I help you with that soup, sir?"

DINER: "What do you mean, help me? I don't need any help."

WAITER: "Sorry, sir. From the sound I thought you might wish to be dragged ashore."

How's That

A man went into a restaurant and said, "Give me a half dozen fried oysters."

"Sorry, suh," answered the waiter, "but we's all out o' shell fish, suh, 'ceptin' eggs."

Please Repeat That

A diner gave his order for oatmeal, toast, scrambled eggs, and coffee.

As the waiter departed the diner called him back. "Bring me waffles, boy, and eliminate my eggs."

The waiter scratched his head. "Says what, boss?"

"Waffles, I said—an' eliminate my eggs."

A stare of suspicion. "Aw right, boss."

Two minutes later, the waiter's perturbed face reappeared down the aisle. "Boss, will you repeat dat order for me? De cook is plumb iggeramus."

"Some oatmeal, toast, scrambled eggs, waffles, and coffee, but eliminate the eggs."

"Yas, suh—dat's what I tol' him."

133

Shaking his head, the waiter left again. After a full five minutes he reappeared, face perspiring. "Boss, couldn't you make it boiled or slurred or fried eggs? De cook says he can't 'liminate yo' eggs—de 'liminator is busted!"

He Won't Do That Again

> *A certain young gourmet of Crediton*
> *Took some* pâté de foie gras *and spread it on*
> *A chocolate biscuit,*
> *Then murmured, "I'll risk it."*
> *His tomb bears the date that he said it on.*
>
> Rev. Charles Inge

She Liked Pickles

> *There was a young lady named Perkins,*
> *Who just simply doted on gherkins.*
> *In spite of advice,*
> *She ate so much spice,*
> *That she pickled her internal workin's.*

Bad Night

> *There was a young man named* **Ted**
> *Who dined before going to bed,*
> *On lobster and ham*
> *And salad and jam,*
> *And when he awoke he was dead.*

FOOTBALL

Risky

The football team had fumbled all afternoon. When a substitute, warming up in front of the bench, dropped a ball, it was too much for a rabid fan.

"Send him in, coach!" he yelled from the stands. "He's ready!"

HIS SISTER: "His nose seems broken."
HIS GIRL: "And he's lost his front teeth."
HIS FATHER: "But he didn't drop the ball!"

FORECASTING

THE CRYSTAL BALL

I used to serve on committees as I suppose all economists do, and twice a year I would sit down and commune with them about the business outlook for the following six months. I did that for a long time.

I stopped it a year or two ago because I found I could guess what would be ahead, and we would always arrive, depending on our state of mind and what was going on immediately then, at a kind of formula. It is a simple formula, and I am not sure it hasn't got a great deal of right in it. Anyhow, I give it to you for your use. We said business was likely to be plus or minus ten per cent difference from what it was in the preceding ten months. It may not be a bad formula.

From an address by Dr. Leo Wolman
Professor of Economics at Columbia University

FORESIGHT

PLEASE BE CAREFUL

The telephone rang in the fire-station office. The chief took up the receiver.

"Is this the fire-station?"

"Yes," said the chief eagerly.

"Well," continued the voice, "I have just had a new rock garden built and I've put in some new plants—"

"Where's the fire?" asked the chief.

"Some of these new plants are very expensive, and—" the voice continued.

"Look here," said the chief at last, "do you want the flower shop?"

"No, I don't," said the voice. "My neighbor's house is on fire, and I don't want you firemen to walk all over my garden when you come here."

FRANK

No Help Needed

A lady was entertaining the small son of a neighbor.

"Are you quite sure you can cut your meat, Herby?" she asked after watching him a moment.

"Oh, yes," he replied. "We often have it as tough as this at home."

FREEDOM

Our Richest Inheritance

Our richest inheritance is the right of every individual to develop ideas.

The tremendous physical achievements of the American people since the birth of our nation, and especially in the last fifty to one hundred years, may blind us to the fact that these physical achievements are a by-product. We have a very high standard of living—and a standard of living is *things*. The American people have wealth on a scale undreamed of a century or two ago. They own things like 200 billion dollars of life insurance, more than 50 billion dollars in savings, accounts, some 60 billion dollars in government bonds, 40 million automobiles, 20 million homes, and farm properties valued at 100 billion dollars. But all of these things are a by-product.

America has been proving—and is still proving on an expanding scale—that if millions of people have individual liberty and freedom of opportunity, they will generate a productive force such as the world has never seen before.

Ernest R. Breech, Executive Vice President
Ford Motor Company

Freedom in Education

A university studies politics, but it will not advocate fascism or communism. A university studies military tactics, but it will not promote war. A university studies peace, but it will not organize crusades of pacifism. It will study every question that affects human welfare, but it will not carry a banner in a crusade for anything except freedom of learning.

L. D. Coffman, Former President
University of Minnesota, 1936

136

THOMAS JEFFERSON AND JOHN ADAMS

When the fiftieth anniversary of the birthday of our country drew near, two great Americans so directly connected with the Declaration of Independence and the sure steps for firm establishment of the Republic—Thomas Jefferson and John Adams —were still living.

John Adams' last years were spent in his beloved New England. Jefferson, too, spent the closing years of his life where he preferred to be—at Monticello. Both continued to give counsel to the people; both helped to steer the Ship of State on an even keel through those formative years.

As the Fourth of July, 1826, was approaching. the citizens of Quincy, Massachusetts, began planning a magnificent celebration. The committee in charge, of course, believed that a public address by the oldest surviving signer of the Declaration of Independence would be appropriate.

But John Adams told the committee he had no desire to make such an appearance. He would, however, propose a toast that could be presented as coming from him.

"I will give you independence forever," he said.

The committee pleaded for more.

"Not a word," said Mr. Adams.

At this time Jefferson lay ill in his bed at Monticello. And, as the people of Quincy had turned to John Adams for an Independence Day oration, the people of Virginia turned to Jefferson for a message. He was too ill to take part in a public ceremony, but he left one deathless word for the nation, one word over his signature.

Historians say, for the last time in his life Jefferson took up his pen and wrote: "Freedom. Thomas Jefferson."

When the Fourth of July, 1826, dawned, the people began joyously celebrating the nation's fiftieth birthday anniversary, with the ringing of church bells and festivities on into the day.

But before this great day was over, on the Fourth of July, exactly half a century from the day on which the Declaration of Independence was adopted, the man who wrote it, and the man who did so much in support of it, Thomas Jefferson and John Adams, died, almost within the hour.

Both passed on leaving to the new United States of America a last message, each of which was a single glorious word. Combined, they gave us and all posterity the admonition: "Freedom and independence forever."

The late Senator Kenneth S. Wherry of Nebraska
Republican Floor Leader of the United States Senate

137

FREE ENTERPRISE

GETTING THINGS DONE THE AMERICAN WAY

Nor can anybody accuse us of lacking imagination or of not having ideas. And they are ideas of a very special kind.

We have an idea, for example, that the American housewife has to work too hard. Somebody gets the idea that the way to fix that is to dream up machinery that will take care of her drudgery. He starts to work on a washing machine. Somebody else gets an idea on how to make it automatic. Somebody else gets an idea on how to make it better and cheaper.

Pretty soon many manufacturers get the idea and start to work on it. The competitive race starts. The trick is to get into the hands of as many people as possible as soon as possible a labor-saving washing machine better and cheaper than the next fellow can dream up.

Others turn their attention to the refrigerator, the sink, the cupboards, the iron, the stove, the tables, the lights, the kitchen floor. And before you can say "Government Security," you have a sparkling thing of push buttons and electricity and paint and polish and efficiency that makes a woman from England want to take off her shoes before she steps inside.

Ernest R. Breech, Executive Vice President
Ford Motor Company

BEFORE IT HAPPENS

The stature of American business is high today. It is too high for us to indulge in petty sniping. Let us not condemn everything as socialistic because it costs money. Let us remember that reformers have a useful function. They are not all moony-minded or profession do-gooders. Let us think of them as gadflies under the saddle of inertia. If they fail to see any solution to inequities in our society except bigger government —why then, gentlemen, isn't it up to this inventive and ingenious system of ours to invent workable solutions the free enterprise way?

If there's a need for better health facilities, the need isn't going to go away because we don't like government control of health. If there's a need for better housing, the need won't disappear because we don't like government intrusion in the real estate business. If there's a need for better schools, the need won't cancel out because we deplore federal control of education.

In short, if there are cobwebs in the free enterprise household, we must find our own brooms to sweep them down, or government will do the sweeping.

The time to lick socialism in America is before it happens.

From an address by D. A. Hulsey, former President,
Chamber of Commerce of the United States,
before the Chamber of Commerce, Salt Lake City

THE MOUSETRAP STORY

Superficial observers think because businessmen have money, or capitalists furnish money, that they are supreme. On the contrary, they are bound to obey unconditionally the "consumer captain's" orders. They cannot determine for long what to produce, how many to produce, or selling prices—the consumers do that. Every businessman knows that if he does not obey the orders of the public, if he does not serve the public by manufacturing what it likes, or offers goods and services for prices it will pay, he will suffer losses, eventually go bankrupt, and be completely removed from the scene. Other men who did better in satisfying the demands of the captains—that is, the consumers—will replace him.

It is we as consumers who decide which companies shall prosper and which shall fail. We as consumers are bosses full of whims and fancies, changeable and unpredictable. When we see something we want and buy it, we do not care an iota about the past merit or vested interests of the person from whom we buy. If something is offered to us tomorrow better or cheaper, or both, we desert our old purveyor.

The old mousetrap story was true a hundred years ago and is true today. If we make the best one, and it is priced right, and we serve a thousand people—we prosper. If we serve a million and do it better than our mousetrap competitors, we prosper a thousand-fold. And not because we are capitalistic. We prosper only because we serve more people better than others, we satisfy their wants, we help them along the way.

The same harsh but fair criterion applies to those who sell their services. Those who work best, work hardest, do more than is expected

139

of them rather than less, cannot help but profit more. All of us know that the most difficult task is getting enough people to do well what is expected of them, and eventually do it better than was expected. Those who keep it up are rewarded with greater opportunities—as well as responsibilities. In other words, it is under the driving power of competition, of freedom of choice that it is possible for each individual to exercise to the fullest his God-given right of liberty, and to reap the just rewards of proper human behavior.

From an address by Hughston M. McBain
Chairman, Marshall Field & Company

FRIEND

OBSERVATIONS ON FRIENDS

"I want someone to laugh with me, someone to be grave with me, someone to please me and help my discrimination with his or her own remark, and at times, no doubt, to admire my acuteness and penetration." So said Robert Burns (1787).

Ambrose Bierce viewed friends more cynically when he said in *The Devil's Dictionary,* "While your friend holds you affectionately by both your hands you are safe, for you can watch both his."

Oscar Wilde explained that "an acquaintance that begins with a compliment is sure to develop into a real friendship."

FRUIT

GREEN APPLES

Fruit out of season,
Sorrow out of reason.
Old English Rhyme

STRAWBERRIES AND CREAM

Goethe said, "One must ask children and birds how cherries and strawberries taste."

FULL

ALL FULL INSIDE

Charles Lamb, English essayist (1775-1834), was returning one afternoon from a dinner party, having taken a seat in a crowded bus. A stout gentleman subsequently looked in, and politely asked, "All full inside?"

"I don't know how it may be with the other passengers," answered Lamb, "but that last piece of oyster pie did the business for me."

FURS

C.O.D.

Bud Collyer asked a woman on "Break the Bank": "How would you order a fur coat if you were in a store without enough money to pay for it then and there?"

The answer he expected was "C.O.D.," but the one he got was "I'd have it sent to my husband's office."

BOTH SKINNED

An intoxicated man was leaning against the window of a furrier when he saw this sign over a denuded tiger: "I was skinned to make a cloak for a woman."

"Shake, old man," said he. "So was I."

GARDEN

HE WILL LEARN

"I am going to start a garden," announced Mr. City Farmer. "A few months from now I won't be kicking about your vegetable prices."

"No," said the grocer, "you'll be wondering how I can sell vegetables so cheap."

GENEROSITY

BOTH ALIKE

A penny was all she dropped into the beggar's hand. "Now, my poor man," she said, "tell me how you lost all of your money."

"Well, I was like you, ma'am," he said. "I was always giving away large sums to the needy."

Schiller, when he had nothing else to give away, gave the clothes from his back, and Goldsmith the blankets from his bed. Tender hands found it necessary to pick Beethoven's pockets at home before he walked out.

E. G. Bulwer-Lytton, 1849

HUMANITY AND GENEROSITY

Humanity is the virtue of a woman, generosity of a man. The fair sex, who have commonly much more tenderness than ours, have seldom so much generosity.

Adam Smith, 1759

GENIUS

AS THEY SAW GENIUS

The public is wonderfully tolerant. It forgives everything except genius.

Oscar Wilde, 1891

Genius is no snob. It does not run after titles or seek by preference the high circles of society.

Woodrow Wilson, 1916

Genius is the clearer presence of God Most High in a man. Dim, potential in all men; in this man it has become clear, actual.

Thomas Carlyle, 1843

Genius, as an explosive power, beats gunpowder hollow.

T. H. Huxley, 1871

PERSEVERANCE

It is said—

That there is hardly a bar of his music which Beethoven did not rewrite a dozen times.

That Bryant rewrote "Thanatopsis" a hundred times.

That Gibbon rewrote his *Autobiography* nine times.

That Plato wrote the first sentence in his *Republic* nine times.

That Vergil spent twelve years writing his *Aeneid*.

A young girl was presented to a professor as a prodigy. The person who introduced her boasted of her proficiency in languages. "I can assure you," said he, "that she can speak and write Latin and Greek."

"These are rare attainments for a young girl," the professor said. "But, tell me, can she skip a rope?"

GENTLEMEN

AND SOME DO

> A man may wear a red necktie, a green vest, and tan shoes, and still be a gentleman.
>
> E. M. Statler, Statler Hotel Service Code, 1921

> If a man is a gentleman, he knows quite enough, and if he's not a gentleman, whatever he knows is bad for him.
>
> Oscar Wilde, 1893

GIFTS

AT THE RIGHT TIME

During a pause in the service the elder leaned over and whispered to the minister: "Remember you were going to say something about the high cost of living."

"I haven't forgotten it," said the minister. "I'll speak of that as soon as the collection has been taken up."

GOD

HE WORKED FOR GOD

For his noble design of the church of St. Peter's in Rome, it is said Michelangelo received only twenty-five Roman crowns, and it was finished in a fortnight. Santo Gallo had been many years employed on his wretched models, and received four thousand crowns for them. This being reported to Michelangelo, far from being mortified or envious, he said, "I work for God, and require no other recompense."

THE POWER OF ONE MAN

Do we believe today that men can so live as to affect genera-
tions yet unborn? Let us turn back the pages of history for
a moment. The time: 1738. It was at Aldersgate Street in
London where the heart of a young Anglican clergyman was
"strangely warmed" by the Spirit of God while listening to the
reading of Luther's comments on faith. And from that Aldersgate Street meeting house, a life was changed; a movement was
born; the kingdom of God was extended around the world!
Yes . . . John Wesley was misunderstood. He had to leave
his own communion. His method was not suited to the
formality of his time. England was reeling like a drunken
man amid her own power, vice, and sin. She was almost on
the verge of collapse. Then, like some mighty giant shaking
the Empire, revivals broke out under the Wesleys. Revival
fires leaped across the Channel to Europe and invaded the new
country, America. This message of "freedom from all sin" and
"holiness unto the Lord" had much to do in the early years
when our own beloved nation was being formed. What was
it? The story of a man who surrendered his will to God and
was changed—and thus empowered, he changed the life of a
nation . . . and a world.

From an address by Dr. S. T. Ludwig
Executive Secretary, Department of Education
Church of the Nazarene, Kansas City, Missouri

MATHEMATICS AND GOD

We hail mathematics as the exact science, yet let us not
forget that mathematics presents one of the best arguments for
God in the orderliness of the universe.

Someone has said that arithmetic is a primer of religion;
algebra is a guide book to divine understanding; geometry is
a textbook of God in expression; physics is God Almighty's
law book of creation, and astronomy is a Bible of religio-
scientific knowledge. No wonder the psalmist burst forth in
his paean of praise and said: "The heavens declare the glory
of God; and the firmament showeth His handiwork."

From an address by Dr. S. T. Ludwig
Executive Secretary, Department of Education
Church of the Nazarene, Kansas City, Missouri

Inevitably, when we forget to count God into our lives we look around for secular substitutes for spiritual values. The other day I came upon a classic bit of advice from a newspaper psychologist. "When you are down in the mouth," he wrote, "wear a red rose." Another gem came from an advertisement: "If your family is drifting apart, buy a television set." The idea seemed to be that Hopalong Cassidy and Arthur Godfrey are God's answer to the distintegrating family of our era. We seem to have the notion, inspired by million-dollar advertising appropriations, that all we need to do to make life glorious is to make it more comfortable or pleasant with gadgets. Just change things outside and everything will be all right inside.

From a sermon by Dr. Harold Blake Walker

CHEERFUL MUSIC

The poet Carpani once asked his friend Haydn how it happened that his church music was always of an animating, cheerful, and gay character. To this, Haydn's answer was, "I cannot make it otherwise. I write according to the thoughts which I feel. When I think upon God my heart is so full of joy, that the notes dance and leap, as it were, from my pen; and since God has given me a cheerful heart, it will be easily forgiven me that I serve him with a cheerful spirit."

GOLF

HONESTY

SANDY: "McPherson's a cheat and I'm not playing golf wi' him again."
ANDY: "How's that?"
SANDY: "Weel, how could he find his lost ball a yard frae the green when it was in my pocket?"

HIS TROUBLE

GOLF PRO: "Now go through the motions without driving the ball."
BEGINNER: "That's exactly the trouble I'm trying to overcome."

Golfer: "Sorry to be late, men. It was a toss-up whether I should come to the club or stay at the office, and—well, I had to toss fifteen times!"

Just Echoes

Two men were playing golf on a course where the hazard on one hole was a deep ravine.

They drove off. One went into the ravine and one got his ball over. The first man said he would go down and play out his ball. He disappeared into the ravine. Presently his ball came bobbing out, and after a time he climbed up.

"How many strokes?" asked his opponent.

"Three."

"But I heard six."

"Three of them were echoes!"

GOOD

How Many Are There

At the end of his life Joseph de Maistre said: "I know not what the life of a rogue may be—I have never been one—but the life of an honest man is abominable. How few are those whose passage upon this foolish planet has been marked by actions really good and useful. I bow myself to the earth before him of whom it can be said, *'Pertransivit benefaciendo'* (He goes about doing good); who has succeeded in instructing, consoling, relieving his fellow-creatures; who has made real sacrifices for the sake of doing good; those heroes of silent charity who hide themselves and expect nothing in this world. But what are the common run of men like? and how many are there in a thousand who can ask themselves without terror, 'What have I done in this world? wherein have I advanced the general work? and what is there left of me for good or for evil?' "

GOSSIP

IT'S DOUBTFUL

"Everyone in town is talking," remarked the wife, "about the Smiths' quarrel. Some are taking her part and some his."

"And," replied her husband, "I suppose a few eccentric individuals are minding their own business."

EXAGGERATION

SUE: "That story you told about Jane isn't worth repeating."

SALLY: "It's young yet. Wait till it grows as others tell it."

HOW TO KEEP FROM GROWING OLD

A suburbanite was sitting at his window one evening. He called to his wife: "There goes that woman Sam Smith is so terribly in love with."

His wife, who was in the kitchen, dropped a plate, rushed through the door, knocked over a lamp and a bowl of goldfish, and ran to the window. "Where?" she cried.

"There," he pointed, "that woman with the blue coat on the corner."

"Don't be silly," she hissed. "That's his wife."

"Yes, of course," he replied casually.

AIN'T IT THE TRUTH

It is perfectly monstrous the way people go about nowadays saying things against one, behind one's back, that are absolutely and entirely true.

Oscar Wilde, 1893

And all who told it added something new,
And all who heard it made enlargements too;
In ev'ry ear it spread, on ev'ry tongue it grew.
Alexander Pope, 1714

IT COULD HAVE BEEN WORSE

Often we complain that someone speaks ill of us. Epictetus had a different view. He said, "If anybody tells you such a one has spoken ill of you, do not refute them in that particular; but answer, had he known all my vices he would not have spoken only of that one."

147

GOVERNMENT

NOTHING IS FREE

Bombarding our ears are words and phrases and ideas that seem to us foreign and full of dangerous foreboding—words like "welfare state," "socialism," "cradle-to-grave security," "pensions for everybody," "deficit spending."

We don't like words like these. We don't like the things they stand for. We like words like "private ownership," "opportunity," "incentive," "thrift," "balanced budgets."

We are disturbed because more and more people seem to like the words and phrases we don't like.

We know very well why they do. Ideas like "security" and "pensions for everybody" soothe the fears of a confused and sometimes frightened world. They offer the hope and promise of all beautiful dreams. They seem to say: "Don't worry. Somebody—probably in 'government'—is about to pull a miracle and you won't have to worry any more—ever. Sit back, take it easy. All of your problems will be taken care of."

There's no denying that such ideas have a lot of appeal. Everyone likes something for nothing. Even a millionaire likes a free pass to a ball game.

Ernest R. Breech, Executive Vice President
Ford Motor Company

RED TAPE

No one knows better than the nearly two and a half million federal employees how many man-years of soul-destructive red tape are represented by such bungling as the government's recent move to buy a fifty-cent booklet published by the U.S. Chamber of Commerce. The press reported, and I quote: "The mailed request to the Chamber was on Order No. (01-600) 52-2274, based on Requisition No. LB 52-107 payable from Allotment No. - - -, and this number actually ran to twenty-six figures. A four-page contract included with the order warned the Chamber about such things as discrimination in employment, patent infringements and the Eight-Hour Law of 1912. Five pages of additional general provisions . . . dealt with contract termination, labor disputes, and the loading, bracing and blocking of freight cars." All for a single booklet! "A pink slip," the story went on, "pointed out that a variation of ten per cent in the quantity ordered would be unacceptable—but paragraph 31 of the provision said such a variation was O.K." Unquote. The Chamber of Commerce decided that "red tape" had already cost the taxpayers enough, and gave the government agency gratis the fifty-cent booklet it wanted—all properly braced and loaded, I hope. The government agency, by the way, was a defense agency, and the booklet it wanted was entitled "Economic Policies for Defense."

William H. Ruffin, President, Edwin Mills, Inc.
Durham, N. C., and former President
National Association of Manufacturers

ONE WAY OF LOOKING AT IT

TEACHER: "Why did we adopt the Constitution of the United States?"
FRESHMAN: "We adopted the Constitution to secure domestic hostility."

HOW'S THAT?

Bill and Jim were discussing the shortage of businessmen in politics. "What we need is good men in politics," said Bill.

"We certainly do. We certainly do," agreed Jim, "and we need them bad, too."

THEY BUY THE BEST

Two vacationists met at a resort and got into an argument about the merits of their respective states. One of them was getting the best of the argument.

Finally, the loser said: "Well, in my state we have the finest governor and the best legislature that money can buy."

THE CORNER STONE

The cornerstone of the Republic our forefathers established was the religious concept: the conviction that every human being is endowed with a soul that is sacred in the eyes of a Sovereign God. From this principle they derived the two basic theses that they employed in setting up our system of popular self-government.

149

First, they concluded that, since God had created man in his own image with the power to distinguish between right and wrong, every individual ought to listen with respect to the opinions expressed by his fellow citizens, and that whatever judgment was expressed by the majority of such divinely created human beings after full and free discussion, was likely to be closest to God's will for all of them. Vox populi, vox Dei—the voice of the people is the voice of God!

Their second thesis was equally logical, namely, that every mortal soul is endowed by its Creator with certain natural inalienable rights that no human agency whatever may justly invade—neither any man called "king," nor any group of men representing a temporary majority called "government." To guard these natural rights, government, in John Locke's words, should be confined to four objectives—the protection of life, property, peace and freedom.

The problem of the founders of this Republic, therefore, was how to combine these two opposing principles—the will of the majority and the rights of the individual—into a workable, durable government adapted to human nature in its manifold economic, intellectual, and spiritual aspects, and to a large population scattered over a big country. They discarded the idea of a pure democracy in which all decisions would be made by the current majority, because they knew historically that pure democracies had never lasted long. They are too susceptible to demagoguery. As Samuel Adams said: "There never was a democracy that did not commit suicide." So they decided on a republic instead, that is, a constitutional representative democracy, so as to make effective the majority will of the people in governing themselves and at the same time not destroy the individual rights that the Creator had conferred upon each person.

H. W. Prentis, Jr., Chairman of the Board
Armstrong Cork Company

The People Will Do the Rest

Our rulers will best promote the improvement of the nation by strictly confining themselves to their own legitimate duties— by leaving capital to find its most lucrative course, commodities their fair price, industry and intelligence their natural reward, idleness and folly their natural punishment—by maintaining peace, by defending property, by diminishing the price of law, and by observing strict economy in every department of the state.

Let the Government do this—the People will assuredly do the rest.

From Lord Thomas Babington Macaulay's "Essay on Southey's Colloquies on Society," published in *Edinburgh Review,* January 1830

FAITHFULNESS

I have been very much impressed with sentiments expressed in a resolution sent out by the Chamber of Commerce of Houston, Texas, a part of which I quote: "If the principles of our great Republic are based on Christianity, as they are; if freedom is preferable to slavery, as it must be; if our leaders—local, state, and national—are the servants of the people and not their masters; then the people are entitled to demand of them honesty in their personal conduct, loyalty to the people and to the principles of decency and constitutional government, faithfulness to their trust (not mere absence of illegality in their conduct of governmental affairs), and, above all, an example of competence in the handling of the people's money, so as to inspire the people to be competent and frugal in the handling of their own."

From an address by Senator Charles W. Tobey

GREAT MEN AND WOMEN

We Americans say that the Constitution made our nation. Well, the Constitution is a magnificent document, and we never would have had a nation without it, but it took more than that to make the nation. Rather, it was our forefathers and foremothers who made the Constitution and then made it work. The government they constructed did get great things out of them, but it was not primarily the government that put the great things into them. What put the great things into them was their home life, their religion, their sense of personal responsibility to Almighty God, their devotion to education, their love of liberty, and their personal character. When their government acted, it drew from profound depths in the lives of men and women where creation's spiritual forces had been at work.

Well, perhaps this has turned out to be a sermon after all.

Coleridge, so the story runs—who sometimes occupied the pulpit—once said to his friend, Charles Lamb, "Did you ever hear me preach?" And Lamb retorted, "I never heard you do anything else."

Voltaire was not supposed to be especially religious, but one day Benjamin Franklin called on him, taking along with him his seventeen-year-old son. As they parted, Franklin asked Voltaire to bless the boy, and Voltaire put his aged hands on the young man's head and said, "My son—God and liberty. God and liberty. Remember those two words."

That needs to be said to America now!

From an address by Dr. Harry Emerson Fosdick

Look to Yourself

Plutarch said to the Emperor Trajan, "Let your government commence in your breast, and lay the foundation of it in the command of your own passions."

Goethe said the best government is "that which teaches us to govern ourselves."

A Flowering of Progress

Once while I was visiting Winston Churchill at Chartwell, he pointed to a luxuriant vine across the face of his house and exclaimed: "Look at that vine, with its lovely, variegated flowers. That is something man cannot do—he can never equal what nature has done there."

I have the same reverent feeling about the human body—another wonder of nature which man cannot equal. I have never believed that natural selection alone could produce something as marvelous as the human system—with all its organs functioning so harmoniously, and with such prodigious powers of recuperation.

Among social institutions, we have devised a close counterpart—our American system of government. No other kind of government has ever produced such a flowering of progress—material, spiritual, and scientific. Unlike some other political systems, our democracy was not born of dogma. It was not arbitrarily and forcefully imposed on the people from on top. It grew out of the people themselves—out of their hopes and ideals, their zest for freedom, their loathing of oppression. It

152

is the supreme expression of the American mind and spirit, and, like that vine in Mr. Churchill's garden, like the human body, it is beyond compare.

From an address by Bernard M. Baruch

GETTYSBURG ADDRESS: MODERN VERSION

One score and nineteen years ago our fathers brought forth upon this nation a new tax, conceived in desperation and dedicated to the proposition that all men are fair game. Now we are engaged in a great mass of calculations, testing whether this taxpayer or any taxpayer so confused and so impoverished can long endure.

We are met on Form 1040. We have come to dedicate a large portion of our income to a final resting place with those men who here spend their lives that they may spend our money. It is altogether anguish and torture that we do this. But in a larger sense, we cannot evade, we cannot cheat, we cannot under-estimate this tax. The collectors, clever and sly, who computed here, have gone far beyond our poor power to add and subtract.

Our creditors will little note nor long remember what we pay here, but the Bureau of Internal Revenue can never forget what we report here.

It is not for us, the taxpayers, to question the tax which the government has thus far so nobly spent. It is rather for us to be here dedicated to the great task remaining before us— that from these vanishing dollars we take increased devotion to the few remaining; that we here highly resolve that next year will not find us in a higher income bracket; that this taxpayer, underpaid, shall figure out more deductions; and that this tax of the people, by the Congress, for the government, shall not cause solvency to perish.

—Author Unknown

IN THE HANDS OF GOD

Before signing the Constitution, George Washington said, "Let us raise a standard to which the wise and honest can repair. The event is in the hands of God."

"Those immortal words," John Fiske said, "should be blazoned in letters of gold and posted on the walls of every legislative hall."

Nothing Free

The government is not an almoner of gifts among the people, but an instrumentality by which the people's affairs should be conducted upon business principles, regulated by the public needs.

Grover Cleveland, 1887

He Forgot

ACCOUNTANT TO FELLOW WORKER: "For a minute this deficit had me worried ... I forgot I was working for the government."

GRAMMAR

Has Grammar Et Too?

"Hiram, Hiram," called his sister as she stood in the doorway and looked toward the group of small boys. "Hiram, come in and eat youself. Paw he's on the table and Maw she's half et."

He Probably Did

A teacher, endeavoring to make a pupil understand the nature and application of a passive verb, said: "A passive verb is expressive of the nature of receiving an action—as, 'Peter is beaten.' Now, what did Peter do?"

"Well, I don't know," said the boy, pausing a moment, "but he probably hollered."

It Makes a Difference

A college freshman met one of his instructors and asked, "What's your guess about Saturday's game? You don't think we'll do too bad, do you?"

"Don't you mean 'badly'?" inquired the professor.

"What's the difference?" asked the frosh. "You know what I mean."

"An 'l-y' can make quite a difference," persisted the professor. Pointing to another student, he explained, "For instance, it makes a difference whether you look at him sternly—or at his stern."

154

GRATITUDE

No Sermon

During the Thanksgiving season a church in Pennsylvania had this notice posted in front of it: "Thanksgiving service will be held in this church at nine o'clock in the morning. The choir will render appropriate selections. There will be no sermon. Let us thank God for our blessings."

From an address by Dr. Harry Emerson Fosdick

GRAVITY

Falls Up

KEN CARPENTER: "You know, gravity is an amazing thing—everything that falls, falls down."

BING CROSBY: "You're wrong, there's one thing that falls up."

CARPENTER: "What falls up?"

CROSBY: "A husband, sneaking up the stairs late at night."

GREATNESS

The Magnanimous Man

"The magnanimous man," Aristotle said, "will behave with moderation under both good fortune and bad. He will know how to be exalted and how to be abased. He will neither be delighted with success nor grieved by failure. He will neither shun danger nor seek it, for there are few things which he cares for. He is reticent, and somewhat slow of speech, but speaks his mind openly and boldly when occasion calls for it. He is not apt to admire, for nothing is great to him. He overlooks injuries. He is not given to talk about himself or about others; for he does not care that he himself should be praised, or that other people should be blamed. He does not cry out about trifles, and craves help from none."

155

HARDSHIP

Schiller produced his greatest tragedies in the midst of physical suffering. Handel, warned of the approach of death, and suffering, composed the great works which have made his name immortal in music. Mozart composed great operas, and last of all his *Requiem,* when oppressed by debt, and struggling with disease. Beethoven produced his greatest works amidst sorrow, when oppressed by almost total deafness. Schubert, after his short but brilliant life, laid it down at the early age of thirty-two; his sole property at his death consisted of his manuscripts, the clothes he wore, and sixty-three florins in money.

CODE OF HONOR

A century ago, so a historian tells us (and I'm quoting now a historian's description of a nurse a hundred years ago), "A nurse is a coarse old woman, always ignorant, usually dirty, often brutal, a messy person in blotched-out, sordid garments, nibbling at the brandy bottle or indulging in worse irregularities." That was a nurse only a century ago.

Then came Florence Nightingale. Her parents were frantic when she wished to become a nurse. Year after year they fought her off from this "disgraceful" occupation, but while at times she was so discouraged that she wrote in her diary, "In my thirty-first year I see nothing desirable but death," she carried on. She was determined to redeem nursing, and she did.

In retrospect, the Crimean War is notable chiefly, I think, not because of the magnificent charge of the Light Brigade, but because of Florence Nightingale.

From an address by Dr. Harry Emerson Fosdick

GROWTH

INTELLIGENCE

It was President Garfield who said, "Do not, I beseech you, be content to enter any business that does not require and compel constant 'intellectual growth.' One may, if necessary, be able to leave his business and enter another where intellectual growth is possible. But, if not, one may read and study and pursue other activities outside his business so he will grow intellectually and not stagnate."

GUEST

POLITENESS

GUEST: "I hope I haven't come too late."
HOSTESS: "No, my dear, you couldn't come too late."

HURRY BACK

An ole guy had his nephew visit him and he wanted him to go home. In fact he wanted him to go home before he took his saddle off his horse. One day the ole fellow was giving the nephew the dog eye and told him, "Boy I don't believe you are ever coming back to see us."

"Why Uncle Si?" the nephew replied.

"Well," the ole fellow said, "I don't believe you are ever going home so you can come back."

Cayce Moore

GUILTY

IF HE HAD THE CHANCE

The jury had been arguing for hours.

At last they straggled back, and the foreman, a mountaineer, expressed the opinion: "We don't think he did it," he said, "for we don't believe he was there; but we think he would have done it if he had had the chance."

HE LOOKS GUILTY

A school board was visiting a school, and the teacher was putting her pupils through an oral test.

"Who signed the Declaration of Independence, Henry?" she asked turning to the first boy.

"Teacher, it wasn't me," whimpered the youngster.

The teacher was about to call on another pupil, but a member of the board was not satisfied.

"Call that boy back," he said. "I don't like his looks. I believe he did do it."

157

HABIT

WHEN THE WHISTLE TOOTS

A great many industrial employers have problems of people wanting to quit on time, when the bell rings. Well, the refinery at Bahrein (Bahrein Island, off the coast of Arabia) has a particular problem in that lots of the men who come to work ride little burros, and when they get off in the morning at the gate they give the burro a slap on the rear end and it goes out and wanders around all day for a blade or two of grass.

Throughout the years, the burros have associated their going home with the tooting of the whistle for knocking off work. So, what happens? Now, when the whistle toots, every burro starts on the double for the gate, and if the man isn't there to mount him and ride home, he goes on home without him. So, the men just drop their tools and run for the gate just as soon as the whistle blows.

Rear Admiral Thomas J. Kelly, U.S. Navy (Ret.)
Former Director, Petroleum Division
National Security Resources Board, Washington, D.C.

HAPPINESS

BEHIND TIME

"How are you this morning?"
"All right."
"Well, then, why don't you notify your face?"

MATTER OF DEGREE

OFFICER: "Are you happy now that you're in the Navy?"
BOOT: "Yes, sir."
OFFICER: "What were you before you got into the Navy?"
BOOT: "Much happier."

"NOTHING AGES LIKE HAPPINESS" (OSCAR WILDE)

One would suffer a great deal to be happy.

Mary Montagu, 1759

Looking for happiness is like clutching the shadow or chasing the wind.

Japanese Proverb

158

Always looking forward to being happy, it is inevitable that we should never be so.

Blaise Pascal, 1670

HARDSHIP

How it Began

The cotton-gin was first manufactured in a log cabin.

McCormick began to make his reaper in a grist mill.

Edison began his experiments in a baggage car on the Grand Trunk Railway as a newsboy.

Ericsson began to construct screw propellers in a bathroom.

Fitch set up in the vestry of a Philadelphia church parts of the first steamboat ever run in America.

Great Obstacles

Pilgrim's Progress was written by John Bunyan during a six-month imprisonment in Bedford Jail.

Robinson Crusoe was written by Daniel Defoe in prison.

Sir Walter Raleigh wrote his *History of the World* during a thirteen-year prison sentence.

The great poet, Dante, worked and died in exile.

David Livingstone, the great Scottish missionary and explorer, died in a negro hut in Central Africa.

Cervantes, who wrote *Don Quixote* in a Madrid jail, was so poor he couldn't even get paper for his last writing, but used scraps of leather.

Milton did his best writing blind, sick, and poor.

His Soul Should See

Timothy Dwight, one-time president of Yale University, looked back upon the failure of his eyes as a kind event within God's providence. The permanent weakness of his eyes altered his habits. He could not read, but he could meditate. He could not study, but he could observe. He could not go on mastering the classics of the world by first-hand investigation, but he could extract information from conversation. Years after the failure of his eyes, he noted that the most useful information comes not from books, but from reading life itself. Ruined eyes did not keep him from being a great teacher and learning what he wanted to know. He found a new gate in the fence that thwarted his path. He echoed the observation of the Blind Plowman: "God . . . took away my sight that my soul might see."

From a sermon by Dr. Harold Blake Walker

He Believed It Could Be Done

Elias Howe got the idea that it was possible to make a machine that would sew. Four years passed. He had a wife and three children to support on nine dollars a week. But the idea of the machine preyed upon his mind. Months were lost in experiment. Finally he had made a rough wood and wire model, but he was out of funds. An old schoolmate agreed to board him and his family, and provide five hundred dollars in return for one-half the patent if the machine merited patenting. In 1845, Howe finally completed his machine and sewed the seams of a suit for himself and one for his financial backer. The machine was a success, and his first model a very good one.

Milton's Paradise Lost

Milton was blind when he composed *Paradise Lost.* His daughters were his secretaries. Nor did they merely write what he dictated. They read to him from day to day whatever authors he might wish to consult for reference, or to relax or invigorate his mind. Reading to their father the Greek and Latin authors must have been very tedious to them, as it is said they did not know these ancient languages very well.

HARVARD

Hahvahd

BILL: "That young man from Harvard is an interesting talker, but what a queer dialect he uses."

HANK: "That isn't dialect, it's vocabulary. Can't you tell the difference?"

HEALTH

SAME EVERYWHERE

His health wasn't too good, so the city-dweller went looking for a place to live in the Southwest. In a small town in Arizona he approached an old-timer sitting on the steps of the general store. "Say," he asked, "what's the death rate around here?"

"Same as it is back East, son," answered the old-timer, "one to a person."

PLENTY OF TASTE

SONNY: "Give me ten cents worth of castor oil, please."
DRUGGIST: "The tasteless kind?"
SONNY: "No—it's for my father."

NOT CONTAGIOUS

OLD LADY: "Little boy, why aren't you in school instead of going to the movies?"
LITTLE BOY: "Lady, I got the measles."

FIRST-AID

SURGEON AT A HOSPITAL: "What brought you to this dreadful condition, an accident?"
PATIENT: "No, sir; I fainted, and was brought to by a fellow who had just studied first aid."

PRESCRIPTION

A well-to-do lady asked the doctor for a cure for gout.
He replied simply, "Live on a dollar a day, and earn it."

HEARING

CAN'T UNDERSTAND ANYWAY

"Grandpa, why don't you get a hearing aid?"
"Don't need it, Son. I hear more now than I can understand.

161

EDITOR: "You didn't spell this word correctly."

YOUNG REPORTER: "Sorry, sir, I spell by ear and sometimes I don't hear so good."

HELP

SUCCOR OR SUCKER?

In describing the disparities between the languages spoken in England and the United States, Bertrand Russell told of a joint Anglo-American war relief rally held in London after the First World War. When the appeal for funds was made, an American in the audience made a very substantial contribution.

The British chairman, deeply impressed, announced the gift to the crowd and then added: "I am sure we are all deeply grateful for this American succor."

He made a hit with the American portion of the audience.

HISTORY

OLD STUFF

The small daughter of the house felt called upon to entertain the scholarly gentleman waiting for her father.

"Once upon a time there was a man named Columbus," she began. "There was a queen too, and she sent him on a voyage in three ships, named the *Nina,* the *Pinta,* an'—an'—"

"The *Santa Maria?*" prompted the professor.

"Yes, and the queen's name was—uh—"

"Isabella?" supplied the professor.

"Say," said the child with sudden suspicion. "I'll bet you've heard this story before."

WELL, DIDN'T HE?

ENGLISHMAN: "That really puzzles me. In my travels through England I've never noticed a hedge like that one. Are you sure George Washington got it from England?"

MOUNT VERNON GARDENER: "Certainly. He got the whole country from England, didn't he?"

COUNT 'EM

TEACHER: "How many wars have we had?"
STUDENT: "Seven."
TEACHER: "Enumerate them."
STUDENT: "One, two, three, four, five, six, seven."

THAT'S ALL

TEACHER: "What did Paul Revere say at the end of his famous ride?"
STUDENT: "Whoa!"

HOARDING

GIVE AND RECEIVE

There are two seas in Palestine. One is fresh, and fish are in it. Splashes of green adorn its banks. Trees spread their branches over it and stretch out their thirsty roots to sip of its healing water. Along its shores the children play.

The River Jordan makes this sea with sparkling water from the hills. Men build their houses near it and birds their nests; and every living kind of life is happier because it is there.

However, the River Jordan flows on south into another sea. Here is no splash of fish, no fluttering leaf, no song of birds, no children's laughter. Travelers choose another route, unless on urgent business. The air hangs above its waters, and neither man nor beast nor fowl will drink.

What makes this mighty difference in these neighbor seas? Not the River Jordan. It empties the same good water into both. Not the soil in which they lie; not the country round about.

This is the difference: The Sea of Galilee receives but does not keep the Jordan. For every drop that flows into it another drop flows out. The giving and receiving go on in equal measure. The other sea is shrewder, hoarding its income jealously. Every drop it gets, it keeps. The Sea of Galilee gives and lives. The other sea gives nothing. It is named the Dead.

Bruce Barton in *The Employment Counselor*

HOME

MAKE HERS CRISP

> *A judge declares that home life needs*
> *Cooperation—who'll deny it?*
> *'Tis hard to bring the bacon home*
> *And then to have to fry it.*
>
> Boston Transcript

HONEST

TEMPTATION

GROCER (to boy standing near box of apples): "Hey! Are you trying to take an apple?"

BOY: "No, I'm trying not to take one."

AS HE SNAPPED HIS SUSPENDERS

The executive was asked what part his company had played in the war effort.

"See that big plane over there," he said, pointing to a very large plane. "Well, we make the clips that hold the blueprints together."

SPIRITUAL CONCEPTS

> No public man can be just a little crooked. There is no such thing as a no-man's-land between honesty and dishonesty. Our strength is not in politics, prices, or production, or price controls. Our strength lies in spiritual concepts. It lies in public sensitiveness to evil.
>
> From an address by Herbert Hoover

HONEYMOON

TEMPUS FUGIT

The man and the girl stood entranced at Niagara Falls. It was the third day of their honeymoon.

"Darling," she whispered, "isn't this heavenly?"

Her husband sighed. "Just think, even if we are fortunate, our married life can hardly last longer than fifty years," he said.

164

"Is that all?" she asked.

"Yes, only fifty years in which to love each other."

"Then kiss me quickly, dear," she said. "We're wasting time!"

HONOR

Often Told, but Still Good

Someone once asked Lincoln whether he did not find the ceremonies of the Presidency irksome.

"Yes, sometimes," said Lincoln. "In fact, I feel sometimes like the man who was ridden out of town on a rail, and said. 'If it wasn't for the honor of the thing, I'd rather walk!'"

One at a Time

When William Penn, the proprietor of Pennsylvania, and the most important man among the Quakers, went to court to pay his respects to Charles II, that merry and observing king took off his own hat and stood uncovered before Penn, who said, "Prithee, friend Charles, put on thy hat." "No, friend Penn," said the king, "it is usual for only one man to stand covered here."

HOPE

He Makes You so Happy

Two women were leaving the theater after a performance of *The Doll's House*.

"Oh, don't you love Ibsen!" cried one excitedly. "He just takes all the hope out of life."

Hope Anchored in God

Without the hope that flows from the Bible, not daring to dream or to trust the future, there is not much use going on. . . . By all the rules of logic, Paul's dream was dead as a dodo when he sat in his prison at Rome and watched the antics of Nero. Paul's gospel was finished and Jesus was only an-

165

other futile prophet whose ways were not fit for the world. The realist, priding himself on his sound sense, would not have gambled his life on Christ. No rational man in his right mind would have dared to hope that what Paul stood for would outlive and outlast the annals of Caesar.

It is hope we need in this tired, troubled, tortured world—hope anchored in the Word of God.

From a sermon by Dr. Harold Blake Walker

HORSES

Just a Yawn

The young fellow thought he could ride, so he mounted the pony. A moment later he painfully picked himself out of the dust. "Man," he cried, "she bucked something fierce."

"Bucked!" said a cowboy. "She only coughed."

HOTELS

We Stayed There

GUEST: "Do you run a bus between the hotel and the railway station?"

MANAGER: "No, sir."

GUEST: "That's strange. My friends said you would get me coming and going."

HOUSEWIFE

Before Electric Appliances

Here lies a poor woman, who always was tired;
She lived in a house where help was not hired.
Her last words on earth were: "Dear friends, I am going
Where washing ain't done, nor sweeping, nor sewing;
But everything there is exact to my wishes;
For where they don't eat there's no washing of dishes."

The Housewife's Epitaph, about 1825

HUMAN BEINGS

Point of View

Two flies were strolling along the ceiling of an apartment. "You know," remarked the first little fly, "human beings are so silly!"

"People are silly?" replied the second fly. "How do you figure that?"

The first fly shrugged his wings. "Just take a look," he said. "They spend good money building a nice high ceiling, and then they walk on the floor."

HUMILITY

Warts and All

Not many men are so outspoken as Cromwell was when he said to the painter, "Paint me as I am, warts and all."

"Pride That Apes Humility"

You've no idea what a poor opinion I have of myself—and how little I deserve it.

W. S. Gilbert, 1887

HUNTING

Confused a Little

Hunter to old guide: "Have you ever been lost in the woods?"
Old guide: "Nope, but I was bewildered once for four days."

HURRYING

Inner Tension

To be sure, much of our tension comes from the pressure of things outside, but not a little of it we make for ourselves. Living and working under pressure, we get into the habit of hurrying. A dining-car waiter felt the truth when he remarked concerning his customers: "Dey's always in a hurry, and dey ain't goin' nowhere but to sit down." The tempo of life

167

around us gets to be a fever within us, until, as Henry Thoreau noted, we become "restless, nervous, bustling, trival," and all tied up with inner tension.

From a sermon by Dr. Harold Blake Walker

HUSBANDS

STILL USEFUL

A White Elephant Party was announced. Every guest was to bring something that she could not find any use for, and yet was too good to throw away. The party would have been a great success, but for an unlooked-for development which broke it up. Eleven of the nineteen women brought their husbands.

HYPOCRISY

"WOE UNTO YOU HYPOCRITES"

There is an old German proverb which says: "When the fox preaches, look to your geese."

Shakespeare in his *Henry VI* described a hypocrite as follows:

I can smile, and murder whiles I smile,
And cry "Content" to that which grieves my heart;
And wet my cheeks with artificial tears,
And frame my face to all occasions.

IDEAS

THE STEAM ENGINE

James Watt, who made possible the modern steam engine, said, "I had gone to take a walk on a fine Sabbath morning, and had passed the old washing-house, thinking upon the engine at the time, when the idea came into my mind that, as steam is an elastic body, it would rush into a vacuum, and if a communication were made between the cylinder and an exhausted vessel, it would rush into it, and might be there condensed without cooling the cylinder." In that idea was the birth of the first practical steam engine.

No Defense Against a New Idea

No army can withstand the strength of an idea whose time has come.

Victor Hugo

An idea that is not dangerous is unworthy of being called an idea at all.

Elbert Hubbard, 1923

IDLE

As They Saw Idleness

It is impossible to enjoy idling thoroughly unless one has plenty of work to do.

Jerome K. Jerome, 1889

Every man is, or hopes to be, an idler.

Samuel Johnson, 1758

Idle people have the least leisure.

English Proverb

Idle men are dead all their life long.

Thomas Fuller, 1732

IGNORANCE

Always Unconscious

One day a smart aleck got into a dentist's chair. The dentist looked at him for a moment, and then said to his attendant, "I don't dare to give him gas."

"Why not?" said the assistant.

"Because we can't tell when he loses consciousness."

Youthful Neglect

Walter Scott, in a narrative of his personal history, gives the following caution to youth:

"If it should ever fall to the lot of youth to peruse these pages, let such readers remember that it is with the deepest regret that I recollect in my manhood the opportunities of learning which I neglected in my youth; that through every part of my literary career I have felt pinched and hampered by my own ignorance; and I would at this moment give half the reputation I have had the good fortune to acquire, if, by doing so, I could rest the remaining part upon a sound foundation of learning and science."

THE ABSENCE OF KNOWLEDGE IS IGNORANCE

Ignorance is voluntary misfortune.

Nicholas Ling, 1597

Ten million ignorances do not constitute one knowledge.

Metternich

From ignorance our comfort flows,
The only wretched are the wise.

Matthew Prior, 1692

Ignorance never settles a question.

Benjamin Disraeli, 1866

If a nation expects to be ignorant and free, in a state of civilization, it excepts what never was and never will be.

Thomas Jefferson, 1816

IMAGINATION

HE ONLY CARRIES A MILLION

FIRST DRUG ADDICT: "Say, have you got twenty million dollars?"
SECOND DRUG ADDICT (thoughtfully): "Not in cash."

EYES THAT WERE OPEN

Galilei Galileo, Italian astronomer (1564-1642), saw the lenses in the eye of an ox and copied them into his telescope.

Johann Wolfgang von Goethe, German author (1749-1832), saw that the core of the apple repeated the blossom, and that the leaf of the tree was a miniature of the oak and elm.

170

Pierre Laplace, French astronomer (1749-1827), saw the Milky Way in the heavens and the rings around Saturn, and with his telescope broke up the milky whiteness into myriads of suns and stars and cosmic systems.

IMMORTALITY

NAPOLEON ON IMMORTALITY

Napoleon, strolling through the gallery of the Louvre one day, attended by the Baron Denon, turned round suddenly from a fine picture which he had viewed for some time in silence, and said to him, "That is a noble picture, Denon."

"Immortal," was Denon's reply.

"How long," inquired Napoleon, "will this picture last?"

Denon answered that with care, and in a proper situation, it might last, perhaps, five hundred years.

"And how long," said Napoleon, "will a statue last?"

"Perhaps," replied Denon, "five thousand years."

"And this," returned Napoleon, sharply, "this you call immortality!"

FRANKLIN'S OWN EPITAPH

The following epitaph was written by Franklin many years previous to his death:

"The body of Benjamin Franklin, printer—like the cover of an old book, its contents torn out and stript of its lettering and gilding—lies here, food for worms; yet the work itself shall not be lost, for it will (as he believed) appear once more in a new and more beautiful edition, corrected and amended by the Author."

IMPOSSIBLE

EXPECTING TOO MUCH

A gentleman who had married a wealthy, but rather homely lady, presented himself with his bride to Gilbert Stuart, requesting the gifted artist to paint the portraits of both. Stuart undertook the task; but when it was finished, the gentleman found considerable fault with the likeness of his wife. The truth was, it was too perfect a copy of the original. Stuart understood the difficulty, and with forbearance quite different from his earlier years, he promised to make an effort to improve the picture. The gentleman called to see it subsequently, but still he hesitated with some dissatisfaction. Stuart, no longer able to endure the man's treatment, rose, and, pacing up and down in his studio in anger, broke out into a soliloquy: "What a miserable life the artist's is! Worried to death with the absurd demands and cavils of his patrons! Here a man brings me a potato, and expects me to make a peach of it!"

INFLATION

ONE CENT

Six-year-old Herby was lecturing little Bill, aged three, on the value of various coins.

"Now this," he said, "is a dime. It will buy two candy bars. This, is a nickel. It will buy only one candy bar."

He brought out a third coin.

"And this," he said with a contemptuous air," is a penny. All it is good for is a parking meter or sales tax."

HIGH COST OF LIVING

JUDGE: "Why did you steal that seventy-five thousand dollars?"
DEFENDANT: "I was hungry."

HOW TO DESTROY A NATION

Lenin said—at least he is reported by the highly placed Lord Keynes as having said—that the best way to destroy the capitalistic system is to debase the currency. Keynes declared that Lenin was absolutely right, and added himself that there was no more subtle or surer way to overturn the existing basis of society than to debase the currency. This method, he said, engages all the hidden forces of economic law on the side of destruction—and please mark and remember these words—"it does so in a way that not one person in a million can diagnose or understand." It is a secretive, sinister, and unending subtraction from possessions gained by industry and thrift.

Rt. Hon. Arthur Meighen, P.C., K.C.
Former Prime Minister of Canada

172

High Prices

The little boy sat gazing into space. His father said, "Junior, a penny for your thoughts."

"Well, to be honest, Daddy," he said, "I was thinking of a dime."

INQUISITIVE

Glad to Tell You

GUEST: "My dear, where did your wonderful string of pearls come from? You don't mind my asking, do you?"

HOSTESS: "Not at all. They came from oysters."

INSULT

Recognized Him

Two farmers were sitting on the porch of the general store when a smart aleck drove up in a flashy convertible.

"Hey, you," yelled the smart aleck, "how long has this town been dead?"

"Can't be long," snapped back one of the natives. "You're the first buzzard we've seen."

Distant Destination

Rousseau, French author and thinker, told Voltaire, French philosopher, he had composed an ode to posterity. Voltaire told him that it would never reach its address. A violent quarrel ensued, and Rousseau became his bitter enemy.

No Other Can

> *A moral, sensible, and well-bred man*
> *Will not affront me, and no other can.*
> William Cowper, 1782

173

INSURANCE

Smart Dog

An Eastern farmer was arguing with a visitor from Kentucky about the merits of his dog, in comparison with the Kentuckian's coon hound. "I'll tell you how smart that dog is," said the Easterner. "When our house burned down, that dog dashed in and rescued my two small children. We knew everyone was out of the house, but the dog tore back into the burning building, and after a long time, came out with our fire insurance policy in his mouth."

"Well, I declare!" said the Kentuckian, "I wouldn't have believed it."

"Yes," replied the Easterner, "and the remarkable part of it was—he had a wet towel wrapped around the policy."

Benefits

Rastus: "Does this lodge yo' belong to have any death benefits?"

Andy: "Yessuh! 'Deed it does. When yo' dies, yo' don' pay any more dues."

Dangerous Life for Pedestrians

A man went to an insurance office to have his life insured.

"Do you drive a car a great deal?" the agent asked.

"No."

"Do you fly?"

"No, no," said the applicant.

"Sorry, sir," the agent said, "we no longer insure pedestrians."

Health

It is estimated that Americans spend between 10 and 11 billion dollars annually for health services. One out of three people are totally disabled every year, and for one out of seven that disability endures five weeks or more. In the span of 12 months, one out of 12 is hospitalized for an average stay of 10 days. Americans lose more than one billion days of work each year on account of sickness.

In the course of an average lifetime, an individual will be

disabled 17 times. Only one dwelling in 400 will be damaged by fire. Only one automobile policy in 33 will result in a loss each year, but one disability insurance policyholder in four will file a claim.

Best's Insurance News, February, 1952

INTELLIGENCE

No Sailor

The teacher was holding an oral exam.

TEACHER: "Willie, tell me what you know about George Washington —was he a soldier or a sailor?"

WILLIE: "He was a soldier."

TEACHER: "Why do you think he was a soldier?"

WILLIE: "I saw a picture of him crossing the Delaware—and anybody who'd stand up in a rowboat ain't no sailor."

Not so Backward

The mother went shopping with her small son. The grocer invited the boy to help himself to a handful of cherries. But the boy seemed backward.

"Don't you like cherries?" the grocer asked.

"Yes," said the boy.

The grocer put his hand in and dumped a generous portion into the little fellow's pocket, which he promptly held out. Afterward his mother asked him why he had not taken the cherries when first invited.

" 'Cause his hand was bigger'n mine," was the answer.

Smart Boy

The teacher read the story of a man who swam a river three times before breakfast.

"You do not doubt that a trained swimmer could do that, do you?" he asked the class.

"No, sir," replied Jimmy, "but I wonder why he didn't make it two or four, and get back to the side where his clothes were."

INTRODUCTIONS

WE HAVE WITH US

I was a guest in the Chicago Athletic Club some few years ago. That is probably one of the best-equipped clubs in the country, if not in the world. I was sitting there in the lounge room admiring the magnificent furnishings, when I noticed a young man come out of the bowling alley, wiping the sweat from his forehead. He sat down beside an elderly gentleman who was reading the newspaper. To make conversation, I suppose, the young man said, "I'm a little stiff from bowling." And to discourage conversation, I suppose, the elderly gentleman looked up from his newspaper and said, "Where did you say you were from?"

Noah M. Mason, Member, Ways and Means Committee, House of Representatives, Congress of the United States

INVESTMENTS

EASY TO DRIVE

FATHER: "I bought four convertibles today."

SON: "Oh swell. Now I can drive one to school."

FATHER: "Sorry, Son, but these are preferred convertibles—and the only place we're driving them is to the bank vault."

THE IMPORTANT FACTOR

CUSTOMER: "I've come back to buy that mutual fund we discussed yesterday."

SALESMAN: "That's fine, I thought you'd be back. Now tell me what was the dominant feature that made you decide to buy? The income feature? the growth factor? or what?"

CUSTOMER: "My wife, sir."

IRRITABLE

SOCRATES AND XANTIPPE

Xantippe, the wife of Socrates, was remarkable for her ill humor and peevishness. She continually tormented him, and one day, not satisfied with her bitter invectives, she emptied a vessel of dirty water on his head. The good man only replied, coolly and philosophically, "I thought that after so much thunder, we should be apt to have some rain."

JOURNALISM

NAPOLEON'S DEFINITION OF A JOURNALIST

The worst recommendation that any man could have, in Napoleon's eyes, was to be a newspaper writer. One of Napoleon's assistants asked for an appointment for a journalist of his acquaintance.

"What has he done?" Napoleon asked.

"He has been a journalist."

"A journalist!" repeated Napoleon. "That means a grumbler, a censurer, a giver of advice, a regent of sovereigns, a tutor of nations."

JUDGE

THIRTY DAYS FOR CONTEMPT

A judge, who was long-winded and pompous, was charging the jury. Suddenly he noticed a juryman asleep. Rapping sharply on his desk, he awakened the sleeper. After glaring at him, the judge said, in a most sarcastic tone: "You're a fine person to have on a jury! Do you think your opinion will be of any value when you go out to determine the fate of the prisoner?"

"Yes, your Honor," said the juryman quietly, "I think so."

"Oh, you do, do you?" shouted the judge. "Tell me, how long have you been sleeping?"

"I don't know, your Honor," was the reply. "How long have you been talking?"

A NEW APPROACH

A culprit was being tried for theft. "This is a serious charge, Andy. You want me to appoint a lawyer to defend you?"

"Naw suh, Jedge, thank you. Every time I done had a lawyer, dey lock me up in de calaboose, an' let de lawyer go free. Dis time, Jedge, I'm gwine to throw myself on de ignorance of de cou't."

There was a clash between the lawyer and the judge. The latter ordered the lawyer to sit down. The lawyer was deaf and didn't hear him and went on talking. The judge fined him ten dollars.

The lawyer leaned toward the clerk of the court and cupped his hand behind his ear. "What did he say?" he inquired.

"He fined you ten dollars," explained the clerk.

"What for?"

"For contempt of court."

The lawyer gave the judge a mean look and thrust a hand into his pocket. "I'll pay it now," he said. "It's a just debt."

JURY

ACCEPTED

The judge was holding court. A prospective juror was being questioned by a lawyer.

"Do you know anything about this case?" the juror was asked.

"No."

"Have you heard anything about it?"

"No."

"Have you read anything about it?"

"No, I can't read."

"Have you formed any opinion about the case?"

"What case?"

"Accepted."

JUSTICE

CLEAR CASE

"I had the right of way when this man ran into me, yet you say I was to blame."

"You certainly were."

"Why?"

"Because his father is mayor, his brother is chief of police, and I'm engaged to his sister."

JUST AND UNJUST

> *The rain it raineth on the just*
> *And also on the unjust fella;*
> *But chiefly on the just, because*
> *The unjust steals the just's umbrella.*
>
> Lord Bowen

KINDNESS

IN HIS FACE

Felix Adler relates that while President Thomas Jefferson was one day horseback riding with a group of younger friends, the party came to a swollen stream. On the bank sat a poor man looking ruefully at the raging flood he was unable to cross. The man watched the others ford the stream on their horses, but said nothing to them. Last came Jefferson. The man, not recognizing him as President, asked if he might mount behind him and cross the stream. Jefferson cheerfully took him across. On the opposite side, someone asked the man why he had not requested the service of one of the other members of the party. He replied, "There are some faces on which is clearly written the answer 'No' to a question you intend to ask. There are other faces on which is written 'Yes.' On their faces was written 'No.' On his 'Yes.'" This man experienced kindness.

Dr. Rolland W. Schloerb, Minister
Hyde Park Baptist Church, Chicago

KINDNESS?

"You call yourself a kind father and yet you haven't sent me a check for a month," wrote the college sophomore.

"That's unremitting kindness," his Dad replied.

KNOWLEDGE

HUMILITY

The humility of General Robert E. Lee, commander of the Confederate Army, is emphasized by the remark attributed to him that he

179

could always learn something of value by talking with a private soldier.

One day Lee found one of his half-starved soldiers under a persimmon tree, eating the green fruit. "Don't you know," said Lee, "that green persimmons are not fit for food?"

"I ain't eating 'em for food," replied the hungry private. "I'm eating 'em to draw up my stomach to fit my rations."

Better Read Them

There is a celebrated reply of Mr. Curran, famous Irish judge (1750-1817), to Lord Clare's curt remark, "Oh, if that be law, Mr. Curran, I may burn my law books."

"Better read them, my lord," was the sarcastic rejoinder.

LABOR

Law and the Constitution

I represent an organization which, I believe, has a good wages, hours, and working conditions as any labor group in the world. We accomplished this by working with industry and within the framework of this government, and by no other method.

I disagree with employers in many parts of the country almost every day, and undoubtedly I shall continue to disagree with them, but I will disagree with them within the framework of our American law and Constitution and in an effort to convince and receive from industry what I honestly believe the men and women of labor are entitled to receive from industry for their labor investment.

From an address by Dave Beck, Executive Vice President
International Brotherhood of Teamsters, Chauffeurs,
Warehousemen and Helpers of America

The Pig Likes It

Cyrus Ching is widely known as a government mediator in labor troubles. He says, "I learned long ago never to wrestle with a pig. You get dirty, and besides the pig likes it."

180

LAND

Hard of Hearing

When the Florida real estate boom was at its height, many an "investor" paid large sums for property that usually was under six feet of water. One victim later surveyed his worthless acres and went back to the promoter who had sold it to him. "You faker," he shouted. "Didn't you tell me I could grow nuts on that property?"

"I did not," said the promoter firmly. "I said you could go nuts on it."

LANGUAGE

No Thanks

Corporal Jones and some other soldiers had been invited to a lady's house for coffee and cakes. Jones was sampling the coffee when his hostess came up to him and said, "There are some nice cookies in the other room, if you'd like them."

"No, thanks, ma'am, I've already got a date with a blonde."

That Makes It All Clear

A precocious five-year-old son of a professor asked his father what was the exact meaning of the verse beginning, "Jack Sprat could eat no fat."

"In simple terms," said the professor, "it means Jack Sprat could assimilate no adipose tissue. His wife, on the contrary, possessed an aversion for the more muscular portions of the epithelium. And so, between them both, you see, they removed or did away with all the foreign substances from the surface of the utilitarian utensil, commonly called a platter. Does that make it clear, son?"

"Perfectly clear," replied the son. "The lack of lucidity in these alleged Mother Goose rhymes is amazingly apparent to one with an intellect above the moronic grade."

De Boids

"De boids choip pretty."

"Those aren't 'boids,' they're birds."

"No foolin'. Dey choip just like boids."

They Don't Talk Right

Northern youngster just back from a trip to the South: "Those Southern kids certainly talk funny. They say 'you-all' instead of 'youse guys.'"

Using Words

The fact is that the use of words has become so important in economics and politics and in other fields that they have invented a word to describe it, "semantics." When I was in Washington I used to hear a good deal about semantics and I used to hear a good many people who were expert in it. Sometimes I thought they were using long words to say very simple things. That was especially true among the many economic wizards who came down there. In any event, this much-abused practice has a solid truth behind it. It must be realized that there are all sorts of ways of expressing a thought and that you can elicit a totally different response from your audience in accordance with the choice of the words you use. In politics we call our machine "an organization," and we call the other fellow's organization a "machine."

James A. Farley

That's Learning 'em English

A man came into the bank to cash a check, then frowned as he looked at the clock. He glanced at his wrist watch then back at the clock and said, "That clock's fast, isn't it?"

"Certainly," replied the teller, "it would fall down if it weren't."

Didn't Lose It

The American visitor to London liked Cockney talk. He would engage them in conversation just to hear the accent.

He was riding on the "underground" one day when he heard the conductor shout, " 'ighbridge next stop. 'ighbridge."

When the conductor passed him the American couldn't resist a little joke. "I beg your pardon," he said, "but didn't you drop something back there?"

"Hi see wot you mean," replied the conductor, "but don't be alarmed. Hi'll pick hit hup hagain when we reach Hoxford Street."

OFFICIAL JARGON

One of the amazing things one learns about official life in Washington is the jargon which has grown up to describe official activities. You don't refer to your office—you refer to your "shop." You do this in your shop—I do this in my shop. You don't delay something which you believe should not be done—you "drag your feet." You don't postpone or slow up a program—you "phase it out." You don't deal with this matter under a certain description—you handle it within a certain "framework," and everything, of course, follows a certain "directive." You don't refer to a mistake in timing or a discrepancy between the objective and the accomplishment— you talk about "slippage" or "a short fall." You don't say that there isn't enough of something to go around—you say it is "in short supply." You don't appoint a group to look into a certain problem—you employ a "task force." You don't refer to the matter at hand as a specific problem—you refer to the assignment as an "ad hoc" detail. You don't conclude or end a job—you "finalize" it.

From an address by Charles Sawyer
When he was Secretary of Commerce

HOW FRANKLIN DID IT

It is no good being able to think straight, however, unless one can express his ideas to the people with whom he comes in contact. Hence, the vital importance of being able to write and speak cogent, fluent English. Poor diction, wordiness, and repetition abound in the average man's speech. Benjamin Franklin tells in his autobiography of the means by which he acquired his effective telling style: He read a passage from the work of some great master of the English tongue, then put it aside and tried to reproduce the thought in his own words. Finally, he compared his effort with the original text and discovered where he had obscured thought, wasted words, or

183

failed to drive straight to the point. A man may be a veritable Encyclopedia Britannica so far as his store of knowledge and his ability to think may be concerned, but all his mental efforts will be of no avail unless he can convey what he knows and thinks to others.

From an address by H. W. Prentis, Jr.,
Chairman of the Board, Armstrong Cork Company

BE CAREFUL

Some foreigners substitute the sound of *d* for that of *th*. A foreign gentleman, being asked how old he was, replied he was *d*irty (thirty); and when asked the age of his wife, he answered she was *d*irty-two (thirty-two).

LARGE

LONG WAY FROM HOME

The bigness of Texas is evident from the map. It is about six hundred miles from Brownsville, at the bottom of the map, to Dallas, which is several hundred miles from the top of the map. The following conversation took place in Brownsville recently between two of the old-time residents:

"Where have you been lately, Hank? I ain't seen you."

"Been on a trip north."

"Where'd you go?"

"Went way up to Dallas."

"Have a good time?"

"Naw—I never did like them Yankees no how."

LAUGHTER

IT WAS A TACTLESS LAUGH

"Have you ever laughed until you cried?"

"Yes, just last night I did."

"How?"

"Dad stepped on a tack. I laughed—he heard me—and then I cried."

LAUNDRY

WHAT! NO SOAP

In some parts of Mexico hot springs and cold springs are found side by side. The women often boil their clothes in the hot springs and rinse them in the cold springs. A tourist remarked to his Mexican friend, "I guess they think Mother Nature is pretty generous."

"No, señor," the other replied. "There is much grumbling because she supplies no soap."

LAW

EXPENSIVE ADVICE

A well-known lawyer was always lecturing his office boy—whether he needed it or not. One day he heard the following conversation between the boy and the one employed next door.

"How much does he pay you?" asked the latter.

"I got five thousand dollars a year," replied the office boy, "twenty-five a week in cash and the rest in legal advice."

HELPLESS

Willie Jones, a sawed-off, beaten-down little man, was arraigned in a Texas district court on a felony charge.

The clerk intoned: "The State of Texas versus Willie Jones!"

Before he could read further, Willie almost broke up the session by solemnly declaring: "Man! What a majority!"

INTERRUPTED

JUDGE: "Can't this case be settled out of court?"

PAT: "That is what we wuz tryin' to do, yer Honor, when the police interfered."

LAWYER

POINT OF VIEW

"Describe to the jury just how the stairs run in that house," the lawyer asked the man who had witnessed a crime.

185

The old man looked dazed and scratched his head for a minute before attempting a reply. "You vant to know how de stairs run?" he repeated.

"Yes, if you please, how the stairs run."

"Vell," ventured the witness, slowly "ven aye bane oopstairs de run down, and ven aye bane downstairs dey run oop."

THIRTY DAYS

A young lawyer was fighting his case brilliantly but felt the judge showed a leaning to the other side. He went so far as to tell the judge so. His Honor rebuked the young lawyer. "Young man," the judge exploded, "you are extremely offensive."

"We both are," the lawyer retorted, "but I am trying to be, and you can't help it."

YOU SCOUNDRELS

"Gentlemen of the jury, the plaintiff called my client, Mr. O'Hara, an Irish scoundrel, as the evidence has shown. Now, Mr. Olson, I ask you, if he had called you a Swedish scoundrel, what would you have done? Or you, Mr. Goldstein, if he had called you a Jewish scoundrel? Or any of you gentlemen, what would you have done, if he had called you the kind of scoundrels you all are?"

NO ARGUMENT

A young lawyer had talked nearly five hours. The jury felt like lynching him. His opponent, an old veteran, arose, looked at the judge and said: "Your Honor, I will follow the example of my friend who has just finished, and submit the case without argument."

LAZY

GUESS THEY WON'T MISS EDDIE

Eddie, the clerk, was inefficient and discourteous. One day when he was absent, the atmosphere was like tranquil summer weather after a thunderstorm, and a customer remarked on the difference.

"Eddie ain't just away," said the proprietor. "He don't work here any more."

"Do you have anybody in mind for the vacancy?"

"Nope," said the proprietor. "Eddie didn't leave no vacancy."

TAKING NO CHANCES

A traveler noticed a farmer was having trouble with his horse. It would start, go slowly for a short distance, and then stop again. The traveler approached and asked: "Is your horse sick?"

"No."

"Is he balky?"

"No. But he is so afraid I'll say whoa and he won't hear me, that he stops every once in a while to listen."

HE REALLY IS TIRED

"Why does your dog howl so?"

"Oh, he's just lazy."

"But why does laziness make him howl?"

"Well," said the dog's owner, "that dog is sitting on a sand burr, and he's too lazy to git off, and he jest sits there and howls because it hurts."

LEISURE

FREEDOM FOR WOMEN

The real authors of emancipated womanhood were not Amelia Bloomer, Lucy Stone, and Susan B. Anthony, but inventors like Eli Whitney, James Hargreaves, and Richard Arkwright.

I hope this does not seem unchivalrous, for undoubtedly these ladies did perform a great service. But if it had not been for the invention of the cotton gin, the spinning jenny, and other textile developments, women would have had little time or concern for equal rights.

The housewife of the eighteenth century was obliged to sit at her spinning wheel turning flax into yarn, weave the yarn into cloth on a home loom, dye it in a kettle and laboriously fashion clothes for herself and her family. Recently we ran a little test on this, and found that the making of a single dress, by these limited methods, would take a woman fifty-six hours, and she had to plan it for sixteen months in advance.

Think of your own wives sitting down today and laying plans for a dress which would be complete in sixteen months.

Fortunately, Whitney's device made it possible to use the short-staple cotton that grew in the South, and made it available to everyone. In ten years following its introduction, annual cotton production in this country jumped from five million to fifty million pounds. Arkwright's and Hargreaves' inventions took the chore of spinning and weaving cloth out of the home, and laid the foundation for the great modern textile industry. This released women from one of their most time-consuming and fatiguing efforts, and gave them the leisure to consider their rights as citizens.

From an address by Harold Brayman
Director, Public Relations Department
E. I. du Pont de Nemours & Company

LIAR

Not if She's Met One

"Do you think a woman believes you when you tell her she is the first girl you ever loved?"

"Yes, if you're the first liar she has ever met."

Just a Fisherman

"Catchin' any?" asked the stranger on the bridge.

"Catchin' any!" answered the fisherman on the banks of the creek. "Why I caught forty bass here yesterday."

"Say, do you know who I am?" asked the man on the bridge.

"Naw, I can't say as I do," answered the fisherman.

"Well, I'm the county fish and game warden."

The fisherman did some quick thinking. After a moment's hesitation, he exclaimed: "Well, say, do you know who I am?"

"No, who're you?"

"I'm the biggest liar in Monroe County."

HE's a Politician

"You seem to be an able-bodied man. You ought to be strong enough to work."

"I know, madam. And you seem to be beautiful enough to go in the movies, but evidently you prefer the simple life."

He got a square meal.

An Innocent Crook

A jury which was directed to bring in a verdict of guilty, because of the prisoner's confession and plea, returned a verdict of not guilty, and offered as a reason that they knew the man to be so great a liar they did not believe him.

LIBERAL

What Is a Liberal?

Carter Glass: "A liberal is a man who is willing to spend somebody else's money."

Unknown author: "One who has both feet firmly planted in the air."

LIBERTY

Freedom and Courage

Pericles observed twenty-four hundred years ago that "the secret of liberty is courage"; not food, not comfort, not money, but just plain old-fashioned fortitude of body, mind, and soul. In thinking about the Four Freedoms that we have heard so much about, I have often wondered what the reactions of the Pilgrim Fathers would have been the day they landed on the rocky, barren coast at Plymouth if Governor Carver had said: Those of you who seek primarily freedom from want, come ashore. Not a man would have stirred. Again, suppose he had said: Those of you who seek primarily freedom from fear in this wilderness full of savages, come ashore. Not a man would have left the ship. But, thank God, impending privation and fear

189

did not daunt those sturdy pioneers. They had known at first-hand what political, intellectual, and spiritual tyranny meant, and they were willing to pay the price for the blessings of such liberty in the New World, no matter what physical suffering was involved. They landed in mid-winter. Before many months had passed, half of their number had died. Yet when the *Mayflower* sailed home in April, as an old historian says: "Not one of the colonists went in her. So sweet was the taste of freedom even under the shadow of death." May it not be written of us in the fateful years ahead, that we lacked that courage of body, mind, and soul, which, when all is said, is the real price of freedom.

H. W. Prentis, Jr., Chairman of the Board
Armstrong Cork Company

INDIVIDUAL LIBERTY

From the moment that Christ held up the idea that prince and peasant alike were in the image of God, and could think God's thoughts in the form of arts, sciences, tools, and laws, all mankind began a great upward march. The fetters were struck from all men. With this idea of individual liberty man found himself. He set forth upon the long journey upward to freedom. Each person is the lord of his own life, and, in the words of St. Paul, "Every man shall give an account of himself unto God."

LIFE

NOT GUILTY

HOTEL CLERK: "Did you take a bath?"
MOUNTAINEER: "No, is one missing?"

LONG LIFE

A traveler in Texas met a cowboy eighty-seven years old. The traveler said: "Tell me, to what do you attribute your old age?"

The cowboy thought for a moment and then spoke gravely. "Well," he replied, "I never stole a horse or called a man a liar to his face."

The early Christians were a revolutionary people. They accepted a doctrine which was considered dangerous to the state and to society. Why do you suppose they were put to death in the arena in Rome? and why was Jesus crucified at Jerusalem? Not for the amusement of the people; not for the satisfaction of their leaders; but because they were considered dangerous, subversive, heretical, and all the rest of it. These early Christians were people willing to constitute a small and unpopular minority. Someone has said of us that we are little more than the resolutionary sons of revolutionary fathers. Whereas they were a revolutionizing influence in society, we try to conform to society, to be like the world in which we live. ... We don't present enough of the adventurous character of the Christian faith to cause men to be challenged by it, or to make them turn to the church in great admiration.

Dr. Edward Hughes Pruden, Minister
First Baptist Church, Washington, D.C.

Living Too Seriously

Take life too seriously, and what is it worth?

If the morning wake us to no new joys, if the evening bring us not the hope of new pleasures, is it worth while to dress and undress? Does the sun shine on me today that I may reflect on yesterday? That I may endeavor to foresee and to control what can neither be foreseen nor controlled—the destiny of tomorrow?

Goethe

What Can You Do?

What can I do? I can talk out when others are silent. I can say man when others say money. I can stay up when others are asleep. I can keep on working when other have stopped to play. I can give life big meanings when others give life little meanings. I can say love when others say hate. I can say every man when others say one man. I can try events by a hard test when others try it by an easy test.

What can I do? I can give myself to life when other men refuse themselves to life.

Horace Traubel

191

WE NEED GUIDEPOSTS

One of the interesting stories which Admiral Byrd has told of his experiences in his south polar expeditions has to do with the experiment that he made of trying to live alone in the frozen wastes about the pole. One problem that he faced was that of getting adequate exercise. The form of exercise he finally adopted was that of walking. This, however, involved the danger of getting lost, since once out of sight of his tent there were no landmarks to guide him back to safety. He solved the problem by driving short stakes in the snow every few yards as the only means of finding his way back.

Such a method of finding one's direction is, of course, not new. Since the advent of the automobile practically every crossroad throughout the nation has signposts to guide the traveler. Likewise the street corners of practically all of our large cities are clearly marked so that even the stranger from afar can find his way.

So in our journey through the world the soul needs reliable guideposts—certain fixed points—in order that one may not lose his way.

Drive in your stakes, then, along the way of life. Here they are—some of them at last: the goodness and love of God, the truth of His World, the faithfulness of Christ, and the assurance that we find through our trust in Him. Following these we shall never lose our way.

Dr. William T. McElroy

A SUMMER'S DAY

Our life is but a summer's day:
Some only breakfast, and away;
Others to dinner stay, and are full fed;
The oldest man but sups, and goes to bed.
Large his account who lingers out the day;
Who goes the soonest, has the least to pay.

Anonymous

WHAT WOULD YOU DO WITH IT?

In a little country community a farmer had a dog who spent part of his time sitting by the side of a large highway waiting for the big red trucks. When the dog saw a truck come around the corner he would get ready, and as it passed him would take out after it down the road.

One day the farmer's neighbor said, "Sam, do you think that hound of yours is ever going to catch a truck?"

"Well, Bill," Sam replied, "that isn't what worries me. What worries me is what he would do if he caught one!"

Many of us in life are like that hound. We run wildly for things which we could not use even if we caught them. It pays to sit down and think about whether one's objectives are worthwhile.

IT'S DANGEROUS

After one of his lectures on mountain-climbing, John Muir, the great naturalist, was approached by a dowager who said, "But Mr. Muir, isn't that dangerous?" To which Muir replied, "Madam, life itself is dangerous; you might die any minute."

From an address by Bower Aly, Professor of Speech
University of Missouri

KEEPS YOU ALERT

A Mexican boy whom I once met had a somewhat unusual but challenging philosophy. He said, "A steady job has many good points, but the way I live means I have to get up early each day and find new jobs every day. It keeps you alert."

BAD BIOGRAPHY

Reader, pass on!—don't waste your time
On bad biography and bitter rhyme;
For what I am, this crumbling clay insures,
And what I was, is no affair of yours!

Anonymous

IT'S A HARD WORLD

MOTHER: "Why are you looking so sad, Billie?"

BILLIE: "Well, it's a hard world. From Monday to Friday I have to go to school. On Saturday I have to take a bath, and on Sunday I have to keep clean. I'm never free."

193

Which sounds longer to you, 569,400 hours or 65 years? They are actually the same in length of time. The average man spends his first eighteen years—157,000 hours—getting an education. That leaves him 412,000 hours from age 18 to 65. Eight hours of every day is spent in sleeping; eight hours in eating and recreation. So there is left eight hours to work in each day. One-third of 412,000 hours is 134,000 hours—the number of hours a man has in which to work between age 18 and 65. Expressed in hours it doesn't seem a very long time, does it? Now I am not recommending that you tick off the hours that you worked, 134,000, 133,999, 133,998, etc., but I do suggest that whatever you do, you do it with all that you have in you. If you are sleeping, sleep well. If you are playing, play well. If you are working, give the best that is in you, remembering that in the last analysis the real satisfactions in life come not from money and things, but from the realization of a job well done. There lies the difference between the journeyman worker and a real craftsman.

From compromise and things half done
Keep me, though all the world deride,
And when at last my job is done,
God keep me still unsatisfied.

From an address by H. W. Prentis, Jr.
Chairman of the Board, Armstrong Cork Company

LITERATURE

ONLY LIKED THE OLD WORKS

When Victor Hugo was an aspirant for the honors of the French Academy, and called on M. Royer Collard to ask his vote, the sturdy veteran professed entire ignorance of his name. "I am the author of *Notre-Dame de Paris, Le Dernier Jour d'un Condamné, Bug-Jargal, Marion Delorme,* etc."

"I never heard of any of them," said Collard.

"Will you do me the honor of accepting a copy of my works?" said Victor Hugo.

"I never read new books," was the cutting reply.

LOAN

On the Telephone

"Hello."

"Hello."

"Is that you, Sam?"

"Yeh, this is Sam."

"It don't sound like Sam."

"This is Sam speaking all right."

"Are you sure this is Sam?"

"Certainly, this is Sam!"

"Well, listen, Sam. This is Bill. Lend me fifty dollars."

"All right. I'll tell him when he comes in."

LOGIC

Is This Clear?

"The sun is all very well," said an Irishman, "but the moon is worth two suns; for the moon gives us light in the night time, when we want it, whereas the sun's with us in the daytime when we have no need for it."

Say That Again

A French professor who was a remarkably ugly man, contended that he was the handsomest man in the world. He proved it thus:

"The handsomest part of the world," said he, "is Europe; of Europe, France; of France, Paris; of Paris, the university; of the university, the college of law; in the college of law the handsomest office is mine; in my office, I am the handsomest man: *ergo,* I am the handsomest man in the world."

A logician said he would prove a scalloped oyster to be better than heaven, and he attempted it by this curious syllogism:

"A scalloped oyster is better than nothing, and nothing is better than heaven: *ergo,* a scalloped oyster is better than heaven."

LOVE

THE PROFESSOR ANSWERS ONE

COED: "Is it natural to shrink from kissing?"

PROFESSOR: "If it were, my dear, most of you girls would be nothing but skin and bones."

From Randolph-Macon's *The Old Maid*

HE DON'T OWE HER NUTHIN'

Joe, thirteen years old, was puzzled over the girl problem, and talked it over with his pal, Willie. "I've walked to school with her three times," he told Willie, "and carried her books. I bought her ice cream sodas twice. Now do you think I ought to kiss her?"

"Naw, you don't need to," Willie decided after thinking a moment. "You've done enough for that gal already."

ACCIDENTS

JIM: "Can you tell me why there are fewer railroad accidents than automobile accidents?"

JOE: "Well, it might be because the engineer isn't always huggin' the fireman!"

GLAD TO MEET YOU

SAILOR: "Hello, Jane, can I see you tonight?"

GIRL: "Sure thing, Bill, come on over."

SAILOR: "But this isn't Bill."

GIRL: "And I'm not Jane, but come on over."

DIFFICULT TO GET GOING

A young man was visiting his girl into the small hours of the morning. The father was becoming impatient and finally remarked, "I can't see why that bird calling on Sophie hasn't sense enough to go home. It's past midnight."

Her little brother spoke up and said: "He can't go, Dad; Sister's sitting on him."

He Knew

LITTLE GIRL: "Papa, what makes a man always give a woman a diamond engagement ring?"

FATHER: "The woman."

Tied and Untied

HE: "Does the moon affect the tide?"

SHE: "No. only the untied."

A Very Punny Joke

" 'I understad he takes her to mystery plays instead of dances.'

'Yes, they love each shudder.' "

H. E. Cook, Director, Federal Deposit Insurance Corporation
Washington, D. C.

The Assurance

A New Haven minister told about a woman who was teaching her three-and-a-half-year-old daughter the Lord's Prayer. The little girl was eager to learn it, but was having a difficult time of it. The mother repeated the first two lines: "Our Father, who art in heaven, Hallowed be Thy Name."

The child solemnly repeated: "Our Father, who art in New Haven, how did you know my name?"

How did you know *my* name? This is the question we fling at the universe in some moment of cosmic loneliness. And yet in the one sentence—"God so loved the world that He gave His only begotten son, that whosoever *believeth in Him* should not perish, but have everlasting life"—is the assurance that whosoever will may avail himself of inclusion in the love which came to fullest expression in Jesus.

Dr. Rolland W. Schoerb, Minister
Hyde Park Baptist Church, Chicago

All Smelled Up

En route to take Carrie out on their Saturday night date, Rastus had stopped at the barber shop to acquire some tonsorial embellishments. When he finally knocked on Carrie's door, she smiled, sniffed emphatically, and said: "Boy, you smell like a barber-pole cat!"

Hard to Please

A young husband admitted to his bride that she was not the first woman he had ever loved. She was selecting a suitable weapon of annihilation from the broom closet, when he gained a reprieve by shouting in terror, "But, darling, I am much harder to please now than I used to be."

Too Nice

A young man, much in love with a young girl, promised to send her one rose for every year of her age.

He ordered the roses, and the florist said, "Oh, he is such a nice man, and a good customer—let's put in an extra dozen roses for him."

The young man still doesn't know why she hasn't spoken to him since.

Honeymoon

"You ought to be ashamed of yourself," the judge began, "assaulting your wife like that. I never saw a worse black eye. Do you know of any reason why I should not send you to prison?"

"If you do," answered the defendant, "it will break up our honeymoon."

Steadfast

"George, will you love me when my hair has turned to gray?"

"Why not? I've loved you through four colors already."

Not So Fast

A bachelor, notorious for his slowness, paid attention for several years to a young lady without coming to the point. The girl's father thought it time to settle the matter. On the bachelor's next visit, the father said:

"Harry, you've been seeing Sue, taking her to picnics and to church, and nothing's come of it. So, now, Harry, I ask you, what are your intentions?"

Harry responded: "Well, answering you as man to man, I'll say there is no cause for you to get excited. My intentions are favorable—but remote."

TIME FLIES

"Daughter," exploded the father, "you can't marry that young fellow. He doesn't make more than two hundred dollars a month."

"Oh, but Daddy," pleaded the girl, "a month flies by so fast when you're in love with each other."

SHE KNOWS MORE THAN HISTORY

The young man sneaked up behind her, covered her eyes with his hands, and announced: "I'm going to kiss you if you can't tell who this is in three guesses."

"George Washington, Thomas Jefferson, Abraham Lincoln," she guessed.

'TIS SWEET

> 'Tis sweet to court, but, Oh! how bitter,
> To court a girl, and then not git her.
>   Anonymous

LOYALTY

DEEP IN THE HEART OF TEXAS

A tall, lanky fellow, wearing a cowboy hat and boots walked nervously into a psychiatrist's office.

"Doc," he said, "please examine me. There must be something wrong. I'm from Texas and don't like it."

AS I WAS SAYING

A number of Confederate prisoners, during the Civil War, were held at one military post under conditions less unpleasant than those in the ordinary military prison. Most of them appreciated their good fortune. One young fellow, though, could not be reconciled to association with the Yankees. He was continually talking about the battle of Chicka-mauga, which had been fought with disastrous results for the Union forces.

When the Union men could stand it no longer, they reported the matter to General Grant. Grant summoned the prisoner.

"See here," said Grant, "I understand you are continually insulting the men here with reference to the battle of Chickamauga. I'm going to give you your choice of two things. You will either take the oath of allegiance to the United States, or be sent to a Northern prison."

The prisoner was silent for some time. "Well," he said at last, "I reckon, General, I'll take the oath."

The oath was administered. Turning to Grant, the fellow then asked if he might speak.

"Yes," said the General. "What is it?"

"Why, I was just thinkin', General," he drawled, "they certainly did give us a licking at Chickamauga."

LUCK

Fool

Husband: "Wasn't I a fool when I married you?"
Wife: "You bet, but fools always have luck."

Soft Landing

A Pullman porter was thrown from his car in the train wreck and flew fifteen feet through the air before he hit head first up against a steel signal. He was dazed and rubbing his head, when the conductor came running up. "Man," cried the conductor, "aren't you killed?"

"No," said the porter getting to his feet, "that steel signal must have broken my fall."

MAGAZINES

Getting a Discount

John and his wife were trying to get up a list of magazines to obtain a club rate. By taking three they would get a discount.

"How are you making out?" a friend asked him.

"Well," John replied, "we can get one that I don't want, and one that she doesn't want, and one that neither wants for two dollars and twenty-five cents."

MAN

ESSAY ON MAN

> *At ten, a child; at twenty, wild;*
> *At thirty, tame, if ever:*
> *At forty, wise; at fifty, rich;*
> *At sixty, good or never.*
>
> Anonymous

MANAGEMENT

THE DINOSAUR

A big institution is always in danger of developing in the direction of the dinosaur—with a very big body and a very small head. I understand the dinosaur lived a long time on this earth, but I don't think any of us would be inclined to use him as a model.

As a matter of principle, I am strongly in favor of turning our attention more and more to the problem of the head—the problem of developing human intelligence and understanding. The development of the individual has always been the source of strength in our country and I believe it is the road to great achievements in any enterprise. It is one of the management problems of our times, it seems to me, to get more and better management *at all levels* and *in all of the parts* of big organizations.

Henry Ford II

MANNERS

COMPANY'S HERE

BILLIE: "I think there's company downstairs."
SUE: "How d'ya know?"
BILLIE: "I just heard Mamma laugh at Papa's joke."

201

Guess That Takes Care of It

A conceited person had rebuked a bootblack on the street for his manners. The boy replied, "My friend, all the polish you have is on your shoes, and I gave you that."

Acting Like a Gentleman

I am reminded of the days when nylons were short, and when our department store friends gave you a slip for the lady to get a pair. One of these slips was sent to the wife of one of the senators. Since she couldn't go downtown, she gave it to her husband to pick up on the way to the shop in the morning.

He got in there, but found two hundred women ahead of him. He stood around on one leg and the other for a while and wasn't getting anywhere fast, the nylons were fading, and he could see an irate wife in the background as he went home that night. Finally, at the end of a couple of hours, he discarded his cane and dignity and waded in the crowd. He stepped on an angry lady's foot, and she said, "What's the matter with you? Can't you act like a gentleman?"

He said, "Well, I've been acting like a gentleman for two hours and now I'm going to act like a lady."

From an address by Owen Brewster
United States Senator from Maine

MARRIAGE

Time to Duck

She greeted her husband affectionately when he returned from the office. "Darling," she said, "you must be tired and hungry. Would you like some nice soup, a sirloin steak, with golden-brown potatoes and green peas, and mushrooms on toast?"

He shook his head and said, "No, let's save the money and eat at home."

She "Learned" Him

"So you and Charlie are married. I thought all the time it was just going to be a flirtation."

"So did Charlie!"

202

He Should Ask Mom

SON: "Pop, why do they rope off the aisles at weddings?"
PAPA: "So the bridegroom can't get away, son."

Experience

YOUNG ACTOR: "I've got a job at last, Dad. It's a new play, and I play the part of a man who has been married twenty years."
FATHER: "Splendid. That's a start anyway, my boy. Maybe one of these days they'll give you a speaking part."

No Improvement Needed

EDNA: "You mustn't be discouraged. In this world there's a man for every girl and a girl for every man. You can't improve on it."
LUCY: "I don't want to improve on it, I just want to get in on it."

No Support

KIND-HEARTED OLD LADY: "Oh, you poor man. Are you married?"
BEGGAR: "Listen, lady, do you think I'd be relying on total strangers for support if I had a wife?"

Not Henpecked

At a certain tavern in the City of Tomah there is a club of men who meet every night. They call themselves the Henpecked Club. Some of them are really henpecked, but some of them are not.

One night a man came to the meeting who had not been there regularly. But he sat down and took a drink and was having quite a nice time.

Suddenly his wife came in the door, walked up to the fellow, grabbed him by the collar and shook him until his teeth rattled.

"What do you mean," she shouted, "by attending this club? You're not henpecked."

Monroe County Democrat, Sparta, Wisconsin

Complete Stranger

The bride was weeping bitterly just before the wedding. Her mother tried to comfort her. "My dear, this is no time to cry. Why, the day I was married was the happiest day of my life."

"But that was different," sobbed the girl. "You married Dad. I'm marrying a complete stranger."

Staying Out Late

Two drunks sat on the curb meditating. One spoke—
"Watsch your wife shay when you shtay out late like thish?"
"Haven't got a wife."
"Then watsch idea of shtaying out so late?"

Complete Outfit

Young man: "I want to buy a diamond ring."
Salesman: "Yes sir. How about one of our combination sets? Three pieces—engagement, wedding, and teething."

Domestic Silence

Sue, the five-year-old, met the caller at the door. "Alice isn't here," she replied to the caller's inquiry about her big sister. "She's gone to her class."

"What class does she go to?" asked the caller.

"Well, Alice is going to get married, you know, and she's taking lessons in domestic silence."

He Knew

When the couple were being married by the clergyman, and the words, "love, honor, and obey," were spoken, the bridegroom interrupted:

"Read that again, suh, read it once moh, so's de lady kin ketch de full solumnity ob de meanin'. I'se been married befoh."

Some Left

Father looked at his wife and then at his son. "That boy has taken money from my pocket!" he stormed.

"Henry," she protested, "how can you say that? Why, I might have done it."

Father shook his head. "No, you didn't; there was some left."

Strange

"John doesn't seem as well dressed as when you married him five years ago."

"That's strange. He's wearing the same suit."

Old Married Couple

"Jack, dear," said the bride, "let us try to make the people believe we've been married a long time."

"All right, honey, but do you think you can carry both suitcases?"

Frank

"Should I marry a man who lies to me?"

"Lady, do you want to be an old maid?"

Peace

In a cemetery in Vermont is a stone, erected by a widow to her loving husband, bearing these words: "REST IN PEACE—UNTIL WE MEET AGAIN."

Another Match

A bereaved husband left orders for a tombstone with the inscription: "THE LIGHT OF MY LIFE HAS GONE OUT."

Before too long he had taken another wife. He remembered the inscription, and thinking it would not be pleasing to his new wife, he asked the stonecutter to adapt it to the new conditions. Then he took his new wife to see the tombstone and found that the inscription read:

> The light of my life has gone out,
> But I have struck another match.

First Time

Liz: "I didn't accept Jim the first time he proposed."

Alice: "No, dear, you weren't there."

Too Infatuated

Wife: "I was a fool when I married you."

Husband: "I guess you were, but I was so infatuated at the time I didn't notice it."

Strange Goings On

Little Ann was all eyes at the church wedding. "Did the lady change her mind?" she whispered to her mother.

"No, dear. What makes you think so?"

" 'Cause she went up the aisle with one man and came back with another."

Couldn't Take It

Jimmy Durante: The Maharajah of Hindustan liked my act so much that as a token of his appreciation he wanted to send me five hundred of his wives. But I turned him down. I couldn't stand the thought of having a thousand nylons hangin' in the bathroom every morning.

A Little Complicated

Mrs. O'Ryan had been absent from her duties for several days. Upon her return her employer asked the reason for her absence.

"Sure, I've been carin' for wan of me sick children," she replied.

"And how many children have you, Mrs. O'Ryan?" he asked.

"Siven in all," she replied. "Four by the third wife of me second husband; three by the second wife of me furst."

Making It Worthwhile

"Yes," said the father to the young man, "I am proud of my daughters and would like to see them comfortably married. I have made a little money and they will not go penniless to their husbands. There is

Mary, twenty-five years old, and a really good girl. I shall give her one thousand dollars when she marries. Then comes Sue, who won't see thirty-five again, and I shall give her three thousand dollars. And the man who takes Dotty, who is forty, will have five thousand dollars with her."

The young man reflected for a moment and then inquired, "You haven't one about fifty, have you?"

NINE CUCKOOS

"I was in a bad predicament yesterday morning," said one husband to another.

"How was that?"

"Why, I came home late, and my wife heard me and said, 'Sam, what time is it?" and I said, 'Only twelve, dear,' and just then that cuckoo clock of ours sang out three times."

"What did you do?"

"Why, I had to stand there and cuckoo nine times more."

DOG'S LIFE

"Your husband says he leads a dog's life," said one woman.

"Yes, it's very similar," answered the other. "He comes in with muddy feet, makes himself comfortable by the fire, and waits to be fed."

SELF-APPOINTED

A young man walked up to the clerk of the court and said that he wanted a marriage license.

"Certainly," said the clerk. "Where's the bride-elect?"

"What d'ya mean, bride-elect?" asked the young man. "There wasn't any election—the gal appointed herself."

AMOS 'N' ANDY

ANDY: "But I still don't see why I need a wife."

KINGFISH: "Andy, I can answer that in one word—companionship. All through de ages everything goes in pairs: Romeo and Juliet, Sears and Roebuck, Walla Walla, Tea for Two, and Double Indemnity!"

She Was No Spendthrift

Boss: "George, how are you getting on?"

George: "Oh, mah wife pesters me asking for money. Ah come home tired to death, nothing but money, money, money. 'Give me a dollar, give me seventy-five cents, give me fifty cents.'"

Boss: "George, what does she do with all that money?"

George: "Ah don't know. Ah ain't gib her none yet."

Which?

Young man: "Would you marry a guy just for money?"

Girl: "Are you gathering statistics or proposing?"

Perfectly Simple

Mr. and Mrs. Smith were known as the ideal couple—never a harsh word between them. Smith, asked how he did it, explained: "Why, it's a very simple arrangement. In the morning she does what she wants, and in the afternoon I do what she wants."

Perfectly Obvious

A party of tourists in New Mexico came upon an Indian riding a pony. A heavily burdened squaw walked beside him.

"Why doesn't the squaw ride?" asked the tourist.

"She got no pony."

A Good Husband Is Deaf and a Good Wife Blind

It is most dangerous nowadays for a husband to pay any attention to his wife in public. It always makes people think that he beats her when they are alone.

Oscar Wilde, 1892

Key to Happiness

A happily married woman was asked what secret she had which made her marriage so successful. "My secret is to do all that pleases him, and endure patiently all that displeases me."

MASS PRODUCTION

We are in a pennies and nickels and dimes business. You may not think so, but we are.

Not long ago, for example, we developed a method for improving the wheels on our cars while cutting the cost of each wheel four cents. That meant an annual saving of ninety-five thousand dollars.

Ford engineers, working with a supplier, found they could improve speedometers by redesigning them and at the same time cut eighty-one cents from the cost of each speedometer. This meant a saving of eight hundred thousand dollars a year.

Believe me, our problem is to cut pennies from thousands of items. That's the only way to get dollars off the finished car.

An automobile is not a single product, but a whole symphony of products. In a Ford De Luxe six, four-door sedan, for example, there are over ten thousand separate pieces, counting every nut and bolt and washer which we buy or manufacture. A penny saved on a part runs into millions of dollars very quickly. Cutting two or three cents from a part—or, better yet, eliminating a part—is an achievement of greatest importance when you are dealing in terms of a million or more cars.

From an address by Ernest R. Breech,
Executive Vice President, Ford Motor Company

MATHEMATICS

SOME PROGRESS

The freshman class in trigonometry was reciting.

"And have you proved this proposition?" asked the professor.

"Well," said the freshman, "proved is a strong word, but I can say that I have rendered it highly probable."

HYPOTENUSE

TEACHER: "What is the line opposite the right angle in a right-angled triangle?"

JOHNNIE: "The hippopotamus."

MEAT

MAKING ENDS MEAT

"Those sausages you sent me were meat at one end and corn meal at the other."

"Yes, ma'am. In these hard times it's difficult to make both ends meat."

THAT EXPLAINS IT

The shoemaker was explaining to a complaining customer the reason for the poor quality of his soles. "All the good leather," he said, "is going into steaks."

MEDICINE

NOT SO FAST

FIRST LITTLE BOY (in hospital ward): "Are you medical or surgical?"

SECOND LITTLE BOY: "I don't know. What does that mean—medical or surgical?"

FIRST LITTLE BOY: "Were you sick when you came, or did they make you sick after you got here?"

HOW'S HE FEELING

The sailor who assisted the doctor was told to give out the medicines by number from the medicine chest. He was told to give a sailor a dose of "No. 5," but not finding No. 5, he gave the man a dose of No. 2 and No. 3.

DOCTOR'S ORDERS

"Try this pill at bedtime," said the doctor. "If you can keep it on your stomach, it should cure you."

Meeting the patient the next day, the doctor asked, "Did you keep the pill on your stomach?"

"I did when I was awake," said the patient, "but when I fell asleep it rolled off."

"Hank," said Joe, "I've got a mule with distemper. What did you give that one of yours when he had it?"

"Turpentine."

A week later they met again.

"Say, Hank, I gave my mule turpentine, and it killed him."

"Killed mine, too, Joe."

MEDITATION

Privilege of Quietness

Fifteen or twenty minutes of quiet meditation and thought each day may bother you at first. It will seem like a waste of precious time. It seemed so to Southey, the British statesman, who thought it was a sin not be active. He was talking on one occasion with a Quaker, describing how his days were filled, what he had to do from hour to hour. "But friend Southey," the Quaker asked, "when dost thou think?" Apparently, it had not occurred to Southey that quiet meditation and thought were important. But Pascal notes that "All the evils of life have fallen upon us because men will not sit quietly in a room." And President Conant, of Harvard University, echoed the same conviction in his observation that all men need "the quiet privilege of an ivory tower."

From a sermon by Dr. Harold Blake Walker

MEMORY

Do You Remember Me?

I would like to add something at this point. It is not a manifestation of good manners for a person to go up to another and challenge him by saying, "Do you remember me?" That puts you at a great disadvantage if you happen to have forgotten. I have found that the best way to meet that situation, when the challenge comes and when I am unable to remember, is to answer frankly that I do not. Such an answer is not always pleasant for me but it is a good reminder to the other person that he should be tolerant and not expect too much of other people's memories. Of course, in my experience that has not happened too often and I am glad that it hasn't; but when I meet it, I meet it frankly.

James A. Farley

FIBBER MCGEE: "Me, I've got a terrific memory. My mind is like a big filing cabinet. If you could look inside my head you'd see a whole line of long drawers."

MOLLY: "Sounds like washday in winter time."

MIDDLE AGE

TIME TO DIET

RED BLANCHARD: "You've reached middle age when your wife tells you to pull in your stomach and you already have!"

MILK

THEY FILL 'EM TOO FULL

"My dear," said the young husband as he took the bottle of milk and held it up to the light, "have you noticed there's never any cream on this milk?"

"I spoke to the milkman about it," she replied, "and he explained the company always fills the bottles so full that there's no room for cream on top."

PAGING MR. PASTEUR

A little boy visited a dairy. When he came home he tried to tell his mother about his trip, but didn't know what the plant was called. Finally, he blurted out: "You know, Mom—the place where they paralyze the milk."

MILLINERY

NO COMPARISON

A husband caught staring at a young lady on the street saved his skin, with no pain except a whopping milliner's bill, by saying, "Dear, I was just thinking how much better that hat would look on you!"

MINISTER

SLIGHTLY CONFUSED

It was the first wedding ceremony for the young minister and he was almost as bashful and embarrassed as the young couple before him. In a brave effort to round out the affair, the minister stammered, "It's all over now. Go and sin no more!"

HER MINISTER

The six-year-old daughter of a clergyman was sick and was put to bed early. As her mother was about to leave her, she called her back. "Mamma, I want to see my papa."

"No, dear," her mother replied, "your papa is busy and must not be disturbed."

"But, Mamma," the child persisted, "I want to see my papa."

The mother again replied, "No, your papa must not be disturbed."

But the little one came back with even more determination. "Mamma," she declared, "I am a sick woman, and I want to see my minister."

SHOULD SIT UP FRONT

"How did you like my sermon yesterday, Mr. Smith?" asked the young clergyman of the small village church.

"Well, pastor, I don't really get a fair chance at those sermons of yours. I'm an old man now, and I have to sit way in the back by the stove; and there's old Mrs. Hendrix, and Widow Grey, and Mrs. Stone and her daughters, and all the rest of them sittin' in front of me, with their mouths wide open, swallerin' down all the best of the sermon, and—well, what gets back to me is purty poor stuff, pastor, purty poor stuff."

CORRECTION, PLEASE

The telephone rang in the newspaper office late Sunday night.
"Is this the religious editor?"
"Yes."

213

This is Reverend Dr. Gray. You have a copy of my sermon for your paper tomorrow?"

"Yes."

"Will you do me the favor to take Daniel out of the fiery furnace and put him in the den of lions?"

DIFFERENCE OF OPINION

"If I were so unlucky," said Smith, "as to have a stupid son, I would certainly, by all means, make him a preacher."

A clergyman, who was present, calmly replied, "You think differently, sir, from your father."

MISERLY

I FORGOT MY POCKETBOOK

It was said of a man who never picked up the check in a restaurant, but permitted his friends to pay the bill, that he never opened his mouth but at another man's expense.

MISTAKE

NOT AS FRESH AS HE WAS

Judge: "You admit that you stole eggs from this store. Have you any excuse?"

Accused: "Yes, I took them by mistake, your Honor."

Judge: "How is that?"

Accused: "I thought they were fresh."

BOTH MAY BE MISTAKEN

Readiness in repartee continually saved Voltaire, French satirist and philosopher. He once praised another writer very heartily to a third person.

"It is very strange," was the reply, "that you speak so well of him, for he says you are a charlatan."

"Oh," replied Voltaire, "I think it very likely that both of us may be mistaken."

MONEY

Where's That Nickel

"Henry!"

"Yes, dear?"

"There's a corner torn off your pay check."

"Yes, dear?"

"Well, what did you spend it for?"

No Improvement

A go-getter saw a lazy Indian chief loafing at the door of his tepee somewhere out west.

"Chief," remonstrated the go-getter, "why don't you get yourself a job?"

"Why?" grunted the chief.

"Well, you could earn a lot of money. Maybe fifty or sixty dollars a week."

"Why?" said the chief.

"Oh, if you worked hard and saved your money, you'd soon have a bank account. Wouldn't you like that?"

"Why?" asked the chief.

"Well," shouted the go-getter. "With a big bank account you could retire, and then you wouldn't have to work any more—"

"Not working now," said the chief.

Inflation

The high school lad had asked for more spending money.

"You don't know the value of a dollar, son," sighed the father.

"Yes, I do," replied the lad. "As of last week it was fifty-one cents, as compared with 1939 standards."

Cost of Living

"Do you know how economists figure out the cost of living?"

"Sure. They take your income—whatever it may be—and add ten per cent."

Stood a Lot

MILT: "Here's the last pair of trousers you made for me. I want them reseated. You know, I sit a lot."

TAILOR: "Yes, and I hope you've brought your bill to be receipted. You know, I've stood a lot."

Changing Times

BOB: "I'm getting stronger."

HELEN: "How do you know?"

BOB: "Because a few years ago I couldn't carry ten dollars' worth of groceries, and now it's easy."

Money Talks

WIFE: "Is it true that money talks?"

HUSBAND: "That's what they say, my dear."

WIFE: "Well, I wish you'd leave a little here to talk to me during the day. I get so lonely."

Nice Work If You Can Get It

The other day Mr. Sam Goldwyn visited the elaborate headquarters of the Ford Foundation in Pasadena. He beheld the beautiful furniture, the expensive rugs, the private swimming pool in back, and the old masters on the walls, and remarked, "Well, if you have to give money away, this is a nice place to do it." If one has to be a chancellor of a university, the University of Chicago is a nice place to do it.

From an address by Dr. Lawrence Kimpton,
Chancellor of the University of Chicago

Holdin' His Own

After seven years of effort on his stony New England farm, the Yankee farmer announced: "Anyhow, I'm holdin' my own. I didn't have nothin' when I come here, and I ain't got nothin' now."

216

GENIUS

JOHNNY: "Teacher said that Mr. Smith was a financial genius. What does that mean?"

DAD: "That he could earn money faster than his family could spend it."

REAL DOUGH

Two tramps were stretched out on the green grass. Above them was the warm sun, beside them a babbling brook. It was a peaceful scene.

"Boy," said the first tramp contentedly, "right now I wouldn't change places with a guy who owns a million bucks!"

"How about five million?" asked his companion.

"Not for five million," drowsed the first tramp.

"Well," persisted his pal, "how about ten million bucks?"

The first tramp sat up. "That's different," he admitted. "Now you're talking real dough!"

TOO BUSY

One time the secretary of a chamber of commerce wired the great Professor Jean Louis Agassiz, scientist and educator, inviting him to speak at their annual banquet on the relation between science and commerce. Busy with his research, Agassiz declined the invitation. The chamber of commerce sent him another message offering a substantial sum of money for the lecture, but Agassiz sent back the following telegram, "I am too busy to make money."

MORTGAGE

A farmer had paid the last instalment on a small farm, and the realtor who sold it to him said, "Uncle Joe, I will make you a deed to the farm now since it has been paid for."

"Boss," he replied, "if it is all de same to you, I had much rather you would give me a mortgage to de place."

The realtor, somewhat surprised, said, "Uncle Joe, you don't seem to know the difference between a mortgage and a deed."

"Well, maybe not," said Uncle Joe reminiscently, "but I owned a farm once and I had a deed and de bank had a mortgage, and de bank got de farm."

MOTHER

STATISTICALLY SPEAKING

Mother wanted to shop; and father, a statistician, agreed to spend the afternoon with their three small children. On the return of mother, father handed her the following statement:

"Dried tears—9 times; tied shoes—10 times; toy balloons purchased —3 per child; average life of balloon—12 seconds; cautioned children not to cross street—20 times; children insisted on crossing street—30 times; number of Saturdays father will do this again—0 times."

MOTION PICTURES

THIS IS HOLLYWOOD

There is no such place as Hollywood. We have no civic center. We have no mayor. A couple of years ago we did get a post office, so our letters could be postmarked "Hollywood, California." Before that we were just "Los Angeles, California." I say of Los Angeles that it's six suburbs in search of a city. That's Hollywood.

From a speech by Hedda Hopper

ALMOST MADE IT

Jack Benny was complaining because he'd never won a movie Oscar. "To win an Academy Award," he explained, "you have to be starred in a serious picture—with no laughs at all. In my last picture I nearly made it."

MUSIC

SUBTRACTION

The teacher was trying to get over the intricacies of subtraction. "You have ten fingers," she said. "Suppose you had three less, then what would you have?"

"No music lessons," Johnny replied promptly.

Busy

"Now that he plays in the band I suppose your boy is busy," said the lady next door.

"Not as busy as I am," said the mother. "I have to help him find A sharp, mend and press his uniform, attend the Band Mothers' meetings, and beat time while he plays the 'Stars and Stripes Forever' on his cornet."

That Goes for a Tuba Too

A preacher was asked if the man who learned to play a cornet on Sunday would go to heaven.

The preacher said, "I don't see why he should not, but I doubt whether the man next door will."

No Future?

London critics once urged a composer to seek another occupation. His name was Beethoven.

Bargain Hunter

An Irishman who asked a teacher of music how much he charged for lessons, was informed, ten dollars for the first month, and eight for the second.

"Then I'll come the second month," said Pat.

What is Music?

What is music? This question occupied my mind for hours last night before I fell asleep. The very existence of music is wonderful, I might even say miraculous. Its domain is between thought and phenomena. Like a twilight mediator, it hovers between spirit and matter, related to both, yet differing from each. It is spirit, but it is spirit subject to the measurement of time. It is matter, but it is matter that can dispense with space.

Heinrich Heine

NAMES

Well Known

"What's your name?"

"Thomas Jefferson."

"That's a pretty well-known name."

"It ought to be. I've delivered milk in this town for three years!"

Old, But Still a Good Story

Policeman (producing notebook): "Name, please."

Motorist: "Aloysius Alastair Cyprian."

Policeman (putting book away): "Well, don't let me catch you again."

Couldn't Fool Him

John Smith witnessed a minor accident. In due time, the police arrived, and one officer asked the witness his name.

"John Smith," said Smith.

"Cut the comedy," said the policeman. "What's your real name?"

"All right," said Smith, "put me down as Winston Churchill."

"That's more like it," said the officer. "You can't fool me with that John Smith stuff."

That's Wright

At a meeting one night,
Messrs. More, Strange, and Wright,
Met to talk, and good thoughts to exchange;
Says More, "Of us three,
"The whole town will agree,
"There is only one knave, and that's Strange."
"Yes," says Strange (rather sore),
"I'm sure there's one More,
"A most terrible knave and a bite,
"Who cheated his mother,
"His sister and brother."
"Oh yes," replied More, "that is Wright."

220

NEATNESS

TROUBLE

A little hillbilly watched a man at a tourist camp making use of a comb and a brush, a toothbrush, a nail file, and a whisk broom.

"Say, Mister," he finally queried, "are you always that much trouble to yourself?"

NEIGHBOR

BUT AT A SNAIL'S PACE

How ingenious an animal is a snail. When it encounters a bad neighbor it takes up its house and moves away.

Philemon, c. 300 B.C.

NERVES

SMART BUTTERFLIES

The patient told his doctor he was so worried about making a speech that he had butterflies in his stomach.

"Take an aspirin," advised the doctor, "and the butterflies will go away."

Whereupon he moaned, "But I took an aspirin, and they're playing ping-pong with it."

"DRY" HUMOR

At a banquet up in Copper Harbor, Michigan, a few weeks ago, we witnessed an excellent demonstration of the old saying that if you get handed a lemon you should just smile happily, and make lemonade out of it.

Just before the main speaker of the evening was to make his speech, one of the jittery ladies who sat next to him upset a glass of water, which landed right in his lap. Facing this situation, we would have gone right up through the ceiling, or down through the floor.

Anyway, the master of ceremonies breezed right ahead and

221

introduced the speaker who, after brushing himself off, dryly opened his remarks as follows:

"I have attended a great many parties and banquets in my day. I vividly recall many little birthday parties I attended when I was only four or five years old, but this is the first time in my life that I ever went to a party when somebody else wet my pants!"

Relph Nuzman, Viola News, Viola, Wisconsin

NEWSPAPER

CONDENSED

The reporter returned from an interview.

"Well," said the editor, "what did Mr. Very Important say?"

"Nothing."

"Well, then, keep it down to a column."

EXTRACT FROM A SCOTCH NEWSPAPER OF 1707

Copy of a painter's bill presented to the vestry for work done in our church:

To filling up a chink in the Red Sea, and repairing the damages of Pharaoh's host.

To a new pair of hands for Daniel in the lions' den, and a new set of teeth for the lioness.

To repairing Nebuchadnezzar's beard.

To cleaning the whale's belly, varnishing Jonah's face, and mending his left arm.

To a new skirt for Joseph's garment.

To a sheet anchor, a jury mast, and a long-boat for Noah's ark.

To giving a blush to the cheek of Eve, on presenting the apple to Adam.

To painting a new city in the land of Nod.

To cleaning the garden of Eden after Adam's expulsion.

To making a bridle for the Samaritan's horse, and mending one of his legs.

To putting a new handle to Moses' basket, and fitting bulrushes.

To adding more fuel to the fire of Nebuchadnezzar's furnace.

Rec'd payment. D.Z.

OBEDIENCE

Orders Are Orders

Jones, a new cavalry recruit, was given one of the worst horses in the troop.

"Remember," said the instructor, "no one is allowed to dismount without orders."

The horse bucked and Jones went over his head.

"Jones," yelled the instructor, "did you have orders to dismount?"

"I did."

"From headquarters?"

"No, from hindquarters."

OPINION

His View Wasn't Good

Resort owner: "Here are some views of our hotel for you to take with you, sir."

Guest: "Thanks, but I have my own views of your hotel."

A Matter of Opinion

"Dr. Porson," said a gentleman to the great Professor of Greek at Cambridge, England, with whom he had been disputing, "Dr. Porson, my opinion of you is most contemptible."

"Sir," returned the doctor, "I never knew an opinion of yours that was not."

OPTIMIST

Give Him Time

In the public schools a boy refused to sew, thinking it below his dignity.

"Why," said the teacher, "George Washington did his own sewing in the wars, and do you think you are better than George Washington?"

"I don't know," said the boy. "Only time can tell."

223

ORPHAN

Her Wish

A Russian school child was asked by his teacher, "Who is your father?"

"Stalin," was the answer.

"Who is your mother?"

"The great Soviet Union."

The teacher smiled because the child was so precocious, and said, "Now, what is your fondest wish?"

"To be an orphan," the child replied.

PAIN

That Will Learn Him

The tired mother ran for the nursery to answer a sudden scream. She found the baby pulling her small boy's hair.

"Never mind, darling," she said. "Baby just doesn't understand that it hurts you."

She had hardly resumed her work when more shrieks brought her to the nursery again. This time it was the baby who was crying.

"Why, Junior," she cried, "what is the matter with the baby?"

"Nothing much," replied junior calmly. "Only now he knows."

PAINTER

Good Resemblance

Whistler (the great painter): "Do you like the portrait of yourself?"

Celebrity: "No, I don't believe I do. You must admit it's a bad work of art."

Whistler: "Yes, but you must admit you are a bad work of nature."

PARENTS

SORRY HE MENTIONED IT

Bill's school report had just come in. It wasn't good.

"I'm losing patience," exclaimed his father. "How is it that young Jones is always at the top of the class while you are at the bottom?"

The boy looked at his father reproachfully. "You forget, Dad," he said kindly, "that Jones has very smart parents."

PAWNSHOP

CORRECT TIME, PLEASE

It was midnight, and Sam was snoring soundly in his room above the pawnshop. Suddenly he awoke. Someone was hammering on the door below. He put his head out of the window.

"Come down here," demanded the caller.

"At this hour?" said Sam indignantly.

"Come down, or I'll break your door in."

Grumblingly Sam stumbled down the stairs. "What is it?" he asked.

"What's the time?" said the caller.

"What!" said Sam. "You wake me up in the middle of the night and ask me the time!"

"Well, you've got my watch, haven't you?"

PAYMENT

SHOULD HAVE PUT IN MORE

In Lancaster County, Pennsylvania, where I have lived for the past thirty years they tell a story about a Pennsylvania Dutch minister who had no regular charge, but who supplied vacant pulpits around the countryside as opportunity offered. One Sunday, accompanied by his little son, he boarded a trolley car and journeyed several miles to a small town where he was scheduled to conduct the service of the morning. As he entered the church he noticed a box in the vestibule bearing the legend,

225

"For the poor"; and although he was himself not blessed with a superfluity of this world's goods, he produced a quarter from his pocket and dropped it in the receptacle. At the conclusion of the service he was escorted from the pulpit by one of the officers of the church who thanked him for his sermon and stated that it was the custom of the congregation to give their supply preachers the contents of the poor box. When he unlocked it, out dropped nothing whatever save the poor minister's own quarter. He pocketed it with a wry smile, and as he and his little son walked back to the trolley station, the boy looked up into his face and said: "You would have gotten more out if you had put more in, wouldn't you, Pop?"

From an address by H. W. Prentis, Jr.
Chairman of the Board, Armstrong Cork Company

PERFECTION

How Samuel Johnson Wrote

Bishop Percy describes how Samuel Johnson, English poet and man of letters, wrote. "He was so extremely short-sighted from the defect in his eyes, that writing was inconvenient to him; for whenever he wrote, he was obliged to hold the paper close to his face. He therefore never composed what we call a poor draft on paper of anything he published, but used to revolve the subject in his mind, and turn, and form every period, till he had brought the whole to the highest correctness and the most perfect arrangement. Then his uncommonly retentive memory enabled him to deliver a whole essay, properly finished, whenever it was called for. I have often heard him humming and forming periods in low whispers to himself, when shallow observers thought he was muttering prayers."

Perfection No Trifle

A friend called on Michelangelo, who was finishing a statue. Some time afterwards he called again, and the sculptor was still at his work. His friend, looking at the figure, exclaimed, "You must have been idle since I saw you last."

"By no means," replied the sculptor. "I have retouched this part, and

226

polished that; I have softened this feature and brought out this muscle; I have given more expression to this lip, and more energy to this limb."

"Well, well," said his friend, "but all these are trifles."

"It may be so," replied Michelangelo, "but recollect that trifles make perfection, and that perfection is no trifle."

PERSISTENCE

ONE STEP AT A TIME

Once, long ago, somebody gave me a pedometer that would tell me how far I had walked. It counted my successive steps, so many hundred steps to a mile. To go a mile required something like two thousand steps taken one by one. I never would have walked a mile if I had contemplated the endless steps to go. Who wants to walk two thousand steps? The vision of two thousand steps means weariness before you start, and the wondering question, "Is it worthwhile to go?"

Sometimes I have the feeling now that we are staggered by two thousand steps ahead. We cannot live today because we fear tomorrow. We cannot bear the burden of the now because we see a rugged road and many steps ahead. And yet, the vision of a tragic road beyond did not deter the Master. I must go on, He said, today and tomorrow and the day following, one step at a time. He was crucified at thirty-three, but He made the eternal now so rich that men called Him Saviour and Lord. There was nothing bright about His future, so far as any man could see, but He went on day after day filling the small moment of the present with the glory of eternity. In the end, the isolated steps He took were quite enough to change the temper of His world and ours.

Harold Blake Walker

IT CAN'T BE DONE?

When nothing seems to help, I go and look at a stonecutter hammering away at his rock, perhaps a hundred times without as much as a crack showing in it. Yet, at the hundred and first blow it will split in two, and I know it was not that blow that did it, but all that had gone before.

Jacob A. Riis

PERSONNEL

EASY MONEY

I am reminded of the story, which is said to have a factual basis, of the hard-boiled head of a large department store. This tough old-timer passed through the packing room one day and saw a boy lounging against a wood box—just whistling. The big boss asked how much he got a week.

"Five dollars," the boy replied.

"Then here's a week's pay," the boss exclaimed. "Take it and get out!"

When the boy was gone, the boss turned to the department head and demanded to know when the boy had been hired.

"We didn't hire him," was the timid reply. "He was just here to pick up a package!"

From an address by Harry A. Bullis

PESSIMIST

POEM FOR PESSIMISTS

My granddad, viewing earth's worn cogs,
Said things were going to the dogs;
His granddad in his house of logs,
Said things were going to the dogs;
His granddad in the Flemish bogs,
Said things were going to the dogs;
His granddad in his old skin togs,
Said things were going to the dogs;
There's one thing that I have to state—
The dogs have had a good long wait.
            —Canadian Fire Insurance Company

PICNIC

NEWS ITEM

"The firemen's picnic was not as well attended as it has been for years. This can be laid to three causes: the change of place in holding it, deaths in families, and other amusements."

PLAGIARISM

AUTHOR

At a famous event at the New York Lambs' Club, Charles Frohman had made a very good speech. There was loud applause at its finish, and then Augustus Thomas jumped up and called: "Author! Author!"

HE LIVES ON AND ON

PROFESSOR: "Did you write this poem yourself?"
STUDENT: "Yes, every line of it."
PROFESSOR: "Then I'm glad to meet you, Edgar Allan Poe. I thought you were dead long ago."

TO A PLAYWRIGHT

> *Your comedy I've read, my friend,*
> *And like the half you've pilfered best;*
> *But, sure, the drama you might mend;*
> *Take courage, man, and steal the rest.*
> Anonymous

PLANNING

THE DIVINE SPARK OF GENIUS

The great progress that the United States has made has come from that limited group of unusual individuals who possess the divine spark of genius. Such individuals cannot be planned for. They emerge from all sorts of odd nooks and crannies where no government group would ever dream of finding them. Can you imagine that a central planning board in Washington would have ever designated an unknown forty-year-old mechanic in Detroit to revolutionize the whole transportation system of the world? Can you imagine a government planning commission appointing a twenty-two-year-old farm boy from Rockbridge County, Virginia, who was neither an engineer nor a college graduate—to devise farm implements

229

that have completely altered the age-old procedure of agricultural production all over the world? Yet Cyrus McCormick was just that boy. And how about Edison—the ex-newsboy and telegraph operator? Would any government planning bureau ever have had the acumen to select such a man to invent the electric light, phonograph, and motion picture?

H. W. Prentis, Jr., Chairman of the Board
Armstrong Cork Company

LAISSEZ FAIRE

It was Jean Baptiste Colbert, finance minister of Louis XIV of France, who in 1661 made the famous statement, *"Laissez faire; laissez passer* (Let it alone; let it pass)," which is now so much criticized by those who believe in economic and government planning. It was quoted by Adam Smith in his *Wealth of Nations* (1776), which work has been considered to have laid much of the foundation of the science of political economy.

POETRY

SIR WALTER SCOTT

When Sir Walter Scott was about ten years old, his mother saw him one morning standing still in the street and looking at the sky, in the midst of a tremendous thunderstorm. She called to him repeatedly, but he did not seem to hear. It is said that at length he returned into the house, and told his mother that if she would give him a pencil, he would tell her why he looked at the sky. She acceded to his request, and in a few minutes he gave her the following lines:

> *Loud o'er my head what awful thunders roll!*
> *What vivid lightnings flash from pole to pole!*
> *It is thy voice, O God, that bids them fly;*
> *Thy voice directs them through the vaulted sky;*
> *Then let the good thy mighty power revere;*
> *Let hardened sinners thy just judgments fear.*

POLITENESS

It Would Take a Hard Storm

"It's raining hard," said the polite host. "Don't you think you ought to stay with us for dinner?"

The guest looked out the window and replied, "Oh, I don't think it's raining quite hard enough for that."

Alphonse and Gaston

Voltaire, French philosopher and satirist, was determined never to be outdone in compliments. He said once to Vernet, the painter, in return for his praise, "Your colors are beautiful and lasting, and your name will be immortal."

"My colors," said Vernet, "are not so durable as your ink," and he was going to kiss Voltaire's hand.

"What are you going to do?" said Voltaire, drawing back his hand. "If you kiss my hand, I must kiss your feet."

POLITICS

"Well, mister," the farmer's wife replied when the census-taker inquired about the political faith of her family, "we-uns is kind o' mixed up. I'm Republican, my husband's a Democrat, the baby's a Wet, the cow's a Dry, and the dog belongs to the Reform Party."

"To the Reform Party?" queried the solicitor.

"Yes, mister," the woman affirmed. "You see, he don't do nothing but set around all day and howl."

Could Be Worse

Asked what he thought of the two candidates for the election, an enlightened voter replied, "Well, when I look at them, I'm thankful only one of them can get elected."

231

Prejudice

Vice President Barkley's favorite story is said to be about President Cleveland, who had some battles with the Senate but got along fine with the House.

He was awakened one night by a servant who said, "There are burglars in the house."

Cleveland replied, "In the Senate, maybe, but not in the House."

Limits

The wife of a politician was making arrangements with the village laundress to do their washing. Now, the politician was extremely fat. He weighed three hundred pounds.

"Missus," said the woman, "I'll do your washing, but I'se gwine ter charge you double for your husband's shirts."

"What is your reason for that, Mandy?" questioned the mistress.

"Well," said the laundress, "I don't mind washing fur an ordinary man, but I draws de line on tents."

Father Is Right

FRESHMAN SON: "I'm registered for Political Economy at the University, Dad."

FATHER: "Why learn to economize in politics? It isn't being done."

Loyal to the Party

PHYSICIAN: "Which ward do you wish to be taken to?"

MALONEY: "Iny one of thim, Doc, thot's Dimocratic."

We Heard That Speech

A sad-looking farmer stood on the steps of the town hall during a political meeting.

"Do you know who's talking in there now?" asked a neighbor, "or are you just going in?"

"No, sir; just come out," said the farmer. "Congressman Blows is talking in there."

232

"What about?" asked the stranger.

"Well," said the farmer, "he didn't say."

That Makes It Easier

POLITICIAN: "My boy says he would like a job in your department."

DEPARTMENT OFFICIAL: "What can he do?"

POLITICIAN: "Nothing."

DEPARTMENT OFFICIAL: "That simplifies it. Then we won't have to break him in."

Applause

Phocion, the great Athenian general, having finished a speech, was applauded by the populace.

"I fear," said he, when he heard their acclamations, "I have said something foolish."

Have any present-day politicians heard this story?

It Takes Brains

"How could you have had brain fever?" asked one politician of another. "It takes strong brains to have brain fever."

"How did you find that out?" was the reply.

And a Closed Mind?

A politician is a person who approaches every subject with an open mouth.

Adlai Stevenson, Governor of Illinois
before the Executives Club of Chicago, June 3, 1952

An Unfurnished House

When Mr. Thomas Sheridan, son of the celebrated English playwright, Richard Brinsley Sheridan, was a candidate for public office, he told his father he would place a label on his forehead with these words, "For Rent," and then he would join the party that made the best offer.

"Right Tom," said the father, "but don't forget to add the word 'unfurnished.'"

233

SANTA CLAUS

No sane local official who has hung up an empty stocking over the municipal fireplace is going to shoot Santa Claus just before a hard Christmas.

Alfred E. Smith, 1933

POPULAR

ALL IN THE FAMILY

It was Commencement at a small women's college, and the father of one of the young women came to the graduation exercises. He was presented to the president, who said, "I congratulate you upon your large and affectionate family."

"Large and affectionate?" he stammered, looking surprised.

"Yes," said the president. "No less than ten of your daughter's brothers have called frequently during the winter to take her to parties, while your eldest son escorted her to the theater at least once a week. Unusually nice brothers they are."

POVERTY

DOLLARS AND CENTS

Charles Goodyear lived in poverty while struggling to make rubber products that would not melt in summer or become brittle in winter. Income from his inventions was great, and he gave it all away. In his later years he remarked, "The advantages of a career in life should not be estimated exclusively by the standards of dollars and cents, as is too often done. Man has just cause for regret when he sows and no one reaps."

The late Senator Kenneth S. Wherry of Nebraska
Republican Floor Leader of the United States Senate

TO GREATNESS

Even after Daniel Webster entered Dartmouth College he was very poor. A friend sent him a recipe to grease his shoes. Webster thanked him but said, "My boots need other doctoring, for they not only admit water, but even peas and gravel-stones." Yet with all his poverty he rose to greatness.

GREATNESS AND MISERY

Homer is the first poet and beggar of note among the ancients. He was blind, sang his ballads about the streets, and his mouth was more often filled with verses than with bread.

The great Cervantes died of hunger.

Milton sold his copyright of *Paradise Lost* for fifteen pounds, and finished his life in obscurity.

John Dryden lived in poverty and distress, and toward the close of his life, was compelled to sell his talent piecemeal in order to exist.

Goldsmith's *Vicar of Wakefield* was sold for a trifle to save him from the law.

Sir Walter Raleigh died on the scaffold.

CHARACTER

Ben Jonson was plain-spoken. When Charles I sent him a slight gratuity during his sickness, Jonson sent back the money with this message, "I suppose he sends me this because I live in an alley: tell him his soul lives in an alley."

POWER

LOSING POWER

As was once said, "First you get power, then you use it, then you abuse it, then you lose it."
From an address by Dr. Harry Emerson Fosdick

"POWER IS PRECARIOUS" (HERODOTUS)

What a dreadful thing it is for such a wicked little imp as man to have absolute power.

Horace Walpole

The imbecility of men is always inviting the impudence of power.   R. W. Emerson

All public power proceeds from God.

Pope Leo XIII

Life is will to power.   F. W. Nietzsche

235

I should like to quote from a private letter written recently by one of the great scientists and educators of America to his friend who, like himself, is one of the senior generation. The writer is Dr. Robert A. Millikan, who paraphrases the writings of two of the great thinkers of the ages and adds his own thoughts as follows:

"You are well aware that your thinking and mine are completely in agreement and further we are also in agreement with Plato in realizing that a pure democracy has never worked and probably never can work. Plato's chapter in the *Republic* on 'How a President Becomes a Tyrant' is one of the most penetrating analyses to be found in literature. You and I both see, as some of our friends do not, that the concentration of power in Washington will ultimately destroy our republic unless it can be held in check. You express a little reserve about the fact that some of our really well-meaning and fine-thinking friends have not yet lived long enough to see the magnitude of the danger that we are running into in the United States. Some think we have already gone so far that we are practically ready for the dictator, who, as Plato says, 'will always appear when democracy goes too far.' Our old friend Montesquieu stated both the danger and the remedy when he said, 'Small republics are destroyed by a foreign power, large republics are destroyed by an inner vice.' Therefore it is probable that mankind would have always had to live under the rule of one man had he not conceived a federal republic, the units of which can preserve self-government and therefore have all the advantages of small republics. In a word, Montesquieu states that *local self-government is the key to the safety of the republican form of government.* I myself do not yet think that the United States is irredeemably lost nor has it developed into a mobocracy. However, you and I agree that we ought to exert every influence in our power to stay the disintegrating tendencies which are here."

From an address by Benjamin E. Young
General Vice President, National Bank of Detroit

PRAISE

Doing All Right Too

My son Bill was a cadet at West Point when we were fighting during the war. Like all sons, he seldom wrote to his

236

parents. Of course, I wanted to know what he thought about how we were getting along over there because it was tough going at times, as you know. Finally, when we captured Rome, I thought to myself, "Certainly, he'll break down and write to his old man," and sure enough he did, and the letter read something like this:

"Dear Dad: It is now June in West Point." (That was enlightening, because it was June in Italy, too.) "I am now a first classman, anxious to get going. I am a cadet sergeant. Yesterday we beat the Navy at baseball."

And he said, "Last night I took a very good-looking blonde from New York to a cadet dance. I'm sorry I cannot write any more. So long. I love you." Signed, "Bill." But down at the bottom of the letter there was a little postscript. He said, "By the way, I see you're doing all right, too."

> From an address by General Mark Clark
> before the Executives Club of Chicago

"Our Praises Are Our Wages" (Shakespeare)

Falsely praising a person is lying.

> St. Augustine

We praise heartily only those who admire us.

> La Rochefoucauld

I praise loudly; I blame softly.

> Catherine II of Russia, 1729-96

The praise of a fool is incense to the wisest of us.

> Disraeli, 1827

Take That and That

> *He who praises in praesentia*
> *And abuses in absentia,*
> *May have the pestilential*
> German Rhyme

PRAYER

Anger and Punishment

Fortunately for me, I was taught to pray from so early a time that I cannot remember going to bed at night without saying my prayers. And only once in all these years have I failed to do so. I remember that occasion very vividly. It was my first night in boarding school, when I was about fourteen years old. And in all the excitement of my room at school and my new roommate, and in the general bewilderment, I forgot to say my prayers.

Well, in the course of time I became a judge. I need not tell you that the toughest part of the judge's work is sentencing the people who are convicted or who plead guilty to the various offenses. I had always wondered what I should do if at the time of sentence some prisoner was impudent to me. It seems so clear that in the stress of such an occasion the judge should not mete out a greater punishment from some feeling of personal pique.

One day this happened to me. Most of you probably do not know about it but the fact is that, with these millions of government checks that go through the mail from day to day, many are placed in mail boxes on the ground floor of walk-up apartment houses and tenements, and they furnish a constant temptation to people in distress or people of naturally predatory instincts. Most of the time they get caught and, as it is a federal offense, they come before the judges of my court.

On this particular occasion a woman who, it was plainly to be seen, would soon become a mother, came before me, and I struggled away with the probation report and with questions and so on, to see what I should do. She suddenly burst out and gave me a tongue lashing that was a work of art. After reflecting for a moment or two, I made up my mind that it would not be right to sentence her that day, and so, over her resounding protests, I put the matter off for a week.

The following Sunday I was sitting in my pew of Saint James Church when the Rector, at a certain point in the services, said that he would pause for a moment or two so that every member of the congregation could make a silent prayer in connection with whatever matter was troubling him. I do not remember that having been done before, but I suppose it has. Anyway, I prayed for that woman just as hard and as fervently as I knew how; and, a day or two later, she was back there in court standing before me. I told her all about what I had been going through; I told her that I had prayed for her in church, just as I have been telling you. I shall not make a long story of it. But the outcome was that I gave her a suspended sentence, and I do not think there is very much chance that she will be in my court or any other court again.

From an address by Harold R. Medina
Judge of the District Court of the United States
Southern District of New York

238

SAINTS

> *And Satan trembles when he sees*
> *The weakest saint upon his knees.*
> William Cowper and John Newton, 1779

"WATCH AND PRAY" (MARK XIII, 33)

> *Who goes to bed and doth not pray*
> *Maketh two nights to ev'ry day.*
> George Herbert, 1633

Work as if you were to live 100 years; pray as if you were to die tomorrow.

Benjamin Franklin

My words fly up, my thoughts remain below.

Shakespeare

> *You may talk about me as much as you please,*
> *I'm goin' to talk about you when I git on my knees.*
> American Negro Song

PREACHERS

TALK

Did you ever read Hegel's definition of love? It is a bit complicated, to say the least. "Love is the ideality of the relativity of the reality of an infinitesimal portion of the absolute totality of the infinite being." A learned judge, while listening to the testimony of a physician on the witness stand, seemed mildly confused when the M. D. stated: "Well, in plain language he died of an edema of the brain that followed cerebral thrombosis, or possible embolism that followed in turn arteriosclerosis of the gangrenous cholecystitis." *The Des Moines Register* was concerned, some time ago, about the wording of a newly enacted law. The editorial stated that laws should be written so plainly that it did not "test" the layman's "ability to unravel an extremely complicated and technically phrased problem in English." All three examples ask for plain words for plain people. A pastor should, by all means, keep his vocabulary within reach of his people. It was Luther who once said

239

something to the effect that he preached to a child in the audience, and if the child could understand, he was certain that the learned doctors would also understand.

Dr. R. R. Belter, President, The Wartburg Synod
United Lutheran Church in America

A BARGAIN

Newell Dwight Hillis, the famous preacher and author, was a minister at The First Presbyterian Church of Evanston, Illinois. Shortly after going there he required the services of a physician. On the advice of one of his parishioners he called in a doctor who attended church very rarely. He proved satisfactory to the young preacher, but he could not be induced to render a bill. Finally Dr. Hillis, alarmed at the inroads the bill might make in his modest salary, went to the physician and said, "Doctor, I must know how much I owe you."

After some urging, the physician replied, "I'll tell you what I'll do with you, Hillis. They say you're a pretty good preacher, and you seem to think I am a fair doctor, so I'll make a bargain with you. I'll do all I can to keep you out of heaven if you do all you can to keep me out of hell, and it won't cost either of us a cent. Is it a go?"

PREJUDICE

OUR PREJUDICES

A fox should not be of the jury at a goose's trial.

Thomas Fuller, 1732

Prejudice is a great time saver. It enables one to form an opinion without getting the facts. That has its advantages, but they are not on the side of intelligence.

Herbert V. Prochnow

PRESS

FREEDOM

No government ought to be without censors; and, where the press is free, no one ever will.

Thomas Jefferson, 1792

240

Why should freedom of speech and freedom of the press be allowed? Why should a government which is doing what it believes to be right allow itself to be criticized? It should not allow opposition by lethal weapons. Ideas are much more fatal things than guns. Why should any man be allowed to buy a printing press and disseminate pernicious opinions calculated to embarrass the government?

Nikolai Lenin, 1920

PRICES

HIT THE CEILING

"You know why they call it a price ceiling?" asked Red Blanchard. "Because when you hear the price you hit the ceiling."

WHITE OR RYE

"I'll take the four-dollar dinner," Red Skelton told the waitress after examining the menu.

"Will you take it," she asked, "on white or rye?"

PRIDE

PERISH THE THOUGHT

"Pardon me, Mrs. Henri de Vere, but has your son ever earned anything by the sweat of his brow?"

"We Henri de Veres never perspire."

"HOW LITTLE ARE THE PROUD" (THOMAS GRAY)

There was one who thought he was above me, and he was above me until he had that thought.

Elbert Hubbard, 1923

WITH STILL GREATER PRIDE

Plato was entertaining some friends. In the room there was a richly ornamented couch. Diogenes came in very dirty, as usual, and getting upon the couch, trampled on it, saying, "I trample upon the pride of Plato."

Plato mildly answered, "But with greater pride, Diogenes!"

Erasmus

241

PRIZES

For Good

Smith's wife had presented him with two boys, and his employer congratulated him.

The following day he was called into the office and was given a silver cup in recognition of the twin blessing he had received. Smith received the gift in an embarrassed manner.

"Thank you very much," he said, turning to his associates. "Is this cup mine now, or do I have to win it three years in succession?"

PRODUCTION

How a Nation Progresses

There are only two systems by which production of the needs of mankind, and distribution of that production, can be carried on—that is, two systems by which a nation can decide what goods it shall produce and where the goods shall go. One is a system of decree from above: this is the socialist way. The other is by operation, on a free market, of the law of supply and demand through the pricing process. If we have a decree from above in respect of production—that is, in respect of supply—we must inevitably have a decree from above in respect of demand. This means control of the whole personal life of a nation; it means the police state. Between these two principles there can only be one sane, enlightened decision—and, truth to tell, this is almost universally recognized today. A thousand times better to have a free market plan under fair and equitable laws democratically passed and enforced, because, first, in that way we avoid the terrific burden entailed in maintaining a vast bureaucracy; and secondly, because it operates with a maximum of freedom and a minimum of force. . . . It rewards efficiency and economy; it punishes laziness and waste, and thus provides incentive, the very mainspring of human progress.

Rt. Hon. Arthur Meighen, P.C., K.C.
Former Prime Minister of Canada

PROFESSION

EMBLEMATIC STONES

It is said that in Brazil members of different trades and professions wear rings to show their vocation. The doctor wears an emerald, the lawyer a ruby, and engineers wear sapphires. Professors are known by their green tourmaline rings, and dentists wear a topaz.

The idea has merit and should be adopted in this country.

A dairyman could wear a milkstone; an undertaker, a tombstone; architects, a cornerstone; and politicians, a blarneystone. Burglars could identify themselves with a keystone; stockbrokers, a curbstone; laundrymen, a soapstone; borrowers, a touchstone; surgeons, a bloodstone; policemen, a pavingstone; cobblers, a cobblestone; beauties, a peachstone; motorists, a milestone; lovers, a moonstone; and club-publication editors, a grindstone.

Scandal Sheet, Graham, Texas

PROFESSOR

THAT'S DIFFERENT

PROFESSOR: "And whatever on earth made you write a paragraph like that?"

STUDENT: "I quoted it from Dickens, sir."

PROFESSOR: "Beautiful lines, aren't they?"

From Dartmouth University
Jack-O'-Lantern

AN ATMOSPHERE OF AWE

A schoolmaster should have an atmosphere of awe, and walk wanderingly, as if he was amazed at being himself.

Walter Baghot, 1879

EDUCATION

If you copy anything out of one book, it is plagiarism. If you copy it out of two books, it is research. If you copy it out of six books, you are a professor.

From an address by
The Rt. Rev. Monsignor Fulton J. Sheen

PROGRESS

Governments Didn't Do It

There were some pretty fine things about the good old days. But personally I don't waste much time yearning for them. I don't miss the livery stable. I can get along without muddy roads and the backyard pump. I can admire the past without wanting to relive it. . . .

Some things about the good old days were not so good.

In 1887, when the United States Chamber of Commerce was born, the obituary columns always gave the cause of death. And about every other death was due to some infectious ailment—typhoid fever or diphtheria, for example. The incidence of deaths from diabetes was also frequent—and of course tuberculosis was a major killer of the day.

Today, a case of typhoid fever in this country is a rare thing. Scarlet fever is substantially controlled, and diabetes is kept in check with insulin. Modern treatment for tuberculosis has greatly reduced its fatalities.

How did this happen?

I can tell you right off the bat how it didn't happen!

It didn't happen through socialized medicine.

In 1887, the horseshoe nail dealers were heavy advertisers in Salt Lake City. Today, the horseshoe nail is virtually in a class with the buggy whip.

How do we account for it?

How did we manage to shift so swiftly from horsepower on the hoof to horsepower under the hood? How did we develop the world's greatest motor industry that provides so many more jobs than ever rode behind the horse?

And the answer is easy.

It didn't happen through government direction of our economy.

In 1887, bacon was eleven cents a pound in Salt Lake City, but your housewives fried it over coal or wood. The popular brand of kitchen range was called the "Early Breakfast." I'll bet it was a good stove, but I'll bet on something else too. Somebody had to get up early to get the "Early Breakfast" going.

What gave us the electric range and the gas stove and the household appliances that we accept as commonplace in 1951?

You know the answer.

We didn't get them through some master plan drawn up in Washington.

From an address by D. A. Hulcy, Former President
Chamber of Commerce of the United States
before the Chamber of Commerce, Salt Lake City

THE GOOD OLD DAYS

George Washington became President in 1789. In that year a woman with her spinning wheel was glad to earn fifty cents a day. The wife of Washington or Adams was not ashamed to spend an hour in the morning and two hours in the afternoon working with the spinning wheel. A farmer's wife could earn a few cents a day for the family she helped to support. Those were "the good old days" before the looms and mills of New England and the South provided clothing for the millions.

THE LAW OF LIFE

All progress is based upon a universal, innate desire on the part of every organism to live beyond its income.

Samuel Butler, c. 1890

HOW NEW IDEAS START

"Can any good come out of Nazareth?"
That is always the question of the wiseacres and the knowing ones. But the good, the new, comes from exactly that quarter whence it is not looked for, and is always something different from what is expected. Everything new is received with contempt, for it begins in obscurity. It becomes a power unobserved.

Feuerbach

"IT WON'T WORK"

When Sir George Stephenson proposed the steam locomotive, the people said, "The roaring steam engine will set the house on fire with sparks," "smoke will pollute the air," "carriage makers and coachmen will starve for want of work." A committee of the House of Commons asked him if it would not be an awkward situation if a cow got on

245

the track with the engine going ten miles an hour. He said, "Yes, very awkward indeed, for the cow."

The English *Quarterly Review* in an article in March 1825, said, "What can be more palpably absurd and ridiculous than the prospect held out of locomotives traveling twice as fast as horses?" The magazine continued, "We trust that Parliament will, in all the railways it may grant, limit the speed to eight or nine miles an hour, which . . . is as great as can be ventured upon."

On October 6, 1829, in a great contest of four locomotives, Stephenson's *Rocket* won with an average speed of fifteen miles an hour, the highest rate it reached being twenty-nine miles an hour.

IN ONE LIFETIME

I am only in my seventies, but think what I have seen. The first bicycle factory in the United States was organized when I was minus one year old. The first telephone exchange in the United States, with twenty-one subscribers, was set up in New Haven, Connecticut, the year I was born. Edison produced his electric light when I was one year old. It was in the year I graduated from college that Wilbur Wright wrote to his father that he was going to a place called Kitty Hawk, in North Carolina, to try a little experiment. "It is my belief," he said, "that flight is possible, and I think there is a slight possibility of achieving fame and fortune from it." What a generation of scientific invention it has been!

Has that saved the world? All this new power in the hands of a race whose ethical character and spiritual culture are no match for their technical civilization? Has that redeemed us? Rather, as another put it, "The road to hell is paved with good inventions."

From an address by Dr. Harry Emerson Fosdick

PROMOTION

IT'S UP TO YOU

The president of a bank was playing golf with an assistant vice president who had made a long drive. The president said, "That's a good drive for an assistant vice president."

"Well," said the assistant vice president, "I'll give it the drive of a vice president if you like, sir."

246

PROPERTY

An old gentleman was extolling the wisdom of Huey Long, pointing out that it was Huey's program to take everything in the state and divide it so that everybody would have an indentical amount. When the visitor said, "But Uncle, even if you gave everybody the same amount on Monday, things would be unequal by Saturday night. A few would have most of it." The old man said, "Yassuh, but I thought they intended to equalize it every Saturday night."

From an address by Dr. Walter R. Courtenay

A NATURAL RIGHT

The right of private property, the fruit of labor or industry, or of concession or donation by others, is an incontrovertible natural right; and everybody can dispose reasonably of such property as he thinks fit.

Pope Pius X, 1903

PROVIDENCE

PROVIDENCE—AN APOLOGUE

The other evening I was a little late in going down to dinner, and this was the reason: I noticed a number of dead bees lying on the floor of the lookout where I am accustomed to work— a sight that I encounter every spring. The poor things had come in through the open window. When the windows were closed they found themselves prisoners. Unable to see the transparent obstacle, they had hurled themselves against the glass panes on all sides, east, north, south and west, until at last they fell to the floor exhausted, and died. But, yesterday, I noticed among the bees, a great drone, much stronger than the bees, who was far from being dead, who, in fact, was very much alive and was dashing himself against the panes with all his might, like the great beast that he was. "Ah! my fine friend," said I, "it would have been an evil day for you had I not come to the rescue. You would have been done for, my fine fellow; before nightfall you would be lying dead, and on coming up-stairs, in the evening with my lamp, I would have found your poor little corpse among those of the other bees. Come, now, like the Emperor Titus I shall mark the day by a good deed: let us save the insect's life. Perhaps in the eyes of

247

God a drone is as valuable as a man, and without any doubt it is more valuable than a prince."

I threw open the window, and, by means of a napkin, began chasing the insect toward it; but the drone persisted in flying in the opposite direction. I then tried to capture it by throwing the napkin over it. When the drone saw that I wished to capture it, it lost its head completely; it bounded furiously against the glass panes, as though it would smash them, took a fresh start, and dashed itself again and again against the glass. Finally it flew the whole length of the apartment, maddened and desperate. "Ah, you tyrant!" it buzzed. "Despot! you would deprive me of liberty! Cruel executioner, why do you not leave me alone? I am happy, and why do you persecute me?"

After trying very hard, I brought it down and, in seizing it with the napkin, I involuntarily hurt it. Oh, how it tried to avenge itself! It darted out its sting; its little nervous body, contracted by my fingers, strained itself with all its strength in an attempt to sting me. But I ignored its protestations, and, stretching my hand out the window, opened the napkin. For a moment the drone seemed stunned, astonished; then it calmly took flight out into the infinite.

Well, you see how I saved the drone. I was *its Providence*. But (and here is the moral of my story) do we not, stupid drones that we are, conduct ourselves in the same manner toward the providence of God? We have our petty and absurd projects, our small and narrow views, our rash designs, whose accomplishment is either impossible or injurious to ourselves. Seeing no farther than our noses and with our eyes fixed on our immediate aim, we plunge ahead in our blind infatuation, like madmen. We would succeed, we would triumph; that is to say, would break our heads against an invisible obstacle.

And when God, who sees all and who wishes to save us, upsets our designs, we stupidly complain against Him, we accuse His Providence. We do not comprehend that in punishing us, in overturning our plans and causing us suffering, He is doing all this to deliver us, to open the Infinite to us.

Victor Hugo

FAITH

I firmly believe in Divine Providence. Without belief in Providence I think I should go crazy. Without God the world would be a maze without a clue.

Woodrow Wilson, 1919

PSYCHOLOGIST

SAY THAT AGAIN, PLEASE

PSYCHOLOGIST: "Now, madam, the best thing to do when children are naughty is quickly switch their attention."
MOTHER: "Switch their what?"

PUBLIC SPEAKING

WE HAVE WITH US TODAY

I was traveling around the country about ten years ago in a play called *Springtime for Henry*. We were playing a city called Detroit, and there is in Detroit a civic club known as the Lions Club. It seemed the Lions Club was short of a speaker, and the manager of the theater came to ask me if I would care to address the assemblage. He told me that it was to be a luncheon, and if I could hold forth for about forty minutes or an hour, it would be a very nice thing, not only for me, personally, but for the theater. Maybe the business would improve.

It was so easy to say, "Why, yes, I'd be delighted." Then you start thinking, "What will I talk about? What is the subject?" What could you say that you could hold forth for forty minutes? Generally, you can say everything you know in about five.

Nevertheless, I went over and sat through a very nice lunch, and listened to a most glowing introduction of myself. I really got fatuous about myself. "And now we will hear from our speaker of the day, Edward Everett Horton." I got up. Well, really, it was deplorable. But I kept going, and eventually I stopped, and there was a sort of "relief" applause. Afterward two ladies made their way up to me and made a remark which had a great deal to do with my future. They said, "Mr. Horton, we were so glad we were here today, becauses all the time you were talking, we kept remembering how wonderful you used to be in silent pictures."

Edward Everett Horton, Distinguished Actor

BIG HORN

An Italian was driving a calf along the highway and an automobile came along and honked the horn. There happened

249

to be a bridge. The calf jumped off the highway and into a stream and was drowned. The Italian shrugged his shoulders and he said, "Too biga de horn for so smalla de calf."

Marriner S. Eccles, former Chairman of the Board of Governors of the Federal Reserve System commenting on an introduction he had received before an address

Honored and Embarrassed

I feel honored and embarrassed in being asked to speak to the Executives Club. I am honored because I have reviewed the names of your past speakers, and I am flattered to be in such a company.

I am filled with the same temerity as the tipsy fellow who approached me some years ago and said, "I know you're a college professor and all that, but I know one thing you don't know. My wife is your wife's laundress, and at this moment I'm wearing one of your shirts."

But this assignment embarrasses me, too. I'm very new at a very large job, and any storehouse of wisdom upon which I might draw for my remarks is still to be built. I am now at the stage of terrified innocence that Nicholas Murray Butler was many years ago when he had been President of Columbia for some six months. He was talking to President Eliot of Harvard who had been in office for some years, and he said to him, "This is a terrible kind of job we have. Have they ever called you a liar?"

"Called me a liar? Man," said Eliot, "they've proved it."

From an address by Dr. Lawrence Kimpton Chancellor of the University of Chicago

Advice

A young preacher who was to give his first sermon said to his bishop, "About what shall I preach?"

The bishop replied, "Preach about God and about twenty minutes."

Dr. R. Worth Frank, President McCormick Theological Seminary

The Chairman Knew the Speaker

When we moved to Manitowoc, Wisconsin, I transferred my Rotary membership from Superior, Wisconsin, to the local

250

club. As is customary, I was invited to address the Manitowoc Rotary Club shortly after becoming a member. The chairman introduced me at some length, telling the members about my previous experience in the school business, my formal education, my hobbies, and finally that I was the father of one son and three daughters. His final statement was, "I suppose that Angus is surprised that I am able to tell you so much about him."

When I rose to speak, I had a wonderful opportunity to break the ice, for I was able to say, "Yes, Bernard is right, I am very much surprised by what Bernard has said, for when I left home I had only one son and two daughters."

Angus B. Rothwell
Superintendent of Public Schools, Manitowoc, Wisconsin

PUBLIC UTILITY

No Profit

"Wanted: Burly beauty-proof individual to read meters in sorority houses. We haven't made a nickel in two years. *The Gas Company.*"

PUN

Game Fathers

The story is told that Sydney Smith and a friend were visiting a school, where a little girl, in reading, several times called "patriarch," "partridge." Sydney Smith observed, "The child seems to be determined to make game of the fathers."

Wit

A professor had in his class a young girl of exquisite beauty. One day a grain of sand happened to get into her eye, and, being unable to extricate it herself, she requested his assistance. As he was observed to perform this little operation with zeal, somebody called out to him, "Do not spoil the pupil."

Cicero said of a man who had ploughed up the ground in which his father was buried, "This is really cultivating one's father's memory."

A punster, being requested to give a specimen of his art, asked for a subject.

Someone suggested, "The king."

"The king is not a subject," he replied.

John Erskine, Scottish jurist, was reproached for his propensity to pun, and was told that puns were the lowest kind of wit.

"True," said he, "and therefore they are the foundation of all wit."

At a time when public affairs were in a very unsettled state, a Frenchman who squinted terribly, asked Talleyrand (famous French minister of foreign affairs, 1797-1807) how things were going on.

"Why, as you see, sir," said Talleyrand.

Worst Pun

Mr. Joseph Addison, English essayist (1672-1718), is guilty of one of the worst puns ever made. He went up to a man carrying a hare in his hand, and said to him, "Is that your hare or a wig?"

An Enemy to Puns

My little dears, who learn to read,
Pray early learn to shun
That very foolish thing indeed
The people call a pun.
Theodore Hook, 1830

PUNCTUAL

Way Ahead of Time

JIM: "My girl was furious with me."

JERRY: "What's the matter?"

JIM: "I was an hour late and she had been ready for ten minutes."

Go Right Ahead

Two men had agreed to fight a duel at 6 A.M.

The one who was a little reluctant to engage in the duel said, "In case I'm a little late in the morning, don't wait, go right ahead and shoot."

252

PUNCTUATION

PUNCTUATION MAKES A DIFFERENCE

A prisoner was charged with robbery in the criminal court. The principal thing that appeared against him was a confession alleged to have been made by him at police headquarters. The document purporting to contain his confession was produced by the police officer, and the following passage was read from it:

"Jones said he never robbed but twice said it was Smith." The meaning attached to it was that, "Jones said he never robbed but twice. Said it was Smith."

The counsel for the prisoner asked to look at the paper. He perused it, and rather astonished the court by asserting that so far from proving the man's guilt, it clearly established his innocence. "This," said the attorney, "is the clear and obvious reading of the sentence:

"'Jones said he never robbed. But twice said it was Smith.'"

This interpretation had its effect on the jury, and the man was acquitted.

PUNISHMENT

SENSITIVE

Little Percy's mother had allowed her precious child to attend public school. She gave the teacher a long list of instructions.

"My Percy is so sensitive," she explained. "Don't ever punish him. Just slap the boy next to him. That will frighten Percy."

SECOND PRIZE

In Montreal at a recent advertising and sales convention, a new contest was announced. First prize was to be a week's visit in Toronto. Second prize was two weeks in Toronto.
The Globe and Mail, Toronto

AFTER DAD TOO

For doing some mischief, Willie has been pursued by his mother, and takes refuge under the bed, where he is held in state of siege until father comes home. The father starts after him, and when his head appears under the bed, Willie calls out, "Hello, Dad, is she after you, too?"

WAIT UNTIL MONDAY

TEACHER: "This makes five times I have punished you this week. Now Henry, what have you got say?"
HENRY: "I'm glad it's Friday."

PURITY

CORRUPTED NO MAN

When Sir Walter Scott, toward the close of his life, was congratulated on the purity of his fiction, he answered, "I am drawing near to the close of my career. I am fast shuffling off the stage. I have been, perhaps, the most voluminous author of the day; and it is a comfort to me to think that I have tried to unsettle no man's faith, to corrupt no man's principles, and that I have written nothing which on my death-bed I should wish blotted."

QUARREL

FOREVER

"Jack and I have parted forever."
"Good gracious! What does that mean?"
"Means that I'll get a dozen roses in about an hour."

NEVER HAPPENS

"We've been married a year and never quarrel. If a difference of opinion arises and I'm right, my husband gives in."
"But what if he's right?"
"That has never occurred."

QUIET

ONLY GOD ABOVE HIM

Somebody once asked Professor Charles Townsend Copeland of Harvard why he lived on the top floor of Hollis Hall, in his small, dusty old rooms, and suggested that he move.

"No," said Copeland, "no, I shall always live on the top floor. It is the only place in Cambridge where God alone is above me." Then after a pause, "He's busy—but He's quiet."

RACE

JUST RIGHT

It has been said that when God first kneaded the clay to fashion the human being, and the first product came out of the oven, it was found that it was underbaked—and it turned out to be the white man. Then God tried again. This time He leaned over backwards, and the product was overbaked and came out as the African. But then at last God tried a third time, and this time He succeeded in turning out the properly baked product—and that is the brown man.

From an address by Minoo R. Masani
Member, Parliament of India

RADIO

ALL THE SAME

GRACIE ALLEN: "I always read on my way downtown and back. That's why I like this little magazine. It doesn't cut out so much of my view when I'm driving."

JANE MORTON: "Good heavens! Don't you watch the traffic signals?"

GRACIE: "Yes, but after you see two or three of them you've seen them all."

MODERN CHILDREN

"Let's play store," said the child. "I'll be storekeeper and you be the customer."

"No, prices are too high," replied the other youngster. "Let's play radio and I'll give away a million dollars."

255

Can You Tune Out the Soprano?

"How is the selectivity on your radio set?"

"Superb. The other day I was listening to a concert but didn't like the trumpet player. So I tuned him out and listened to the rest of the band."

Is Anyone Unhappy About It?

An elderly person dragged his radio into a repair shop.

"What's wrong with it?" asked the mechanic.

"Ah dunno, it's jess outta commotion."

RAILROADS

The 12:05 Train

In the dimly lit railroad station, one face stared grimly into another. The man's face was tense and strained, the other face deathly white, with two slender hands pressed against it. It was those hands that held the man's horrified gaze.

"Heavens!" he groaned, in misery.

For the other face was the face of his watch, and those little hands told him that he had missed the last train home!

You May Sleep

Some time ago I addressed a group of men in New York. It was a New York Central Day.

Behind where I was standing, they had placed a New York Central banner indicating that it was New York Central Day. But on that banner it said: "The New York Central Railroad: a water level route. You may sleep."

From an address by Gustav Metzman
President of the New York Central Railroad

He Has an Electric Train at Home

A little old lady hobbled up to the dispatcher and asked him what time the train for Cleveland would leave.

256

"Two-two," he replied rapidly, "Two-two."

She looked at him over her spectacles. "My," she said, "a big man like you still likes to play choo-choo train."

RAIN

UNUSUAL WEATHER

"Doesn't it ever rain around here?" the tourist asked the native in Arizona.

"Rain? Rain? Man, there's bullfrogs in this town over five years old that ain't learned to swim yet!"

REAL ESTATE

CONFESSION

"Harry, whatever induced you to buy a house in this undeveloped section?"

"One of the best men in the real estate business."

REASON

NO FAIR

"I can stand brute force, but brute reason is quite unbearable. There is something unfair about its use. It is hitting below the intellect."

Oscar Wilde, 1891

REFERENCES

OTHERWISE O.K.

WIFE: "I've been asked for a reference for our last maid. I've said she's lazy, late for work, and impertinent. Can I add anything in her favor?"

HUSBAND: "You might say that she has a very good appetite and sleeps well."

257

REFLECTION

WITH SORROW

When I look upon the tombs of the great, every motion of envy dies; when I read the epitaphs of the beautiful, every inordinate desire forsakes me; when I meet with the grief of parents upon a tombstone, my heart melts with compassion; when I see the tombs of the parents themselves, I reflect how vain it is to grieve for those whom we must quickly follow; when I see kings lying beside those who deposed them, when I behold rival wits placed side by side, or the holy men who divided the world with their contests and disputes, I reflect with sorrow and astonishment on the frivolous competitions, factions, and debates of mankind.

Addison

BABBLE

They only babble who practice not reflection,
I shall think—and thought is silence.

Sheridan

REFORM

OBSERVATIONS ON REFORM

Necessity reforms the poor, and satiety reforms the rich.

Tacitus

The best reformers the world has ever seen are those who have commenced on themselves.

H. W. Shaw

He who reforms himself has done more toward reforming the public than a crowd of noisy, impotent patriots.

Lavater

Reform, like charity, must begin at home.

Carlyle

258

RELAXATION

How the Great Have Played

Socrates often played with children.

Tycho Brahe, Danish astronomer, diverted himself with polishing glasses for all kinds of spectacles.

Balzac amused himself with a collection of crayon portraits.

Dr. Samuel Clarke used to amuse himself by jumping over tables and chairs.

Dr. Jonathan Swift, English poet, exercised by running up and down the steps of the deanery; and even in his later days, when his constitution was almost broken, he was on his legs about ten hours a day.

Shelley took great pleasure in making paper boats, and floating them. The *New Monthly* has the following curious anecdotes on this subject: "So long as his paper lasted, he remained rivetted to the spot, fascinated by this peculiar amusement. All waste paper was rapidly consumed, then the covers of letters, next letters of little value; the most precious contributions of the most esteemed correspondents, although eyed wistfully many times, and often returned to his pocket, were sure to be sent at last in pursuit of the former squadrons. Of the portable volumes which were the companions of his rambles, and he seldom went out without a book, the fly leaves were commonly wanting ... But learning was so sacred in his eyes that he never trespassed further upon the integrity of the copy; the work itself was always respected."

RELIANCE

By the Sweat of Thy Brow

When a person is thrown upon his own resources, there is a strong possibility that it will help him to grow and to develop his mind, self-reliance, patience, courage, and character. One of the kindest laws ever made by God was the law: "By the sweat of thy brow thou shalt eat thy bread." There is an old Greek proverb which says, "The youth who daily lifts the calf, after three years can lift the full grown ox."

RELIGION

The Biblical Texts Chosen by Presidents

It might be well for America to be reminded, in the words of Calvin Coolidge, that "Our government rests upon religion. It is from that source that we derive our reverence for truth and justice, for equality and liberty, and for the rights of mankind. Unless the people believe in these principles, they cannot believe in our government. There are only two main theories of government in the world. One rests on righteousness, the other rests on force. One appeals to reason, the other appeals to the sword. One is exemplified in a republic, the other is represented by despotism. The government of a country never gets ahead of the religion of a country. There is no way by which we can substitute the authority of law for the virtue of man. Of course we can help to restrain the vicious and furnish a fair degree of security and protection by legislation and police control, but the real reforms which society in these days is seeking will come as a result of our religious convictions, or they will not come at all. Peace, justice, humanity, charity—these cannot be legislated into being. They are the result of Divine Grace."

Our Presidents, when they took the oath of office, placed their hand upon some particular verse or chapter, and in so doing, seemed to say, in effect, what Coolidge stated above ... Those men chose these texts on the day they took over the highest office of the land. We give you those texts which we have. They have been culled from various sources. Robert C. Gooch, Chief of the General Reference and Bibliography Division of The Library of Congress, was kind enough to supply most of them.

George Washington—*The History of the Centennial Celebration of the Inauguration of George Washington,* by Clarence W. Bowen, states that the pages upon which he took the oath were: left hand page, two pictures illustrating Gen. 49:13-15; right hand page, Gen. 49:13 to 50:8.

John Quincy Adams—Ps. 127:1.

Martin Van Buren—Prov. 3:17.

Abraham Lincoln—Matt. 7:1; Matt. 18:7; Rev. 16:7.

Andrew Johnson—Prov. 21.

Ulysses S. Grant—Isa. 11:1 (2nd Term).

Rutherford B. Hayes—Ps. 118:11-13.

James A. Garfield—Prov. 21:1.

Chester A. Arthur—Ps. 31:1-3.
Grover Cleveland—Ps. 112:4-10 (1st Term).
Benjamin Harrison—Ps. 121:1-6.
Grover Cleveland—Ps. 91:12-16.
William McKinley—2 Chron. 1:10 (1st Term).
William McKinley—Prov. 16:21-22 (2nd Term).
Theo. Roosevelt—Jas. 1:22 (2nd Term).
Wm. Howard Taft—1 Kings 3:9-11.
Woodrow Wilson—Ps. 119:43-46 (1st Term).
Woodrow Wilson—Ps. 46 (2nd Term).
Warren G. Harding—Micah 6:8.
Calvin Coolidge—John 1.
Herbert Hoover—Prov. 29:18.
F. D. Roosevelt—1 Cor. 13 (At the beginning of each of the
four terms).
Harry S. Truman—Ex. 20:3-17; Matt. 5:3-11.

Dr. R. R. Belter, President, The Wartburg Synod
United Lutheran Church in America

ONLY LIP SERVICE

Two Southern church-goers were discussing a third, who was known
as a great shouter and testifier for the Lord.

"Ah tells you," said one, "dat man talks mo' good in five minutes
dan he can do in a whole yeah."

FIRE IN THE PULPIT

Sunday was the great day of the week in the American colonies.
The clergyman was the best-informed man in each community. Everybody went to church, even in the coldest weather. The women and
children were allowed hot soapstones and even a floorstone. A Deacon
Sewall once wrote in his journal one Sunday afternoon, "Though the
ink in the bottle from which I write is now freezing in this room beside
the fire, I suffered no cold whatever in church today." The fire must
have been furnished by the pulpit. Church lasted all day.

DUTY

It is said of the Duke of Wellington that when a certain chaplain
asked him whether he thought it worth while to preach the Gospel

261

to some of the people of Asia, Wellington replied, "What are your marching orders?"

The chaplain replied, "Go ye into all the world, and preach the Gospel to every creature."

"Then follow your orders," said the Duke. "Your only duty is to obey."

REPARTEE

Cause and Effect

A thin man met a fat man in the hotel lobby.

"From the looks of you," said the fat man, "there must have been a famine."

"Yes," was the reply, "and from the looks of you, you must have caused it."

Didn't Possess Either

M. Lalande, the astronomer, dined one day at the house of Récamier, the banker. He was seated between the celebrated beauty, Madame Récamier, and Madame de Staël, equally distinguished for her wit. Wishing to say something agreeable to the ladies, the astronomer exclaimed, "How happy I am to be thus placed between wit and beauty!"

"Yes, M. Lalande," sarcastically replied Madame de Staël, "and without possessing either."

RESOLUTIONS

Too Often Dies the Same

At thirty man suspects himself a fool,
Knows it at forty, and reforms his plan;
At fifty chides his infamous delay . . .
Resolves; and re-solves; then dies the same.

Young, 1742

RESOURCES

No man can lay claim to being educated unless he has stowed away in his mind a certain mass of information about men and things. In my own case I have never had occasion to use for any practical purpose what little I ever knew about binomial theorems, integral calculus, the periodic law in chemistry, the Mendelian theory of inheritance, the choral odes in Greek tragedies, the scanning of Latin verse, the quantitative theory of money, the intricacies of Anglo-Saxon roots, the history of the Hyksos kings in Egypt, or the details of the plot of *Othello*—but all have affected my enjoyment of life and I am sure have aided me in developing any bit of mental resourcefulness or imagination that I may possess. To quote Dr. Lowell, former President of Harvard University: "The real thing we want is not knowledge but resourcefulness; what I mean is that the art which creates things, both great and small, is not the capacity for solving problems. . . . The real art of life consists in finding out what is the question to be solved, and the person who can find out what problem is to be solved is the man who really makes contributions to life. How can resourcefulness be acquired? Do it by pumping into a man information? No, not at all. There is only one thing which will really train the human mind, and that is the voluntary use of the mind by the man himself. You may aid him, you may guide him, you may suggest to him, and, above all, you may inspire him; but the only thing that is worth having is that which he gets by his own exertions, and what he gets is proportionate to the effort he puts into it. It is the voluntary exercise of his own mind, and I care very little about what he exercises it upon."

From an address by H. W. Prentis, Jr.
Chairman of the Board, Armstrong Cork Company

RESPONSIBILITY

It was the crying need today for a rejuvenation of our spiritual values and a nation-wide recognition of our individual responsibility that prompted the Episcopal House of Bishops to make a stirring appeal a few months ago, which I quote:

"There is no man who cannot see his present duty, and to do it at this significant moment in history is a rare privilege given to us by God. Nothing can take the place, in our life together, of integrity and character, and we must remember in the fear of God that we are threatened not only by outward forces but by any lack of responsibility from within."

"Every man," said the House of Bishops, "who lives irresponsibly today, who seeks his own security or gain without counting the cost to others; every politician who plays recklessly on the present crisis for partisan advantage or his own advancement; every injustice in our common life; every hypocrisy in our democratic profession—weakens us and makes us less able to fulfill the role laid upon us.

"Even though we cannot see the pattern of the future," continued the Bishops, "we can see the duties that lie at hand and the value of hard and self-denying work in the present. We, too, in our day, by what we do, can help to shape the course of history."

William H. Ruffin, former President, National Association
of Manufacturers, and President, Erwin Mills

Everyone Wants a Prize

There are in every society those who have no wish to stand on their own feet as responsible citizens, and creative coworkers with God, if they can persuade a benevolent government to give them a prize of one sort or another. The contest for prizes has become a great American game popularly known as "subsidy." I recall the days when I was trying to teach my three boys to play baseball. The two older boys agreed that their small brother ought to have a subsidy, a handicap. So, when we played ball, he got four strikes instead of three. That one strike subsidy remained in effect for some months, until it assumed the proportions of a vested right. Even when the little brother got to the point of hitting the ball all over the lot, he still assumed he ought to have four strikes. There came a day, however, when his older brothers rebelled and insisted on three strikes or none. Surprisingly enough he did as well on three strikes as he had done on four. He had overcome the need for a subsidy!

Our country today is full of people who want four strikes. The labor lobby in Washington wants four strikes for labor against three for industry. The manufacturers would get four strikes to labor's three if they could. Farmers want four strikes against three for the consumers. Renters want four strikes against three for owners. Manufacturers want four-strike tariffs against three strikes for foreign competition. . . . The trouble is that the four strikes have become a vested right. Nobody wants to play the game on even terms.

From a sermon by Dr. Harold Blake Walker

RESTAURANT

NOT HERE

CUSTOMER: "What would you eat if you were me?"
WAITER: "Hash, but not here."

ISLANDS IN THE THOUSAND ISLAND DRESSING

CUSTOMER: "I can't find any chicken in the chicken pie."
WAITER: "Do you expect to find a dog in the dog biscuit?"

JUST SO IT'S WITHOUT

A customer stopped in a restaurant late one evening, and ordered a cup of coffee.

"Without cream," he added, as the waitress headed for the kitchen.

Presently the waitress came scurrying back, empty-handed and apologetic. "I'm sorry, sir," she said. "There is no more cream."

"Very well," said the disappointed man, "I'll take it without milk."

IT'S UP TO YOU

A cafeteria owner had the following sign posted:

COURTEOUS AND EFFICIENT SELF-SERVICE.

WE KNOW THE WAITER

MAN AT RESTAURANT TABLE TO WAITER: "What's my offense? I've been on bread and water for two hours."

RESURRECTION

FAITH

What reason have atheists for saying that we cannot rise again? Which is the more difficult—to be born, or to rise again? That what has never been, should be, or that what has been, should be again? Is it more difficult to come into being than to return to it?

Blaise Pascal, 1670

REWARD

TEXAS

A Texan who goes to church and is good thinks that when he dies he will be allowed to stay in Texas.

RHEUMATISM

WEATHERMAN

Some men ('gainst rain) do carry in their backs
Prognosticating aching almanacs;
Some by a painful elbow, hip or knee
Will shrewdly guess what weather's like to be.

John Taylor, 1637

RICHES

HEAVY RICHES

If thou art rich, thou art poor;
For, like an ass whose back with ingots bows,
Thou bear'st thy heavy riches but a journey,
And death unloads thee.

Shakespeare, 1604

RIGHT

DANGEROUS

Nicolaus Copernicus, famous astronomer, did not publish his book until he was on his deathbed. He knew how dangerous it is to be right when the rest of the world is wrong.

Thomas B. Reed, 1885

Cannibals have the same notions of right and wrong that we have. They make war in the same anger and passion that move us, and the same crimes are committed everywhere. Eating fallen enemies is only an extra ceremonial. The wrong does not consist in roasting them, but in killing them.

Voltaire

RIGHTEOUSNESS

A NEW AMERICA

What we need—what we must have—is a revival of the application of the life and teachings of the Master of Men. Until that virtue lives in America again, I tremble for America's future.

Up in New England we had a poet. He is dead now. His name was John Greenleaf Whittier. He had a home up near Squam Lake. He was a simple man and a great man, a Quaker, and he wrote some wonderful things in poetry. In one poem, called "Problems," he commented on the ills of the nation, and he closed with this: "But solution, there is none, save in the rule of Christ alone." No truer words were ever spoken, friends. There is the answer!

When the hearts of men and women are touched, they take their inspiration from the Master of Men, and then we will have a righteous and a new America, and we will have in this nation a nation in which "dwelleth righteousness," before God. It is high time.

So, fathers and mothers of America—wake up! Make that home a great trust for the children God has entrusted to you. Teach them to put first things first, and know that "a man's life consisteth not in the abundance of the things which he possesses."

Churches, wake up, over America! Not in rituals or creeds lies the salvation of the world, but rather in living out the teachings of the Master of Men, seven days each week, remembering always the test Jesus gave when He said, "By their fruits ye shall know them."

Politicians, wake up! Remember the words of Grover Cleveland: "Public office is a public trust." Be a trustee to conserve the people's—all the people's interests.

From an address by Senator Charles W. Tobey

ROUTINE

You're in the Army Now

An old army sergeant was told to look after a plot of grass in front of the administration building. The sergeant appointed a private to water the plot each afternoon at three o'clock.

One day, during a thunderstorm, the sergeant came into the barracks and caught the private doing bunk fatigue.

"It's three o'clock," roared the sergeant, "and you're supposed to be out there watering the grass."

"But, Sergeant," the private said, "look at the rainstorm."

"That's no excuse," the sergeant bellowed. "Haven't you got a raincoat?"

RULES

Rules Are Rules

There was a loud knock on the door. The doctor, who had just settled himself for a nap, got up. "What is it?" he asked the man at the door.

"I've been bitten by a dog," said the man unhappily.

"Well, don't you know that my hours of consultation are between twelve and three?"

"Yes," groaned the patient, "but the dog didn't know. He bit me at twenty to four."

SABBATH

Misery of War

One of the miseries of war is that there is no Sabbath, and the current of work and strife has no cessation. How can we be pardoned for all our offenses?

Robert E. Lee, 1861

268

And Then Some

A salesman summed up his success in three words: "AND THEN SOME."

"Most of the differences between average people and top people can be explained in three words. The top people did what was expected of them—AND THEN SOME!

"They are thoughtful of others; they are considerate—AND THEN SOME! They meet their obligations and responsibilities fairly and squarely—AND THEN SOME! They are good friends to their friends—AND THEN SOME! They can be counted on in an emergency—AND THEN SOME!"

The Reason

INVESTIGATOR: "Don't you know you can't sell insurance without a license?"

SALESMAN: "I knew I wasn't selling any, but I didn't know the reason."

Honest

SALESMAN: "Boy, I want to see someone around here with a little authority."

OFFICE BOY: "Well, I have about as little as anyone. What is it you want?"

Good Salesman

A farmer walked into the office of the general manager of a railroad and asked for a free pass to Chicago and return. The general manager reasoned with him as follows: "Suppose I dropped in on you some time and asked you to drive me to the next town and back, what would you think of me?"

"I'd think you were awfully cheeky," replied the farmer. "But, if I were driving to town anyway and you asked me for a ride, what would you think of me if I refused?"

A Good Day

FIRST SALESMAN: "Gee, Albert, I had a marvelous day—made a lot of friends for the company."

SECOND SALESMAN: "Me, too, Harold—I didn't sell anything either."

Perfect Job

A salesman joined the police force. After several months a friend asked, "How do you like being a policeman?"

"The pay is good and the hours are satisfactory," he answered, "and best of all—the customer is always wrong."

No Trade

Deep in the Ozarks, a carpet sweeper salesman knocked at the door, and was presently confronted by a man.

When he began his sales talk, the prospect interrupted with, "Don't waste your breath. I got a carpet sweeper."

The salesman was ready for his reply. "Good," he said. "Then I can make you a generous allowance on your old sweeper in part payment on a splendid new model."

The prospect seemed tempted, then shook his head. "No," he said, "I can't make that kind of a deal. After all, I took her for better or wuss."

She'll Do All She Can

Charles Schwab, who was known as a great industrialist, told a story of a neighbor who wanted to sell him a cow.

"I've got a cow I want to sell you, Charlie," the neighbor said.

"Would she fit into my herd?" asked Schwab.

"No; I don't know that she would."

"Does she give lots of milk?"

"No; I can't say she does, but she's a kind, gentle, good-natured old cow, and if she's got any milk she'll give it to you."

Go Easy

IRATE SALESGIRL TO DISAGREEABLE CUSTOMER: "Go easy, madam. The days when I used to insult customers are still fresh in my mind."

Two men were traveling on a train. One asked his fellow traveler for a match to light his pipe. Shortly they began talking.

"What's your line of business?" asked the first.

"It may sound strange," said the other gentleman, "but I'm a pepper seller."

The first man threw out his hand. "Shake," he said. "I'm a salt seller."

NOBODY HOME

SALESMAN: "Sonny, is your mother at home?"

LITTLE BOY: "Yes, sir."

SALESMAN (after knocking in vain): "I thought you said your mother was at home?"

LITTLE BOY: "Yes, sir, but I don't live here."

SALESMANSHIP

TIME IS MONEY

One morning when Franklin was busy preparing his newspaper for the press, a man stepped into the store and spent an hour or more looking over the books. Finally taking a book in his hand, he asked the clerk the price.

"One dollar," was the answer.

"One dollar," said the browser, "can't you take less than that?"

"No, indeed; one dollar is the price."

Another hour had nearly passed, when the browser asked, "Is Mr. Franklin at home?"

"Yes, he is in the printing office."

"I want to see him," said the man.

The clerk immediately informed Mr. Franklin that a gentleman was in the store, waiting to see him. Franklin was soon behind the counter, and the man with the book in hand addressed him thus: "Mr. Franklin, what is the lowest you can take for that book?"

"One dollar and a quarter," was the answer.

"One dollar and a quarter! Why, your young man asked for only a dollar."

"True," said Franklin, "and I could better afford to have taken a dollar then, than to have been taken out of the office."

The man seemed surprised and wishing to end the discussion of his own making, said, "Come, Mr. Franklin, tell me what is the lowest you can take for it?"

"One dollar and a half."

"A dollar and a half! Why, you offered it yourself for a dollar and a quarter."

"Yes," said Franklin, "and I had better have taken that price then, than a dollar and a half now."

The man paid the price, and went about his business—if he had any —and Franklin returned into the printing office.

The Hen's Still on the Nest

HOUSEWIFE: "Are these eggs strictly fresh?"

GROCER (to his clerk): "Feel those eggs, Bill, and see if they're cool enough to sell yet."

Good Idea Too

Hans decided to sell vacuum cleaners from house to house. Calling on his first lady prospect, he proceeded to put the machine and its gadgets through their various paces.

Finally he came to the grand finale—the bug killer.

"You see," he explained, "ven you see a bug in your house, you get out de vacuum gleaner and put dis attachment on. Den you put in de insect powder. Den you turn on de machine and point it at de bug. In no time, he's dead."

"But, why go to so much trouble?" asked the housewife. "If I see a bug, I just step on it and it's dead."

Hans was thoughtful for a moment. Then he said: "Ya, dot's a good idea too."

SANTA CLAUS

NOT SURE

A small boy looked critically at a department store Santa. The boy asked, "Are you really Santa Claus?"

"Ho, ho," said Santa. "If I'm not really Santa, just why are you here?"

The small boy replied, "Because I'm not taking any chances."

SCHOLAR

VALUE OF THE SCHOLAR

I do not know who first questioned the value of the scholar's life: it may have been one of Socrates' disciples who watched his master drink the hemlock. Surely no calling has been so much questioned—and despaired of—since that memorable event; and just as surely none has contributed so much to western civilization. What is the nature of this calling? Archimedes might have come down to us as a military strategist on the strength of the wonderful engines he contrived for the defense of Syracuse. But, says Plutarch, "he possessed so high a spirit, so profound a soul, and such treasurers of scientific knowledge, that though these inventions had now obtained for him the renown of more than human sagacity, he yet would not deign to leave behind him any writing on such subjects; but . . . placed his whole affection and ambition in those purer speculations where there can be no reference to the vulgar needs of life studies whose superiority to all others is unquestioned, and in which the only doubt can be whether the beauty and grandeur of the subjects examined, or the precision and cogency of the methods and means of proof, most deserve our admiration." The scholar, says Emerson, is the "delegated intellect" of mankind. In the degenerate state he becomes a "mere thinker, or still worse, the parrot of other men's thinking. . . . In the right state he is Man Thinking." To whom else do we owe our progress from savagery? To whom else do we pin our hopes of ending our periodic reversions to savagery and putting our engines of destruction to creative use?

From an address by Alfred Whitney Griswold
President of Yale University

273

MISPLACED SISTER

An Indiana boy told his teacher that his sister had the measles. The teacher became excited.

"You go home, Johnny," she said, "and don't come back until your sister is well."

Johnny left in a hurry. After he had gone, another boy held up his hand and said, "Teacher, Johnny's sister what has the measles is in Boston."

ATTENTION

The teacher was trying to show that children are not attentive. He said, "Now, children, tell me a number to put on the board." Some child said, "Thirty-six." The teacher wrote sixty-three. He asked for another number, and twenty-six was given. He wrote sixty-two. When a third number was asked, a child who apparently had paid no attention called out: "Sixty-six. Change that, you crook!"

OUT OF THE MOUTHS OF BABES

The Sunday-school class was composed of three-year-olds. The teacher asked: "Do any of you remember who St. Matthew was?" No answer.

"Well, does anyone remember who St. Mark was?" Still no answer.

"Surely some of you must remember who Peter was?"

The little faces were full of interest, but the room was quiet. Finally a tiny voice came from the back of the room.

"I fink he was a wabbit!"

PRACTICAL MATHMATICS

SON: "I don't wanna study arithmetic."

DAD: "What, a son of mine doesn't want to grow up and be able to figure out baseball scores and batting averages?"

Give one word for "love of mankind"—Woman.
An interjection is a sudden explosion of mind.
A myth is a female moth.
During the war my father was repotted dead!
The feminine of bachelor is lady-in-waiting.
The Gorgons looked like women—only more horrible.
An epicure is a poet who writes epics.
Chaliapin is a great comedon.
Immortality is running away with another wife.
Henry Ford invnted perpetual motion.
A Sinecure is a disease without a cure.
A spinster is a bachelor's wife.
Ambiguity means having two wives living at the same time.
An interpreter is a thing you take temperatures with.
Extempore is a disease in dogs.
Cossacks are things which ladies wear.
The Pilgrim Fathers were Adam and Eve.
Nearly at the bottom of Lake Michigan is Chicago!
Certain areas of Egypt are cultivated by irrigation.
An oasis is a futile spot in a desert.
Green Bay is the center of the canning industry.
People go about Venice in gorgonzolas.
Water is melted steam.
Water is turned into a viper when it gets too hot.
A molecule is a girlish boy.

School Board Journal

Ask Father

Mother was absent from the dinner table; so Beata, aged seven, sat in her chair and pretended to take her place. Father was watching the child's solemn, matronly airs with ill-concealed glee, when her brother challenged her position with the remark, "So you're mother tonight? Well, if you're mother, tell me—how much is six times nine?"

Calmly and without hesitation, Beata retorted, "I'm busy; ask your father!"

Next Question

TEACHER: "Can you tell us what the blood does?"
STUDENT: "The blood flows through the elementary canal into the

abdominal canopy. It is also putrefied in the lungs by inspired air. The heart beats, and that stirs up the blood and digests the food."

ACCOMMODATING

TEACHER:"Why does cream rise to the top?"
STUDENT: "So the people can get it."

POOR FATHER

TEACHER: "Use abominable in a sentence."
STUDENT: "My father takes exercises every morning to stretch his abominable muscles."

CORRECT

TEACHER: "Give the amount of imports and exports of coffee in any one year."
BRIGHT BOY: "1942. None. None."

NEXT QUESTION

HISTORY TEACHER: "Tell us all you know about Nero."
JOHNNIE: "The less said about Nero the better."

TEACHING IS GOOD AT BOTH ENDS

FATHER: "Aren't you ashamed of being at the bottom of the class?"
SON: "No, Dad, They teach the same thing at both ends."

SCIENCE

THE RAPIDITY OF CHANGE

Science has done an amazing amount in a relatively short time in other fields. The laws of thermodynamics, which led to the development of the internal combustion engine, were developed largely during the nineteenth century. It was only about sixty years ago that the foundation of the radio art began to be laid by pure research into electric discharges in high vacuums. It was only a little more than a half century ago that X-rays were discovered so that the whole structure of nineteenth century physics had to be rebuilt on new lines. The discovery of radio activity, the development work in electron theory, and the research which led to atomic fission have all come since then.

Henry Ford II

The Business of Scientists

Their business is not with the possible, but the actual—not with a world which might be, but with a world that is. They have but one desire—to know the truth. They have but one fear—to believe a lie.

John Tyndall, 1870

SCOTCH

Thanks

A Scotsman went to a hospital to give blood to an ailing man. The transfusion was successful. The grateful man sent the Scot fifty dollars.

Later a second transfusion was necessary and again the Scot was called upon. Again he was rewarded, but this time with twenty-five dollars.

A third transfusion became necessary. Again the Scot responded. The transfusion was once more successful.

But by that time the sick man had so much Scotch blood in his veins that he wouldn't give anything but a "thank you."

SEARCH

No One Specially

As the microbe said to the microscope, "Are you looking for anyone in particular?"

SEASICKNESS

No Round Trip

A businessman was on his way to Europe and was experiencing real seasickness. Calling his wife to his bedside, he said in a weak voice, "Jane, my will is in the Reliable Trust Company's care. Everything is left to you, dear. My stocks you will find in my safe-deposit box." Then he added, "And Jane, bury me on the other side. I can't stand this trip again, live or dead."

277

SECURITY

No Man Is an Island

You are not allowed to say that you do care for the welfare of other people, for the answer of John Donne is the final answer of all time: "No man is an Iland, intire of it selfe." You are not allowed to say that for your part you want a life of security and repose, for there comes Justice Oliver Wendell Holmes' sharp reminder that "security is an illusion, and repose is not the destiny of man." So live, therefore, and so perform your part that free men across the future years will look back and say, "Here was a generation that did not seek security, but looked for opportunity."

Dr. W. Norwood Brigance, Professor Speech
Wabash College, Crawfordville, Indiana
and Past President of the Speech Association of America

SELF-ESTEEM

Well, It Ain't Exactly Difficult

It is easy for every man, whatever be his character with others, to find reasons for esteeming himself.

Samuel Johnson, 1750

To love one's self is the beginning of a life-long romance.

Oscar Wilde, 1894

SELFISH

Guess Who?

BRAGGART: "Sweet, I have brought something for the one I love. Can you guess what it is?"

WIFIE: "Yes. A box of cigars."

He Liked Himself

Barthe, a French playwright, was remarkable for selfishness. He was strangely insensible to the wants and woes of others.

Calling upon a friend, whose opinion he wished to have on a new comedy, he found him in his last moments, but notwithstanding asked him to read the play.

"Consider," said the dying man, "I have hardly more than an hour to live."

"Ay," replied Barthe, "but this will occupy only half that time."

SELF-PRAISE

Your Merits

> *If you wish in this world to advance*
> *Your merits you're bound to enhance;*
> *You must stir it and stump it,*
> *And blow your own trumpet,*
> *Or, trust me, you haven't a chance.*
>   W. S. Gilbert, 1887

SELLING

No Samples

A salesman boarded the train and took a roomette. He carried with him only a small grip, and the porter inquired of his other luggage.

"I have none," said the man.

"I thought you were a salesman," said the porter.

"That's right, I am. But I don't need a lot of luggage. I sell brains."

The porter scratched his head and said, "Well, you are the first salesman that ever rode this train without samples."

SEMANTICS

Say That Again

"English is a funny language."

"Why so?"

"I heard a man talking of a political candidate the other day, say: "If he only takes a firm stand when he runs, he'll walk away with the election."

279

NATURE IS PECULIAR

"Queer, isn't it?"
"What's queer?"
"Why the night falls—"
"Yes."
"But it doesn't break."
"No."
"And the day breaks—"
"Yes."
"But it never falls."

SENTIMENT

SENTIMENT AND SAUCE

One day in spring, Sir Walter Scott strolled forth with Lady Scott to enjoy a walk around Abbotsford. In their wandering they passed a field where a number of ewes were enduring the frolics of their lambs.

"Ah!" said Sir Walter, " 'tis no wonder that poets, from the earliest ages, have made the lamb the emblem of peace and innocence."

"They are, indeed, delightful animals," returned her ladyship, "especially with mint sauce."

SERMONS

HOW TO PREACH

A preacher, popular with his congregation, explained his success. It was a silent prayer he offered each time he took the pulpit:

Lord, fill my mouth with worthwhile stuff,
And nudge me when I've said enough.

H. E. Cook, Director
Federal Deposit Insurance Corporation
Washington, D.C.

How's That?

The parson who conducts chapel services at a certain college frequently comes to his duties in a drowsy condition which, combined with his mechanical delivery and his fondness for alliteration, sometimes results in peculiar performances.

Recently he was praying for the improvement of his youthful listeners in his usual sing-song voices, when they were suddenly brought to attention by the following: "And so we plead that the inefficient may be made efficient, the intemperate temperate, and the industrious dustrious."

Broad Acquaintance

Said the lady, shaking hands with the preacher after the service, "Wonderful sermon! Everything you said applies to somebody or other I know."

You Better Listen

My Bishop's eyes I've never seen
Though the light in them may shine;
For when he prays, he closes his,
And when he preaches, mine.
                              Anonymous

Calm Delivery

A celebrated preacher, who was remarkable in the first period of his ministry for a boisterous mode of preaching, suddenly changed his whole manner in the pulpit, and adopted a mild delivery. One of his brethren, observing it, inquired of him what had induced him to make the change. He answered, "When I was young, I though it was the thunder that killed the people; but when I grew wiser, I discovered that it was the lightning; so I determined in future to thunder less, and lighten more."

SERVANTS

RESPECT

"Out West we treat the help just like the rest of the family."

"Well, in New York, if we want them to stay, we have to treat them with respect."

ORDERS ARE ORDERS

HOUSEWIFE: "Why didn't you come?"

MAID: "I didn't hear you ring."

HOUSEWIFE: "Well, the next time you don't hear me ring, please come and tell me."

SERVICE

COMPLAINT

A man and two children entered a restaurant and ordered three plates and three glasses of water. When the waiter brought the order, the man took some sandwiches from his pocket, unwrapped them, and atfer passing each of the children one, began to eat.

The manager, who had been watching, rushed over. "What do you think you're doing?" he exploded.

"And who are you?" inquired the diner.

"I'm the manager."

"Good," said the man. "I was just going to send for you. Why isn't the orchestra playing?"

NOT CULTURED PEARLS

DINER: "Waiter, I want some oysters, but they mustn't be too large or too small, too old or too tough, and they mustn't be salty. I want them cold and I want them at once."

WAITER: "Yes, sir. With or without pearls?"

SICKNESS

Oops, I'm Sorry

There was a young girl named O'Neill,
Who went up in the great Ferris wheel;
But when halfway around
She looked at the ground,
And it cost her an eighty-cent meal.

SILENCE

He Never Learns

VISITOR: "Has your baby learned to talk yet?"

DAD: "Yes, we're teaching him to shut up now."

VISITOR: "I guess you know it takes a baby approximately two years to talk—and between sixty and seventy-five years to learn to keep his mouth shut."

Pipe Down

TALKATIVE LADY: "A big man like you might be better occupied than in cruelly catching little fish."

ANGLER: "Perhaps you are right. But if this fish had kept his mouth shut, he wouldn't be here."

She Enjoys the View

A nature enthusiast was climbing a mountain and overtook an old native. The enthusiast began to talk about scenery in gushing phrases. The native paid no attention to him. Provoked by this irresponsiveness, the enthusiast said, "You don't seem to care for this magnificent scenery?"

The native replied, "I enjoy it; I don't jabber."

Socrates and His Pupil

A young man, who was a great talker, was sent by his parents to Socrates to learn oratory. On being presented to Socrates, the lad spoke so incessantly that Socrates was out of all patience. Socrates asked him double his usual fee.

"Why charge me double?" said the young fellow.

"Because," said the orator, "I must teach you two sciences—the one to hold your tongue, and the other how to speak."

The Cloak of Silence

God has given to man a cloak whereby he can conceal his ignorance, and in this cloak he can enwrap himself at any moment, for it always lies near his hand. This cloak is silence.
Bhartrihari, about 625

SINGER

Longfellow on Crooners

When he sang, the village listened;
All the warriors gathered round him,
All the women came to hear him.
Henry W. Longfellow in Hiawatha, 1855

He Listened to the Radio and TV in 1766

Man was never meant to sing;
And all his mimic organs e'er expressed
Was but an imitative howl at best.
John Langhorne, 1766

SLEEP

We Heard that One

A congressman, back home from Washington, was telling a few of his constituents about a dream he had. "I was sitting in the House," he said, "and must have dozed off. Soon I began dreaming that I was on the floor, making a speech. And, brother, I was."

Do As I Say, Not As I Do

I have, all my life long, been lying till noon; yet I tell all young men, and tell them with great sincerity, that nobody who does not rise early will ever do any good.

Samuel Johnson, 1773

SOCIALISM

EQUALITY

Dr. Samuel Johnson remarked, "Your levellers wish to level down as far as themselves, but they cannot bear levelling up to themselves."

SOCIETY

As They Saw It

Society has gone to the dogs: a lot of nobodies talking about nothing.

Oscar Wilde, 1895

High society is for those who have stopped working and no longer have anything important to do.

Woodrow Wilson, 1915

Society is now one polish'd horde,
Form'd of two mighty tribes, the bores and bored.

Byron, 1823

SOLDIERS AND SAILORS

SMART GUY

SERGEANT: "All right, you dumbbells, fall out!"
Every soldier fell out except one rookie.
SERGEANT: "Well."
ROOKIE: "There were a lot of them, weren't there, Sarge?"

SYMPATHY

An admiral, watching a new recruit labor eagerly but clumsily on the quarterdeck, asked: "How long have you been in the Navy, son?"

"Two months," the boy replied. "How long have you been in?"

The admiral was taken slightly aback but he good-naturedly answered: "Thirty years."

"It's tough, ain't it?" the youngster said sympathetically.

No Complaints

The army officer received a complaint about the issue of bread. "Soldiers should not make a fuss about trivialities, my man," he said. "If Napoleon had had that bread when he was crossing the Alps, he'd have eaten it with delight."

"Yes, sir," said the corporal, "but it was fresh then."

Ingenious

The admiral was examining the young officer. "Suppose there was a bad wind, what would you do?"

"I'd drop an anchor."

"But suppose it was ten times worse than you expected?"

"I—I'd drop another anchor."

"Suppose it was even ten times worse than that. What would you do?"

The young man tried to think of something bright. At last he said "I'd drop another anchor, sir."

"Man," roared the admiral, "where would you get all the anchors?"

"From the same place, sir, where you would get all the wind."

Come Clean

Whenever one of the higher ranking officers had a birthday, the mess sergeant celebrated by having a cake baked.

However, when it came time to test the cake to see if it was ready to take from the oven, one cook shouted, "One of you guys see if the cake is done. Just stick a knife into it and see if it comes out clean."

No one paid any attention to the private and a little later a cook shouted, "Did the knife come out clean?"

"You bet it did," said the private. "It came out so clean, I stuck all the other dirty knives into it too."

Duty

I am a man under authority, having soldiers under me; and I say unto this man, "Go," and he goeth; and to another, "Come," and he cometh; and to my servant, "Do this," and he doeth it.

The Centurion in St. Matthew

SPECULATE

Is That Right?

Nosey neighbor: "Did the men from the Public Gas Company come to your house today?"
Young child: "Yes, they came to speculate the meter."

SPEECHES

Listener's Choice

A man who was to give a speech appeared with a bandage on his chin. After the speech he explained that while shaving he had concentrated on his speech and cut his chin.

A listener said, "What a pity you didn't concentrate on your chin and cut your speech."

Ah Says, "It's Moider"

"Now, I'm not saying that we Southerners are without fault, much, much fault in our pronunciation—not to speak of our grammar! We slur our words, drawl them out, we cut them short, and substitute vowel sounds 'something awful!' We say, for example—'sump'n,' 'readin,' and 'wawder.' We say 'Aintchergoner, 'whatchergohndoodernight' and 'dontcherreckin.' We say 'poah, 'thaink,' and 'goner.' We say a million things perhaps incorrectly. But, put it altogether, and it sounds more like American than does de lingo what dem guys uses what come from de Noith."

He Wasn't Asked Back

A Commencement speaker was addressing the graduating class of a large Eastern college for women. He began his remarks with the salutation, "Young ladies of '53." Then in a horrified aside he added, "That's an awful age for a girl!"

Impossible

SPEAKER: "Remember, there's nothing in the world that's impossible to accomplish."

LISTENER: "Ever try pushing toothpaste back in the tube?"

He Had Everything

The lecture was over and three persons walked home together discussing it.

"I tell you," said one enthusiastically, "our speaker can dive deeper into the truth than any other lecturer I ever heard."

"Yes," said the second man, "and he can stay down under longer."

"Yes," said the third, "and come up drier!"

Sounds Logical?

Victor Borge says that the reason most after-dinner speakers are men is that "women can't wait that long."

Clearness of Thought

It is related of David Crockett, American frontiersman, that on his arrival in Washington, he heard Daniel Webster, and afterwards meeting him somewhere in the Capitol accosted him: "Is this Mr. Webster?"

"Yes, sir."

"The great Mr. Webster, of Massachusetts?"

"I am Mr. Webster of Massachusetts."

"Well, sir," continued Mr. Crockett, "I had heard that you were a great man, but I don't think so. I heard your speech and understood every word you said."

Observing

Groucho Marx had a drama student on his show, "You Bet Your Life." "What did you study?" Groucho asked.

"Speech projection, diction, proper breathing, and things like that," said the boy.

"What do you think of my diction?" asked Groucho.

"I notice you drop your 'ngs' occasionally," he replied.

Groucho took a quick look around and observed, "I guess I'll have to start wearing suspenders *and* a belt!"

FLEA, FLY, FLEW

> *The fly and the flea*
> *Flew up the flue*
> *Said the fly to the flea*
> *"What shall we do?"*
> *"Let us fly," said the flea;*
> *"Let us flee," said the fly.*
> *So they fluttered and flew*
> *Through a flaw in the flue.*

ENOUGH SAID

Gladstone finished a long speech in which he had attacked the policies of Disraeli. The premier then rose and said, "The man needs no reply. He is inebriated by the exuberance of his own verbosity."

VERY MOVING SPEECH

BILL: "Jones gave a very moving speech last night."

HANK: "I'm surprised."

BILL: "Yes, before he had finished, half the audience had moved out into the hall."

THAT EXPLAINS IT

OSCAR WILDE: "And so you Philistines have invaded the sacred sanctums of art!"

A BYSTANDER: "I suppose that's why we are being assaulted with the jawbone of an ass."

THE HUMORIST

> *He must not laugh at his own wheeze:*
> *A snuff-box has no right to sneeze.*
>
> Keith Preston

Impromptu

It is extremely difficult to give a good impromptu speech. As Menage said in substance many years ago, "I believe for my own part, that no impromptu speech is good except one that has been prepared."

They Agreed

A professor who was to give a lecture on nuclear physics found he had an audience of only two or three persons. He commented at the beginning of his address: "Plato, when delivering lectures in Athens, sometimes had Aristotle for his only hearer; on which occasion he was accustomed to proceed with his lecture as usual, remarking that when he had Aristotle for a hearer, he had the better half of Athens. On the same principle I may congratulate myself on my audience this evening."

Randolph in the United States Senate

John Randolph, United States Senator and brilliant orator (1773-1833), was brilliant in retort.

"Isn't it a shame, Mr. President," said he one day in the Senate, "that the noble bulldogs of the administration should be wasting their precious time in worrying the rats of the opposition?" Immediately the Senate was in an uproar, and he was clamourously called to order. The presiding officer, however, sustained him; and, pointing his long skinny finger at his opponents, Randolph screamed out, "Rats, did I say?—Mice, mice?"

When Speeches are Long

Most speeches to an hour-glass,
Do some resemblance show;
Because the longer time they run,
The shallower they grow.

The Bedrock

Group talk and collective decision make up the bedrock of the American way of life. From the family unit meeting its inevitable day-to-day problems to the federal unit making its essential day-to-day judgments, discussion, debate, and decision exemplify democracy in the process of being, and doing, and succeeding. If this is true, then three things rank high in importance in education for democracy: (1) our students must be taught to appreciate these speech activities at their vital value, (2) they must learn the verbal skills and techniques of these activities, and (3) they must be given ample opportunity to practice these skills and become proficient in their use.

From an address by Arthur Eisenstadt
in charge of Public Speaking
Newark College of Arts and Science, Rutgers University

Applause

I always consider applause at the beginning of a lecture a manifestation of your faith. If it comes in the middle, it is a sign of hope. And if it comes at the end, it is always charity.

From an adress by
The Rt. Rev. Monsignor Fulton J. Sheen

In Conclusion

I was out in Los Angeles to address a convention, and I had one of those prepared speeches. The night before, three or four of the fellows came up to my hotel room, and we indulged in a little game of bridge, and the man who was dummy picked up the speech and looked it over. He suddenly said, "Well, here's the best part of it."

I sort of straightened up and said, "I wonder what that is?"

He turned to the last page, where it started out, "In conclusion."

From an address by Leroy A. Lincoln,
Chairman of the Metropolitan Life Insurance Company

One at a Time

Henry IV of France passed through a small town where the people had assembled to congratulate him on his arrival. Just as the principal magistrate had commenced his tedious oration, an ass began to bray. The king, turning toward the place where the noisy animal was, said gravely, "Gentlemen, one at a time, if you please."

SPEED

But Hurry

"Is it true that an alligator in these swamps won't hurt you if you carry a torch?"

"Dat all depends on how fas' yo'all carry it."

SPELLING

To his son who was attending college, the deacon of a church wrote: "Dear Henry: I suggest that you add penmanship to your other courses; at least, long enough to learn that the small 'e' and 'l' are not the same height. Until your mother deciphered your last letter for me, I was sure that you and the other young man sharing your room both had coeds—not colds."

Some Test

"I had a hard time. First, I got angina pectoris and then arteriosclerosis. Next I got tuberculosis and phthisis. Then they gave me hypodermics. Appendicitis and tonsillectomy gave way to aphasia and hypertrophic cirrhosis. I also had diabetes and indigestion, besides gastritis, rheumatism, lumbago, and neuritis. It was the hardest spelling test I've ever had."

Be Specific

Boss: "How do you spell Mississippi?"
Stenographer: "Which one, the river or the state?"

SPENDTHRIFT

On Foot

She was a spendthrift, and finally her husband could stand it no longer.

"Dotty," he said, "you're driving me to the poorhouse."

"Driving, nothing," she answered. "You'll have to walk. The finance company took the car this morning."

STATESMEN

General Romulo in the United Nations

As one who has been in the United Nations since 1945, you can understand that I am not averse to speaking, which reminds me of the lectern that we have in the General Assembly of the United Nations. It is one of those products of American ingenuity, donated by Mr. Thomas Watson of I.B.M. to the United Nations. It has several gadgets. If you are as short as I am, you push a button to the left and the lectern goes down. If you are as tall as James McCarthy of Notre Dame, you push a button to the right and it goes up. It has two clocks—one that shows the time of the day, and the other which shows how long you have been speaking. American ingenuity did not foresee how long the speeches in the United Nations can be, because that clock should have been a calendar. You may, therefore, open your wallets and get out your calendars because it is a delegate of the United Nations who is addressing you today.

Which reminds me that in the United Nations, as you must have read in the papers, I have had a lot of disagreements with a certain delegate by the name of Vishinsky, and one day he really got mad. I attacked a Greek resolution which the Soviet delegation presented in Paris. I called it cynical; I called it an insult to the intelligence of the General Assembly. And my good friend, Vishinsky, was really mad. So, as soon as I sat down, he asked for the floor. He said, "Mr. President, this small man, Romulo, who spreads noise wherever he goes, represents an insignificant little country like the Philippines. He dares attack Russia! He reminds me of that Russian proverb, 'His ambition is worth a ruble, but his ammunition is only worth a cent.'" And he kept on abusing me.

Well, of course, as soon as he sat down, I asked for the floor, and I said, "Mr. President, I have just been abused personally, which is no surprise to any of the delegates here because that is how the Soviet delegation has been acting since 1945. The distinguished delegate of the Soviet Union, its Foreign Minister, said that I am a small man and that I spread noise wherever I go. I would like to remind him that we are the little Davids here who must fling our pebbles of truth between the eyes of the blustering Goliaths and make them behave, and," I said, "as to my representing an insignificant little country, may I remind Mr. Vishinsky that here, in the United Nations, I like to believe while we occupy a humble place, it is a place of honor. And, as to my ambition being worth a ruble, when my ammunition is only worth a cent, may I also remind him that with the present rate of exchange the cent is worth more than the ruble."

Which also reminds me of a very heated debate that I had with the Foreign Minister of the Ukraine, Mr. Manuilsky. He went to the platform one day and began to abuse me and he said, "What is the matter with the delegate from the Philippines is that he looks at all these international questions with the spectacles bought from these American optometrists."

So, as soon as he said that, I asked for the floor. And I pulled out my glasses and said, "The distinguished Foreign Minister of the Ukraine has just said that I bought my glasses from an American optometrist. It isn't so; I bought them from a Russian optometrist by the name of Burdisky, and that is why when I put on my glasses my vision is many times blurred."

From an address by General Carlos P. Romulo
Ambassador of the Philippines to the United States
before the Chicago World Trade Conference

STATISTICS

SAFE RISK

"You wrote a policy on a ninety-two year-old man!" gasped the insurance branch manager.

"Sure," replied the new and elated salesman. "Our statistics show that few men die after ninety-two."

STEALING

TEACHER, SUCH LANGUAGE!

TEACHER (trying hard to unfasten coat for a little pupil): "Did your mother hook this coat for you?"

LITTLE PUPIL: "No, ma'am. She bought it."

STENOGRAPHER

Now Everything is Clear

SUE: "When I applid for a job the manager had the nerve to ask if my punctuation was good."

SALLY: "What did you tell him?"

SUE: "I said, I'd never been late for work in my life."

STRENGTH

He Should Know

EDGAR BERGEN: "I'm a little surprised that you are looking for a book on health. You look quite strong."

MORTIMER SNERD: "My doctor says I'm as strong as a horse. And he oughta know—he's a horse doctor."

STUBBORN

Unpopular

Ezra was inspecting an obstreperous young mule that was proving more troublesome than useful. Turning to his grandchildren, who had joined him to watch the animal, he said, "Chillun, dat jackass should be a warnin' to you 'gainst de habit ob kickin'."

"What you mean, Grandpappy?" rejoined the oldest of the group.

"Why," explained Ezra, "de better he does it de more unpopular he gits to be."

He Walks Backwards

In West Virginia a mountaineer was having difficulties in persuading his mule to proceed.

"What's the matter with your mule?" inquired a passerby. "Is he stubborn?"

"Stubborn!" said the mountaineer. "Mister, that critter is so stubborn that when his hind legs are pushing his front ones are walking backwards."

STUPID

A SLIGHT DIFFERENCE

SUE: "I thought I heard him say that I had a thick head of hair."
MAE: "He didn't mention your hair."

GUESS WHO?

One day Bill came away from a sale with a live parrot. "Now, I wonder why I bought this stupid bird?" he muttered.

"Stupid?" said the parrot. "Who's stupid? Who do you think was bidding against you?"

SUCCESS

PERSISTENCE

You can't win all the time in any line of endeavor. The best baseball team in the world loses from 50 to 60 games a season. Frank Woolworth worked hard to save his first $50, and then saw 3 of his first 5 chain stores absolutely fail. Cyrus H. K. Curtis lost over $800,000 on the *Saturday Evening Post* before he could make it pay a single dollar of profit. DuPont worked 11 years and spent $27 million before the first pound of Nylon was sold. Frank Munsey's remarkably successful career, after repeated failures, might be tersely described as: "40 failures, 40 successes, 40 millions." Abraham Lincoln suffered one failure after another—was badly defeated in 5 different elections—and finally became our country's greatest man.

R. Perry Shorts, President, Second National
Bank & Trust Company, Saginaw, Michigan

MAKING HAY

"Jones seems to be a successful man. I suppose he made hay while the sun shone."

"Not only that, but he made it from the grass that other people let grow under their feet."

296

Three Kinds

There are three kinds of employers: those who *make* things happen, those who *watch* things happen, and those who *do not know* things are happening.

Hard Job

I am the captain of my soul;
I rule it with stern joy;
And yet I think I had more fun,
When I was cabin boy.

Keith Preston

One of the Atlas Boys

"Whither so hurried, my good little man?
"Can life be so terribly fleeting?"
"I'm rushing along as fast as I can
"To a chamber of commerce meeting!"

William A. Philpott, **Jr.**

Cut the Criticism

I hate those guys
Who criticize
And minimize
Vigorous guys
Whose enterprise
*Has helped them **rise***
Above the guys
Who criticize.

Anonymous

SUGGESTION

Adding a Little Weight

Bill, who had just agreed to take Sam to dinner and was afraid the bill would be large, said, just as they were about to give their order to the waiter, "Putting on a little weight aren't you, Sam?"

POLITENESS

Little Billie was given a piece of bread and butter, and politely said, "Thank you."

"That's right, Billie," said the lady. "I like to hear little boys say 'thank you.'"

"Well," replied Billie, "if you want to hear me say it again, you might put some jelly on it."

SUNDAY-SCHOOL

TO THE FOOT OF THE CLASS

An instructor in sunday-school that paid considerable attention to Bible history, dwelt on the phrase, "And Enoch was not, for God took him." This was repeated many times in connection with the death of Enoch. He thought even the dullest pupil would answer correctly when asked: "State in the language of the Bible what is said of Enoch's death."

This was the answer he got: "Enoch was not what God took him for."

MAYBE SHE ISN'T ALONE

The children had been told they must not appear at Sunday-school the following week without their application blanks properly filled out with names of parents, addresses, date and place of birth. On Sunday morning Susie arrived, the tears streaming down her cheeks.

"What is the trouble?" the teacher inquired, seeking to comfort her.

"Oh," sobbed the little girl, "I forgot my excuse for being born."

TACT

WHAT'S IN A NAME

"I've decided on a name for the baby," said the expectant mother. "I shall call her Minerva."

The young husband didn't care very much for her selection but, being a tactful fellow, he was too wise to object verbally.

"Fine," he agreed. "That's a beautiful name. The first girl I ever loved was called Minerva, and the name revives happy memories."

There was a brief pause, then: "We'll call her Lucy," said the wife.
"I think I like that better."

DISCRETION

An employer wanted a tactful but honest man. To each of three
applicants he put this question: "Do you think I'm right in believing
two and two make five?"

The first man said: "I think you're wrong."

The second man said: "I'm sure you have a good reason for thinking
so, sir."

The third man got the job.

He said: "Did you say you believe two and two make six?"

"No," the employer answered. "I said five."

"Oh," said the third man, "that's more like it!"

TO THE HEAD OF THE CLASS

A boy had returned from a birthday party. His mother, fearful re-
garding his manners, asked, "Are you sure you didn't ask Mrs. Jones
for a second piece of cake?"

"Oh, no, mother. I only asked her for the recipe so you could make a
cake like it, and she gave me two more pieces!"

WINNING FRIENDS

The confidential confession of Jean Racine, the great French
dramatist, to his son is remarkable. "Do not think that I am sought
after by the great for my dramas; Corneille composes nobler verses
than mine, but no one notices him. I never allude to my works when
with men of the world, but I amuse them about matters they like to
hear. My talent with them consists not in making them feel that I
have any, but in showing them that they have."

DIPLOMAT

A group of men were conversing when one asked another to comply
with a certain request and received the reply, "Emphatically, No!"
Another one of the group said, "You should reply like a diplomat.
When a diplomat says No, he means Maybe. If he says Maybe, he
means Yes; if he says Yes, he is no diplomat. Or in case a lady is asked

for a kiss, if she says No, she means Maybe; if she says Maybe, she means Yes; if she says Yes, she is no lady. Or take the prospect asked to take a life insurance policy. If he says No, he means Maybe; if he says Maybe, he means Yes; if he says Yes, he has a heart murmur!"

TASTE

TIMES CHANGE

Our tastes change as we mature. Little girls like painted dolls; little boys like soldiers. When they grow up, girls like the soldiers and the boys go for the painted dolls.

TAXES

THEY PICK US CLEAN

Joey Adams, the TV-radio comedian, honeymooning in Paris, wasn't too impressed with his first glimpse of the Eiffel Tower. He called it, "The Empire State Building—after taxes!"

MEETING THE EMPLOYER

A mild little man walked into an income tax inspector's office, sat down and beamed on everyone.

"What can we do for you?" asked the inspector.

"Nothing, thank you," replied the little man. "I just wanted to meet the people I'm working for."

OVERSIGHT

"And now, gentlemen," continued the congressman, "I wish to tax your memory."

"Good heavens," muttered a colleague, "why haven't we thought of that before?"

TOO SMALL TO BE PRACTICAL

VOTER: "Senator, has the government ever thought of leveling off the Appalachian Mountains?"

SENATOR: "Yes, we think it's a good idea except it doesn't cost enough to be practical."

A wrestling match had been held in Turkey, and it was followed by a banquet. In this particular instance the winner was an enormous Turk. They came to the fish course of the dinner. I might say they raise enormous lemons in Turkey. This big Turk took a lemon to squeeze over his fish. He cut a little gash in it with his knife, squeezed the lemon up and down over his fish, and the juice all flowed out. Then he turned it inside out with one hand and squeezed it again until there was nothing left but the pulp, which he threw over his shoulder.

Sitting next to him was a little wizened-up guy who must have weighed a hundred and ten pounds, with a squeaky voice. Up to this time the big Turk had paid no attention to him. Well, the little guy didn't bother to cut the lemon at all. He gave it one mighty squeeze and the juice flowed out of the lemon and there was nothing left but the pulp, which he threw over his shoulder.

The big Turk amazed at the accomplishment, turned to the little, wizened-up guy and said, "Say, I haven't noticed you before. Are you a wrestler or prize-fighter?"

The little guy said, "No, I'm a tax collector."

From an address by Eric Johnston

TAXICAB

We've Thought So

A patron wearing a hearing aid entered a cab and the driver remarked, "Those things any good?"

The patron replied, "I would be lost without it."

"Must be tough to be hard of hearing," sympathized the cabbie. "Oh, well," added the cabbie, "nearly all of us have something the matter one way or another. Take me, for instance. I can hardly see!"

TEACHER

The Goal

One hundred and thirteen years ago a young lawyer of Boston gave up his practice to become secretary of the first state board of education. His name was Horace Mann. He said: "When giving up the law to enter education, henceforth, the next generation will be my client." That is the prospective of the Christian college. That is the goal of the Christian teacher. All that we want to accomplish will not be finished today or tomorrow, or in the next decade. But if our foundation is right, we can stand on that platform without fear and proclaim eternal truths that will outlast time.

From an address by Dr. S. T. Ludwig
Executive Secretary, Department of Education
Church of the Nazarene, Kansas City

TEACHING

SMART LAD

TEACHER: "Correct this sentence: 'Girls is naturally better-looking than boys.'"

PUPIL: "Girls is artifically better-looking than boys."

PROFESSOR

POLICE SERGEANT: "So you say you're a professor, eh?"

PRISONER: "Yes, sir."

PATROLMAN: "That ain't so, Sarg! I searched his pockets and found money in them."

A POLITICIAN?

TEACHER: "What do we call a person who keeps on talking when people are no longer interested?"

PUPIL: "A teacher."

AND THE SAME TO YOU

"Dear teacher," wrote little Johnny's mother, "kindly excuse John's absence from school yesterday afternoon, as he fell in the mud. By doing the same you will greatly oblige his mother."

TEARS

WOMAN'S WEAPON

> *Trust not a woman when she cries,*
> *For she'll pump water from her eyes*
> *With a wet finger, and in faster showers*
> *Then April when he rains down flowers.*
>
> Thomas Dekker, 1604

TELEPHONE

HE'S LISTENING

MAN OUTSIDE TELEPHONE BOOTH: "Excuse me, but I'm in a hurry! You've had that telephone twenty minutes and not said a word!"

MAN INSIDE BOOTH: "Sir, I'm talking to my wife."

IS THAT CLEAR?

MAN: (at telephone): "Zilch! Zilch! Z! Z! No, not C! ABCDEF-GHIJKLMNOPQRSTUVWXYZ!"

WRONG NUMBER

Groucho Marx had a telephone operator as a guest on his radio program.

"Are you married?" Groucho asked.

"No," was the reply.

"That's terrible," said Groucho. "A telephone girl without a ring. I'll put in a plug for you. Why aren't you married?"

"I'm not in a hurry."

"Yes," said Groucho, "she's a telephone operator all right."

PERFECTLY CLEAR

LORD TEMPLETON: "I really think our English way at the telephone is better than saying 'Hello' as you do in the United States."

YANKEE: "What do you say in England?"

LORD TEMPLETON: "We say, 'Are you there?' Then, of course, if you are not there, there is no use in going on with the conversation."

303

TELEVISION

A Long, Long Time

TEACHER: "If a man saves two dollars a week, how long will it take him to save five hundred dollars?"

BOY: "He never would. After he got two hundred and fifty dollars he'd buy a television set."

TEMPER

We've Met Him

In the course of a hot-tempered telephone conversation with a high-powered executive, a junior executive remarked, "Take it easy, will you? If you're not careful you will get ulcers."

To which the producer snarled back, "I don't get ulcers. I give them."

THEATRE

Scalped

"Father, why are the men in the best seats bald-headed?"
"They bought their tickets from scalpers, my child."

Sometimes

DRAMATICS TEACHER: "What is a plagiarist?"
STUDENT: "A plagiarist is a person who writes plays."

Some Pan Out

An editor met the late Sir James Barrie, the famous author of *Peter Pan,* at a dinner.

"Sir James," he said, "I suppose some of your plays do better than others. They are not all successes, I imagine."

Barrie said confidentially, his eyes twinkling, "No, some Peter out and some Pan out."

304

Hard to Do

A very dull play had to close after one week of performances. A critic said, "The only reason it wasn't hissed is that the audience couldn't hiss and yawn at the same time."

Silence

"Have you noticed the absence of comment upon my last play?" asked the author. "I am the victim of a conspiracy of silence. What would you do about it?"

"I'd join it if I were you!" his friend replied.

Happy Ending

"Did that new play have a happy ending?"

"Sure, everybody was glad it was over."

He Should Be Haunted

"Shakespeare haunts him night and day," someone said of a not-too-successful Shakespearean actor.

"It's no wonder," said a theater-goer, "for he has most cruelly murdered Shakespeare in every character of his he ever played."

THINKING

"To Think Is to Live" (Cicero)

> *Yond Cassius has a lean and hungry look;*
> *He thinks too much: such men are dangerous.*
> Shakespeare, 1599

THRIFT

He Knew

LITTLE WOMAN: "They have no car, no television set, no piano. I can't imagine what they do have!"

HUSBAND: "A bank account, perhaps?"

Name One

WIFE TO HUSBAND: "All right, I admit I like to spend money. But just name one other extravagance."

$12,000 Worth of Tools

Let us see what thrift has done for us. Five million thrifty citizens saved an average of $10,000 each, making a pool of about $50 billion. This great sum finances the 100 largest manufacturing corporations in the United States. These concerns employ about 4 million workers at an average wage of $3,500 each or a total of nearly $14 billion a year. The 5 million savers who created the 4 million jobs received in dividends about one-sixth the amount paid to the workers.

It is hard to save. We all want to spend all we earn and it is difficult to keep some of it back for the purchase of tools and better equipment in order to increase future production. Nevertheless $12,000 had to be saved in order to create each one of those 4 million good jobs.

Some day you may see advertisements in the paper reading as follows:

"Workers wanted; salary $3,500. If applicant brings $12,000 worth of tools, he will receive an extra $600 or a total of $4,100 per year."

Surely no one would object to paying the worker who brought to his job $12,000 worth of equipment or capital, an extra $600. That would be little enough reward for all the patience, industry, and self-denial necessary to save $12,000. If less reward were offered, would anyone save?

From an address by Howard E. Kershner,
President of Christian Freedom Foundation, Inc.

TIME

TAKE TIME!

Take time to work—
  It is the price of success.
Take time to think—
  It is the source of power.
Take time to play—
  It is the secret of perpetual youth.

306

Take time to read—
　It is the fountain of wisdom.
Take time to be friendly—
　It is the road to happiness.
Take time to laugh—
　It is the music of the soul.
Take time to dream—
　It is the road to greater vision.
Take time to give—
　The day is too short to be selfish.
Take time to love and be loved—
　It is the privilege of the gods.

The Employment Counselor

Why Hurry

The engineer was seeking local support for a highway in Latin America, and attempted to explain it to the natives. He asked a native: "How long does it take you to carry your goods to market on a donkey?"

"Three days," was the reply.

"That's the point," said the engineer. "With our road you could take your goods to market and be back home in one day."

"Good, señor," answered the native. "But what would we do with the other two days?"

Ere Long

The following quaint epitaph is copied from a churchyard in Finsbury, near Chatham, England:

> *Time was I stood as thou dost now,*
> *And viewed the dead as thou dost me:*
> *Ere long thou'lt lie as low as I,*
> *And others stand to look on thee.*

Daylight Saving Time?

> *In winter I get up at night*
> *And dress by yellow candle-light*
> *In summer, quite the other way,*
> *I have to go to bed by day.*

From Bed in Summer by R. L. Stevenson, 1855

TIPS

SURPRISE

NEW GUEST: "I can't understand why they call this hotel 'The Palms.' I've never seen a palm near the place."

OLD-TIMER: "You'll see them before you go. It's a pleasant little surprise the staff reserves for guests on the last day of their stay here."

WE'VE HAD IT HAPPEN

The bill for his lunch in the dining car was $1.45 and the diner pulled out two one-dollar bills. The waiter brought in change, a fifty-cent piece, and a nickel. The guest looked up at the waiter. With a grunt of annoyance the guest pocketed the half dollar and, to his astonishment, the waiter grinned widely.

"That's all right, sir," he chuckled. "I just gambled and lost. Just gambled and lost!"

TOASTMASTER

RIGHT

Two little boys had just returned from a dinner and were rehearsing what they had seen and heard.

"You can be the mastoid of ceremonies," said the smaller.

"But a mastoid is a pain in the ear."

"That's right."

THE STARTER

The toastmaster, in a prelude to his introductions, said, "I am what is known as a toastmaster—the punk that sets off the fireworks."

HOW'S THAT?

As I listened to the introduction I thought how much better off I was than the speaker introduced by the chairman at a club meeting who said, "Our audience today is made up of two

308

groups——those who have heard the speaker before, and those who have not heard him. Those in the second group look forward with considerable pleasure, I am sure, to hearing what he has to say."

From an address by Edwin O. Griffenhagen, Senior Partner
Griffenhagen & Associates, Chicago

WE ARE PLEASED TO HAVE WITH US

Pray let me tell you here and now—
Although I've seen a purple cow—
A sadder sight and more absurd
Is he who stands and takes a bow,
Resumes his seat without a word!
No thing in nature, you'll allow,
No scene you've seen, no sound you've heard,
No act is quite so minus wow
As his who stands and takes a bow!

William A. Philpott, **Jr.**

TOASTS

TRUE OF MOST OF US

Drink not to my past, which is weak and indefensible;
Nor to my present, which is not above reproach;
But, let us drink to our futures, which, thank God, are immaculate.

Leone P. Forkner

TOBACCO

MALES IN MEDITATION—PEW!

Some master minds in self-delusion
Believe to smoke a pipe
Helps them to think!
Not me—I've come to this conclusion:
To suck a pipe is tripe—
I only stink!

William A. Philpott, **Jr.**

309

TOURIST

ALL TIED UP

A couple, on a visit to the city, were reading the notice of the meal hours in the hotel:

Breakfast 7 to 10
Luncheon 11 to 3
Dinner 5 to 9

Ruby turned to her husband and said, "John, I don't see how in the world we are going to get time to see the city."

TOYS

WANTED TO BE SHOWN

A boy with a penny tightly clutched in his hand entered the toy shop and drove the proprietor to distraction asking to see everything without ever making up his mind.

"Look here," the proprietor said finally, "what do you want for a penny—the whole world with a fence around it?"

The boy replied without hesitation, "Let's see it."

TRADITION

OLD IDEAS

> It is an instinct with me personally to attack every idea which has been full grown for ten years, especially if it claims to be the foundation of all human society. I am prepared to back human society against any idea, positive or negative, that can be brought into the field against it.
>
> George Bernard Shaw

TRAFFIC

ANYWAY, A TICKET

"Well, Miss," said the traffic cop to the perfectly sweet motorist. "I suppose you know why I stopped you?"

"Don't tell me," she replied. "Let me guess. Yes, I know! You want to sell me a ticket to the Policemen's Ball."

TRANSPORTATION

THE PAST—THE PRESENT!

Let me tell you of an interesting visit I had with a banker from Pennsylvania. He has lived to that ripe age which so often carries absorbingly interesting personal episodes in our changing economy. In 1904 he purchased an automobile in Hartford, Connecticut, the city in which the model was manufactured. He drove the car back to his home in Pennsylvania. It took thirty-nine days to make that return trip, and en route he had to hire horses or mules on twenty-two occasions. Today, that same distance can be made with an automobile in five hours. Think what the phenomenal growth and success of our country, in the past fifty years, owe to this revolution in transportation—and transportation is a keystone in any nation's economy and success.

H. F. Quinn, Assistant Chief
National Bank Examiner, Washington, D.C.

THE TIME WILL COME

The time will come when people will travel in stages moved by steam engines, from one city to another, almost as fast as birds fly, fifteen or twenty miles an hour.

Oliver Evans, 1813

TRAVEL

TRAVEL YEARS AGO

Years ago it took six days to go from New York to Boston. The stage coach started at three in the morning and drove until ten every night. Now one goes by airplane in approximately one hour. In the early days it took two days to travel from New York to Philadelphia. In 1769 Benjamin Franklin was asked by the Continental Congress to go to London with a message from the colonists to the King. At daylight, one stormy March morning, Franklin stepped into the stage coach that stopped before his house on Chestnut Street, in Philadelphia. It took two days for that fast mail to reach New York. The stage coach driver had the lines around his shoulders, and he knit mittens while he drove.

The agent for the ship suggested that Franklin have a carpenter nail up a partition for a private cabin. He also told Franklin to buy flour, ham, and bacon, and have them put on board. Franklin found a sailor who agreed to cook his food. The Captain said he had given word that the boat would sail by Saturday, but if Franklin got there by Monday, he would be on time. Franklin started in April and arrived in London, July 27.

The passengers went at once to church; bells were rung to celebrate the arrival; and the passengers fell to their knees in prayers of thanks to God.

TRIBUTE

Some Men Shine

Some men shine at speakin'
Others write or sing,
Chap I'm thinkin' of
Couldn't do a thing.

Ain't no public speaker,
Couldn't sing a note,
Never saw in print
Anything he wrote.

Quiet sort o' feller—
Friendly and sincere,
Gives a hearty handclasp
Radiates good cheer.

Always lookin' after
Them that's feelin' blue,
Sick, or hurt, or troubled—
Glad to do it, too.

Docs and sawbones, likely,
Play a useful part,
But sympathy and sunshine
Right from out the heart

Beat the best prescriptions
Known to medic lore—
Nuthin' half so helpful
When you're sick and sore.

Here's a cheer for Jones,
Who with his Committee—
Spreads a lot of sunshine
Throughout our boomin' city.

By C.P.J. in the Chicago Rotarian as a tribute to
Byron O. Jones for his work among the sick and troubled

WE ALL HAVE OUR TROUBLES

So, naturalists observe, a flea
Hath smaller fleas that on him prey;
And these have smaller still to bite 'em,
And so proceed ad infinitum.

Jonathan Swift, 1712

TRUTH

FIRST MOTHER: "Are you bothered much by your children telling fibs?"

SECOND MOTHER: "Not so much as by their telling the truth at very inappropriate times."

GUILTY

"Brothers," said the preacher, "the subject of mah sermon today is liars. How many in dis congregation have read the sixty-ninth chapter of Matthew?"

Nearly every hand went up.

"You is just de people ah wants to preach to," the reverend said. "Dere is no such chapter."

LAWYER

"Judge, I don't know what to do."

"Why, how's that?"

"Well, I swore to tell the truth, but every time I try, some lawyer objects."

313

Ain't Nothing So

There is no lead in a lead pencil.
(It is graphite, a form of carbon.)
The coffee berry is not a berry.
(It is a seed.)
There is no rice in rice paper.
(It is made from patch or wood pulp.)
There is no tea in beef tea.
(It is an extract of beef.)
There is no soda in soda water.
(It is water charged with carbonic acid gas.)
The whale is not a fish.
(It is a mammal.)

Is It True That He Lies?

There was a famous problem among the Stoics, which ran thus: "When a man says, 'I lie,' does he lie, or does he not? If he lies, he speaks the truth; if he speaks the truth, he lies." Many profound works were written on this problem.

True or False

Protagoras, the fifth century B.C. Greek philosopher, maintained that all is illusion, and that there is no such thing as truth. But Aristotle refuted him by the following dilemma: "Your proposition is true or false; if it is false, then you are answered; if true, then there is something true, and your proposition fails."

UNITED STATES

America's Greatness

Why is America great? It is not our population, as we have only six per cent of the population of the world. It is not our area, which is only a tiny speck on the world's surface. It is not our natural resources, which are being rapidly depleted by the obligations we have undertaken. It is our individual freedom, and the free enterprise system is the vital spark that stimulates every American to gain such reward as his own industry and capacity make him worthy of.

Harry F. Byrd, United States Senator from Virginia

UNIVERSITY

IT AIN'T EASY

The use of a university is to make young gentlemen as unlike their fathers as possible.

Woodrow Wilson, 1914

VANITY

VICES

Sheridan once said, "They talk of avarice, lust, ambition, as great passions. It is a mistake; they are little passions. Vanity is the great commanding passion of all. This excites the most heroic deeds, and impels to the most dreadful crimes. Save me from this passion, and I can defy the others. They are mere urchins, but this is a giant."

WELL READ

Robert Burns was one day in a very fine private library of books, which the proprietor seemed to value more for their bindings than for their internal value. Burns, after some few hours' conversation with the owner, wrote the following verse and left it on the library table:

Free through these books, ye maggots, seek your winding,
But, for the owner's sake, O, spare the binding.

VERSATILITY

ACCOMPLISHMENT

Consider the versatility of William Gladstone (1809-1898), British prime minister, who could speak to an audience at Corfu in Greek, at Florence in Italian, with Bismarck in German, with the French leaders in French, and to his own people in English.

315

VERSE

A punster one day observed that anything might be turned into rhyme, or doggerel; where at a friend, pointing to a board in the street, on which were painted the words, "This house to be sold," exclaimed, "Come, then, turn that into rhyme!" upon which the other redeemed his pledge by writing with chalk on the board:

This house to be
S O L D

VICE PRESIDENT

The late Vice President, Charles G. Dawes, once said that the Vice President of the United States had only two duties: (1) to listen to the speeches of Senators, and (2) to look at the newspaper each day to see whether the President was in good health.

VIOLIN

THE CAT AND THE HORSE

> *A squeak's heard in the orchestra,*
> *The leader draws across*
> *The intestines of the agile cat*
> *The tail of the noble hoss.*
>
> G. T. Lanigan, 1875

VIRTUE

AND TOWELS

If he does really think that there is no distinction between virtue and vice, why, sir, when he leaves our houses let us count our spoons.

Samuel Johnson, 1763

The practical thing we can do if we really want to make the world over again is to try out the word "Old" for a while. There are some Old things that made this country.

There is the Old Virtue of religious faith.

There are the Old Virtues of integrity and the whole truth.

There is the Old Virtue of incorruptible service and honor in public office.

There are the Old Virtues of economy in government, of self-reliance, thrift, and individual liberty.

There are the Old Virtues of patriotism, real love of country and willingness to sacrifice for it.

These Old ideas are very inexpensive. They even would help win hot and cold wars.

I realize that such suggestions will raise the cuss word "Reactionary." But some of these Old things are slipping badly in American life. And if they slip too far, the lights will go out of America, even if we win these cold and hot wars.

Think about it.

From an address by Herbert Hoover
former President of the United States

VISION

FORESIGHT

Perhaps you have heard the story of Christopher Wren, one of the greatest of English architects, who walked one day unrecognized among the men who were at work upon the building of St. Paul's cathedral in London which he had designed. "What are you doing?" he inquired of one of the workmen, and the man replied, "I am cutting a piece of stone." As he went on he put the same question to another man, and the man replied, "I am earning five shillings twopence a day." and to a third man he addressed the same inquiry and the man answered, "I am helping Sir Christopher Wren build a beautiful cathedral." That man had vision. He could see beyond the cutting of the stone, beyond the earning of his daily wage, to the creation of a work of art—the building of a great cathedral. And in your life it is important for you to strive to attain a vision of the larger whole.

From an address by Mrs. James Bush-Brown
Director, Pennsylvania School of Horticulture for Women

317

WAGES

EXPERIENCE

An employer, interviewing an applicant, remarked, "You ask high wages for a man with no experience."

"Well," the prospect replied, "it's so much harder work when you don't know anything about it."

$1.65 PER HOUR

"And just what are you making?" the visitor asked as he toured the factory.

The worker looked at him a moment, shifted his tobacco quid, and said, "Dollar sixty-five an hour!"

WAR

SOMETHING ENDED

Permit me to take you back, briefly, to the summer of 1914. It was a beautiful summer. A great calm, undisturbed by any news, lay over most of the world. Everybody in Europe was on vacation. The house parties in England were never nicer. On the continent the spas were filled with the rich and fashionable. An old aristocracy blended with a new plutocracy in a fine harmony of fun and relaxation. Millions of the middle class swarmed through the art galleries and up the green valleys of Switzerland. They feared no evil. And then, as history says, a shot was fired at Sarajevo. War. It was incredible. It was a bad dream. It was a sudden insanity which would pass. But it didn't. In that beautiful summer of 1914, something ended forever—something very great and wonderful. That something has various names. You might call it the Nineteenth Century. Or you might call it the Age of Enlightened Evolution. Or you might just call it Europe, or perhaps more exactly, the European System. Anyway, it ended forever.

From an address by Henry Luce, Founder and Publisher of Time, Life, and Fortune magazines

The Cost of War

War is never bashful in its demands. It does not ask, "What will you give?" It dares to state, "You can keep only what I do not need."

Let us realize that, according to the *Congressional Record,* the last war cost us 400 billion dollars. Dr. Nicolas Murray butler says that would "have provided a $2,500 house, with $1,000 worth of furniture, and five acres of land for every family in the United States, Canada, Australia, England, Wales, Ireland, Scotland, France, Belgium, Germany, and Russia; besides a five million dollar library and a ten million dollar university to every city of 20,000 or more in the countries named; and there would still be a large sum of money left over." It costs $55,000 to kill a man. How much does the average Christian give to help win the world for Christ?

Dr. R. R. Belter, President, The Wartburg Synod
United Lutheran Church in America

The Cost of War

The 1,550 U.S. merchant ships sent to the bottom during World War II were capable of carrying in a single trip enough wheat to feed the people of Greece for eight years. Our own armed forces alone used up enough cotton and wool to make 650 million dresses and 160 million suits of clothes—enough to clothe all the people in Greece for 20 years. Enough steel was used up by the U.S. alone to make 230 million automobiles—one for every man, woman, and child in North and South America. The money spent on tanks alone by the U.S. Army would have paid for 20 million electric refrigerators, 85 million bathtubs, or 140 skyscrapers the size of the Empire State Building in New York. The wire used by our armed forces in communications and electronic equipment would have stretched around the world 200 times.

Henry Ford II

WATER

"No More Ice Waiter"

Full many a man, both young and old,
Is brought to his sarcophagus
By pouring water, icy cold,
Adown his warm esophagus.

Anonymous

319

WEALTH

He Knew

A porter was asked why rich men usually give smaller tips than poor men.

"Well, sir," he answered, "the rich man don't want nobody to know he's rich, and the poor man don't want nobody to know he's poor."

Long Story

A young man called one evening on a rich old farmer to learn the farmer's story of how he became rich.

"It's a long story," said the old man, "and while I'm telling it, we might as well save the candle." And he blew it out.

"You needn't go on," said the youth. "I understand."

Sorry, Sir

A rich oil tycoon was in one of New York's big hotels. The indifference of the staff to his wealth irritated him. He decided to do something about it.

At breakfast the next morning he said to the waiter, "Bring me five dollars' worth of bacon and eggs."

The waiter shook his head. "Sorry, sir," he replied, "but we don't serve half portions in this hotel."

Couldn't Speak

Sandy, whose cottage was situated in a hidden valley near the sea, had stumbled upon a large smuggling operation. The leader of the smugglers was inclined to deal with the Scot in a persuasive fashion— with a little hush money.

"My friend," said the head of the smugglers, "if I put a hundred-dollar bill over each of your eyes, you couldn't see, now, could you?"

"Nae," replied Sandy, "and if ye'll put a thousand-dollar bill over my mouth, I couldna speak, either!"

The deed was done.

AFTER TAXES

TEACHER: "How many make a dozen?"
SAM: "Twelve."
TEACHER: "How many make a million?"
SAM: "Very few."

WHAT EVERY HUSBAND KNOWS

Women control the purse strings in this country.

They own: 70 per cent of private wealth; 55 per cent of savings accounts; 50 per cent of stocks in industrial corporations; and 44 per cent of public utilities. They inherit: 68 per cent of all estates. They buy: 80 per cent of all consumer goods.

In at least one field, however—grocery shopping—the trend seems to be reversing. If it's any consolation to the men, they are now purchasing at least 25 per cent of the groceries bought every week. This figure was revealed in a nation-wide survey of newspaper food editors made by J. H. Sawyer, Chicago newspaper representative.

Four major reasons are cited for this switch from female to male food shopping: (1) the shorter work week; (2) the growth of supermarkets; (3) the increase in evening shopping; and (4) the continuing shortage of domestic help.

According to the survey, women grocery shoppers outnumber the men by a wide margin early in the week. On weekends, though, when 70 per cent of food shopping is done, men equal women shoppers in many cases.

Advertising Newsletter (U.S. Chamber of Commerce)
November 1951

RABELAIS AND HIS WILL

The celebrated Rabelais, French satirist, is said to have made the following will: "I owe much. I possess nothing. I give the rest to the poor."

WEATHER

HE FOUND THE TROUBLE

The weather forecaster hadn't been right in three months, so his resignation caused no surprise. But his alibi for resigning did.

"I can't stand this town any longer," he wrote. "The climate doesn't agree with me."

321

WE AGREE

TEACHER: "What do we mean by climate?"
STUDENT: "Climate is what we have all the time, and weather is what we have only a few days."

SMOG

An American returned from his trip abroad.
"How was the weather in London?" a friend asked.
"Dunno. So foggy I couldn't tell."

UNUSUAL

There was a young man of Quebec
Who was frozen in snow to his neck.
When asked, "Are you friz?"
He replied, "Yes, I is,
But we don't call this cold in Quebec."
Rudyard Kipling

WEDDING

FATHER OF THE BRIDE

Usher, passing collection plate at church wedding: "Yes, ma'am, it *is* unusual, but the father of the bride requested it."

WHOLESALE

A GREAT MAGICIAN

"I have a great act, Sam. Out of the air I pick two hundred lighted cigars. I puff on them. Then I swallow them."
"You mean you swallow two hundred lighted cigars? How can you do it?"
"It's easy," said Sam. "I buy 'em wholesale."

WIFE

THEY OFTEN ARE

BILL: "He concedes that he's a self-made man."
SAM: "Maybe, but his wife's the power behind the drone."

322

WOMEN

THE VOICE OF EXPERIENCE

A school advertised: "Short Course in Accounting for Women."
Next day the director of the school received a note which read:
"Gentlemen: There is NO accounting for women."

DEFINITIONS

One woman talking . . . a monologue.
Two women talking . . . a cat-a-logue.

POINT OF VIEW

The luggage-laden husband stared miserably down the platform at
the departing train. "If you hadn't taken so long getting ready," he
sadly admonished his wife, "we should have caught it!"

"Yes," she replied, "and if you hadn't hurried me so, we shouldn't
have so long to wait for the next one!"

TOOK TIME

"Where have you been for the last two hours?" demanded the
minister's wife.

"I met Mrs. Jones on the street and asked her how she was feeling,"
sighed the weary pastor.

SLOW PLEASE

Two women were preparing to board the air liner. One of them
turned to the pilot and said, "Now, please don't travel faster than sound.
We want to talk."

TACT

HOUSEWIFE: "Why should a big, strong man like you be out
begging?"

HOBO: "Lady, it's the only profession I know in which a gentleman
can address a beautiful woman like you without an introduction."

He Had Experience

"How do you manage when the phone rings while you are in the bathtub?" asked Mr. Dough.

"It's simple," replied Mr. Know. "I put off taking a bath until my wife calls one of her friends. Then, of course, I have plenty of time to finish without being interrupted."

Only Two?

> Two things make woman slow, we find,
> In going any place;
> For first she must make up her mind
> And then her face.
>
> Keith Preston

Smile When You Say That

> When man and woman die, as poets sung,
> His heart's the last part moves—her last, the tongue.
>
> Benjamin Franklin

Man's Equal

If God had designed woman as man's master, He would have taken her from his head; if as his slave, He would have taken her from his feet; but as He designed her for his companion and equal, He took her from his side."

St. Augustine, *De Civitate Dei*

They Call Her Blessed

Who can find a virtuous woman? for her price is far above rubies. . . . Her husband is known in the gates, and he sitteth among the elders of the land. . . . Strength and honor are her clothing, and she shall rejoice in time to come. She openeth her mouth with wisdom, and in her tongue is the law of kindness. She looketh well to the ways of her husband, and eateth not the bread of idleness. Her children arise up and call her blessed; her husband also, and he praiseth her.

Proverbs of Solomon

CLINGING VINE?

"The brain-women," said Oliver Wendell Holmes, "never interest us like the heart-women."

SO THAT'S THE REASON

> *Do you not know I am a woman?*
> *When I think, I must speak.*
>> Shakespeare, about 1601

WORDS

HE WEIGHED HIS WORDS

An average English word is four letters and a half. By hard, honest labor I've dug all the large words out of my vocabulary and shoved it down till the average is three and a half. . . . I never write *metropolis* for seven cents, because I can get the same price for *city*. I never write *policeman,* because I can get the same money for *cop*.

> Mark Twain, in a speech in New York, 1919

WORK

IT TAKES EFFORT

"The world is my oyster" is a saying Americans have lived by. But the idea has gotten around these days that the oyster is served on the half-shell. It isn't. It has to be opened, and that is a tricky proposition.

> Ernest R. Breech, Executive Vice President,
> Ford Motor Company

UNFAIR COMPETITION

BOSS: "Why are you going to quit? Are the wages too low?"
BILL: "The wages are okay, but I'm keeping a horse out of a job."

WOOD WOULDN'T DO

A tramp called at a home and asked for a handout.
"And how would you like a nice chop?" asked the kindly housewife.
"That all depends," said the tramp. "Is it pork, lamb, or wood?"

Out of Work

PASSERBY (to picket carrying a blank sign): "What's the idea?"
PICKET: "I'm looking for a sponsor."

Useful Life

"Just what have you done for humanity?" asked the judge before pronouncing sentence on the pickpocket.

"Well," said the confirmed criminal, "I've kept three or four detectives working regularly."

That Explains It

Personnel manager interviewing applicant for job:
"How long did you work in the other place?"
Fifty-five years."
"How old are you?"
"Forty-five years."
"How could you work fifty-five years when you are only forty-five years old?"
"Overtime!"

Mother Knows What's Best

Aunt Betty came up the walk and said to her small nephew, "Good morning, Willie. Is your mother in?"

"Sure she's in," replied Willie. "D'you s'pose I'd be workin' in the garden on Saturday morning if she wasn't?"

The Boy's Got Something

"My boy," said the successful man lecturing his son on thrift, "when I was your age I carried water for a gang of bricklayers."

"I'm proud of you, Father," answered the boy. "If it hadn't been for your work and thrift, I might have had to do something of that sort myself."

Too Much Free Time

A hired man who had worked hard in the fields from dawn until dark, day after day, and who had been obliged to finish his chores by electric light, said to the farmer at the end of the month, "I'm going to quit. You promised me a steady job."

"Well, haven't you got one?" was the reply.

"No," said the hired man. "There are two or three hours every night when I don't have anything to do except waste my time away sleeping."

BRAINS

Two old fellows were talking about a neighbor.

"He works too hard."

"He is under a heavy strain. I look for him to blow his brains out."

"Well if he does, he'll sure be a crack shot."

Cayce Moore

REWARDS WITHOUT WORK

Have we bequeathed youth lackluster ideas? Bernard Iddings Bell blames our generation for the weird philosophy of youth which says:

Give me the prize without the training,
The reward without the quest,
Wages without work,
A master's prestige without a master's skill,
A trade without apprenticeship,
Easter without the cross,
Heaven without probation.

Isn't it time to stop expecting something for nothing, or that a "rich uncle" whose surname is "Sam" will bail us out at every turn? Isn't it time again to teach some good old-fashioned Americanism?

Dr. Eva Anderson, Chelan County Member of
Washington State Legislature

WORLD

BAD SHAPE

In one of our grammar schools the teacher asked a class one day, "What is the shape of the earth?"

A small boy raised his hand and said, "My father says it's in the worst shape it ever was."

I suspect it is.

From an address by Dr. Harry Emerson Fosdick

All's Right or Riot

In the good old days when optimism was in flower, Browning sang, "God's in his heaven, all's right with the world." An American has altered that last line—"All's riot with the world."

From an address by Dr. Harry Emerson Fosdick

WORRY

Cooperating

Uncle Joe was always cheerful in spite of having had more than his share of life's troubles. Albert Edward Wiggam, the author, asked him how he had managed to remain so cheerful and calm.

"Well, I'll tell you," replied Uncle Joe. "I've just learned to cooperate with the inevitable."

It's a lesson we must all learn.

Inspection News

YOUTH

"Youth Supposes; Age Knows" (Welsh Proverb)

Young men think old men are fools, but old men know young men are fools.

George Clapman, 1605

Accomplishment

Galileo was only eighteen when he discovered the principle of the pendulum by observing a swinging lamp in the cathedral in Pisa.

Peel was in the British Parliament at twenty-one.

Elizabeth Barrett Browning knew Greek and Latin at twelve.

Gladstone was in Parliament before he was twenty-two, and by twenty-four was Lord of the British Treasury.

Lafayette was general of the whole French Army at twenty.

ZEAL

"Zeal Is Fit Only for Wise Men" (Thomas Fuller)

The greatest dangers to liberty lurk in insidious encroachment by men of zeal, well-meaning but without understanding.

Mr. Justice Louis D. Brandeis, 1928

Index

329

331

333

334

335

Painters, 14, 46, 47, 76, 222, 224
Painting, 27, 28, 69
Pantheon, 25
Parachutists, 60
Parents, 225
Parrots, 44, 296
Passions, 315
Paternalism, 103
Patience, 259
Patients, 98–100
Patronage, 233
Pawnshops, 225
Payment, 225–226
Peace, 136
Peasant, 190
Pedestrians, 174
Penn, William, 165
Pennsylvania Dutch, 225–226
Pensions, 148
People, the, 150–151
Pep talk, 50
Perfection, 226–227
Perserverance, 14, 142
Persistence, 227, 296
Personal character, 56–57
Personnel, 228
Pessimists, 228
Philosophers, 47
Photographs, 59
Physicians, 27, 83, 97–100, 210–211, 240
Pickets, 326
Pickles, 134
Pickpockets, 326
Picnics, 228
Pies, 77
Pigs, 30, 111, 124, 125, 180
Pilgrim Fathers, 61, 189–190
Plagiarism, 229, 243
Plagiarist, 304
Planning, 229–230
Play, 194, 259

Plays, 304–305
Poetry, 230
Poets, 76, 235
Poker, 101
Police state, 242
Politeness, 79–80, 116, 133, 231, 298
Politicians, 151, 164, 233, 267
Politics, 231–234
    businessmen in, 149
Poor, the, 74
Popularity, 234
Portraits, 167, 171–172, 224
Posterity, 46
Poverty, 234–235
Power, 235–236
Praise, 231, 236–237
    of self, 279
Prayer, 64, 197, 237–239, 280
Preachers, 62, 70, 71, 74, 82, 84, 213–214, 225–226, 239–240, 250, 280–281, 313
Precociousness, 181
Prediction, 34, 135, 311
Prejudice, 74, 232, 240
Presidents, 108
    favorite Biblical texts, 260–261
    on public debt, 89
Press, free, 240–241
Prestige, 56
Prices, 241
Pricing process, 242
Pride, 79, 167, 241
Princes, 28, 47, 190
Princeton, 67
Prizes, 49, 242, 253, 264–265, 266
Prodigy, 143
Production, 242
    mass, 53, 209
Professional men, 54
Professions, 243
Professors, 13, 68, 104, 181, 217, 243, 250

343